The
Headman
Was a
Woman

The *Headman* Was a *Woman*

The Gender Egalitarian Batek of Malaysia

Kirk M. Endicott
Dartmouth College

Karen L. Endicott

WAVELAND
PRESS, INC.
Long Grove, Illinois

For information about this book, contact:
Waveland Press, Inc.
4180 IL Route 83, Suite 101
Long Grove, IL 60047-9580
(847) 634-0081
info@waveland.com
www.waveland.com

10-digit ISBN 1-57766-526-0
13-digit ISBN 978-1-57766-526-7

Printed in the United States of America

7 6 5 4 3

Contents

Preface

This book describes the gender concepts, roles, and relations among the Batek, a hunting-gathering and trading people living in the rainforests of Peninsular Malaysia.[1] It is based on research spanning over three decades, from 1971 to 2004. In this book, however, we focus particularly on the years 1975–76 because that was the period during which we carried out our longest joint fieldwork and because the Batek at that time were living relatively undisturbed by logging and government programs. (We examine the changes that have taken place since 1976 in chapter 6.) We have written our description in the past tense to avoid implying that Batek culture is and always will be the way it was in 1975–76. However, this does not mean that the Batek culture we describe has now disappeared. Research by Dr. Lye Tuck-Po from 1993 onward shows that Batek in Pahang state are maintaining their basic values and practices in spite of changing circumstances (Lye 1997, 2004). We expect Batek living inside or close to Malaysia's National Park (Taman Negara) to continue following the general way of life described in this book for a long time to come.

Our primary aim in the book is to provide a basic description of the Batek way of life, focusing on their gender beliefs and practices. We are well aware, however, that ethnographic descriptions are summaries of numerous statements and observations that are shaped by the authors' views of what is relevant to the topic, how the various beliefs and practices fit together, and why they take the form they do. Our description, then, is also an explanation—our understanding of Batek gender. Our explanation is not the only one possible. We invite others to apply their own theories and analyses to this material. We see this ethnography as a preliminary step in a process of scholarly discussion of the wider significance of the Batek case for social science.

Our other aim is to help preserve knowledge of the Batek way of life in the late twentieth century for future generations of Batek. As Batek experience the impact of development and Malaysian government assimilation programs, their memories and oral traditions will inevitably fade and change.

We hope that our written descriptions and photographs will help future generations of Batek preserve their history, identity, and sense of self-worth. Anthropologists are painfully aware of how easily people can become cut off from their past. In 2004, Kirk briefly visited a number of Batek groups with whom he had lived and studied since 1971 and presented them with albums of photographs of themselves and their relatives—many of them now dead—taken between 1971 and 1990. They were thrilled. One man made a point to tell Kirk how happy they were to see pictures of their long-dead relatives and to be reminded of those earlier times.

A note about our use of personal names. Most Batek have at least three names: a "true" or "flesh" name, which is concealed from outsiders after a person reaches adulthood; an "outsider" name, which is used in the presence of non-Batek; a teknonym, consisting of the term "mother-of" or "father-of" followed by the true name or outsider name of one of that person's children, which is used in everyday conversation; and sometimes one or more nicknames derived from their personal characteristics. In this book we refer to people by their outsider names. (We use English spellings for the names of people, deities, and ethnic groups, approximating how they are pronounced. Apostrophes indicate glottal stops.) We use pseudonyms whenever revealing people's identities could cause them embarrassment or harm. One further complication is that Batek avoid mentioning the names of the dead, out of fear that the person's ghost will be offended and may cause the speaker to become ill. Regrettably, many of the people we knew are now dead. For the sake of future generations of Batek who might wish to learn about their ancestors, we have chosen to call even the dead by their outsider names. However, we advise readers not to mention these names when speaking to Batek people.

Numerous photographs of Batek are available at www.keene.edu/library/orangasli and www.flickr.com/photos/tplye.

This book is a product of a long-term collaboration among numerous Batek and ourselves. All royalties from this book, after taxes, go to the benefit of the Batek and other Orang Asli (Aborigines of Peninsular Malaysia).

Note

[1] When we use the term "Batek" without qualification, we are referring to the people we have called Batek De' (*dɛʔ*) and Batek 'Iga' (*ʔigaʔ*) in some previous publications. Other peoples commonly called Batek include the Batek Teh (*təh*) (an offshoot of the Mendriq) of the lower Lebir River, the Batek Te' (*tɛ̃ʔ*) of the lower Lebir River and the Besut River in Trengganu, the Batek Tanum (or Mintil) of the Tanum River in Pahang, and the Batek Nong (*nɔŋ*) of the Ceka River in Pahang.

Acknowledgments

Numerous people and organizations have contributed to our research and to this book. Above all, we give our heart-felt thanks to our many Batek friends and acquaintances who graciously allowed us to observe and participate in their lives and patiently answered our many questions. It is entirely due to their help and goodwill that we were able to live in the rainforest and learn about their way of life. We wish especially to acknowledge the late Tanyogn and Langsat and their children and the late Penghulu Sele' and Soli' and their children, our main mentors and guardians during our studies.

Our fieldwork was supported by many agencies over the years. Kirk's fieldwork in 1971–73 was financed by the U.S. National Institute of Mental Health and the University of Malaya. The Australian National University supported our joint fieldwork in 1975–76 and Kirk's research in 1981. Our 1990 research was made possible by a Fulbright-Hays award, a grant from the Joint Committee on Southeast Asia of the American Council of Learned Societies and the Social Science Research Council (funded by the Ford Foundation and the National Endowment for the Humanities), and the Claire Garber Goodman Fund of Dartmouth College. Kirk also received a grant from the Goodman Fund for his return trip in 2004. We also received valuable institutional support from Harvard University, the University of Malaya, the Australian National University, Dartmouth College, and the Institute for Environment and Development (LESTARI) of Universiti Kebangsaan Malaysia. We are very grateful to these agencies and institutions.

We thank the Economic Planning Unit of the Prime Minister's Department, the government of Kelantan state, and the Department of Orang Asli Affairs (JHEOA) in Malaysia for permission to do the research. We also thank the many staff members of the JHEOA who went out of their way to help us, including Dr. Baharon Azhar Raffie'i, Encik Jimin Idris, Encik Mohd. Ruslan Abdullah, Encik Osman Idris, Encik Jaafar Abdul Rahman, Mr. Howard Biles, Encik Ahmad Khamis, Dr. Mohd. Tap Salleh, Encik Nik Hassan, Encik Abd. Ghani Abdullah, Encik Mahmood Mohamed, Dr. Malcolm Bolton, Dr. Peter Schindler, and Encik Abu Bakar. Also, the former Director-General of the National Museum (Muzim Negara), Encik Shahrum Yub, and his staff were unfailing in their assistance.

Many dear friends in Malaysia and Singapore provided help and hospitality. We are grateful to Mette Lauritsen, Brian Lunn, Jack and Louise Shively, Nordin Ariffin and Halimah Ab. Rahman, Ben and Michiko Stone, Peter and Jan Schindler, Wong Chew Meow, Wazir Jahan Karim and Razha Rashid, Colin Nicholas, and Lye Tuck-Po. Our special thanks go to Geoffrey Benjamin and Vivienne Wee, Ken and Dalia Connell, Hood Mohamad Salleh and Maherani Modh. Ishak, and Mohd. Ruslan Abdullah and Musli Mustafa Hakim for taking us into their homes for weeks at a time!

We also wish to thank our academic advisors and mentors. Professor Rodney Needham of the University of Oxford and Professors James Fox and Evon Vogt of Harvard University supervised Kirk's doctoral research. Professors Davydd Greenwood and Thomas Gregor grounded Karen in anthropology at Cornell University, and Professor Anthony Forge directed her graduate studies at the Australian National University. We also received valuable advice in Canberra from Drs. Nicolas Peterson, Rhys Jones, and Betty Meehan. In addition, Dr. Geoffrey Benjamin, now at Nanyang Technological University in Singapore, has acted as an informal mentor and constant source of help and advice since the beginning of our interest in Orang Asli. Professor Robert K. Dentan of the University at Buffalo and Professors Shuichi Nagata and Richard B. Lee of the University of Toronto have also offered welcome advice and encouragement over the years.

This book has passed through many versions before arriving at its current form, and we have had valuable input from numerous colleagues and students along the way. It is based in part on Karen's M.A. thesis, "Batek Negrito Sex Roles" (Australian National University, 1979). We thank Professor Forge for his guidance during the research and writing of the thesis, Shirley Hayes for her support during the writing, and the outside examiners, Professor Needham and Dr. Lenore Manderson, for their valuable criticisms and suggestions. We also thank the numerous colleagues who read parts or all of earlier drafts and gave us valuable feedback, including Geoffrey Benjamin, Vivienne Wee, Shuichi Nagata, Peter Reynolds, Nicole Sault, Cathy Winkler, Corry van der Sluys, Barbara Nowak, Rosemary Gianno, Dale Eickelman, Robert Welsch, Celia Erlich, Marilyn Lord, Shirley Campbell, Christine Helliwell, and Lye Tuck-Po. We especially thank Dr. Lye, who carried out fieldwork with the Batek of Pahang state beginning in 1993, for freely sharing her findings and ideas with us. We have also benefited from the suggestions of the many Dartmouth students who read earlier drafts of the book in Kirk's "Hunters and Gatherers" course. We thank especially Jane Langdell Robinson '95 and Adam Levine '08, who served as research assistants. And we are grateful to Jeni Ogilvie at Waveland Press for her careful and insightful editing of our manuscript and to senior editor Tom Curtin for his excellent advice and encouragement. These colleagues and students do not necessarily agree with all our interpretations and conclusions, however. For those we alone are responsible.

Orthography

The spelling system used here uses symbols from the International Phonetic Alphabet as adapted by Geoffrey Benjamin for writing the Aslian languages of the Austroasiatic language stock. Each symbol represents one phoneme. In the following list we give the approximate American English values of most of the vowels and a few of the consonants. (We have had to use German and Cockney English for two of the sounds.)

a pronounced like "a" in "car"
ə pronounced like "a" in "above"
e pronounced like "a" in "way" (but without the i-offglide)
ɛ pronounced like "e" in "desk"
i pronounced like "ea" in "beat"
o pronounced like "o" in "vote"
ɔ pronounced like "o" in "hot"
u pronounced like "oo" in "boot"
ʉ pronounced like "ü" in German "Hütte"
c pronounced like "ch" in "church" (but with the blade of the tongue)
k pronounced like "k" in "kid" (not aspirated in terminal position)
ŋ pronounced like "ng" in "singer" (but "gn" in terminal position)
ɲ pronounced like "ny" in "banyan"
ʔ glottal stop, pronounced like "t" in Cockney English "battle"

A tilde (~) over a vowel indicates phonemic nasality. Stress in Batek words falls on the final syllable, even in words borrowed from Malay.

Malay words are spelled according to the "new orthography" (*ejaan baharu*), which was officially adopted by the governments of Malaysia and Indonesia in 1973, except in direct quotations from older sources.

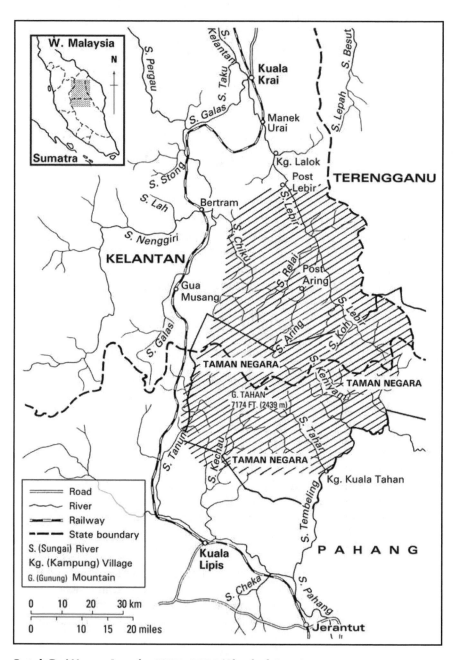

Batek De' Home Area in 1975–1976 (Shaded Area)

Chapter 1

Encountering the Unexpected

Going to the Batek

The day dawned bright and deceptively cool. From the veranda of the resthouse where we had spent the night, we looked out over the town of Kuala Krai, in the east coast state of Kelantan in Peninsular Malaysia. It was mid-September 1975. Patches of fog still hung over the playing field of a school at the foot of the hill. Huge cobwebs glistened between the power lines leading up the road to the resthouse. On our left the road from the state capital Kota Bharu, on the coast, swept across our view in a gentle curve and disappeared behind the buildings of the town. The road continued between rows of Chinese shops, past small government buildings, and finally ended at the head of a long flight of concrete steps that descended to the main boat landing on the Kelantan River.

Soon our friend Halimah, a teacher at the local high school, arrived in her car to take us to the train station. We loaded our equipment and drove into town, where we stopped outside the Eng Fong Medical Hall, a family-owned general goods shop. Our friend Wong Chiew Meow had let us assemble our supplies at his family store. Kirk hailed a goods "trishaw," a three-wheeled vehicle with a cargo platform in front and a bicycle in back, and we loaded it with our bags of rice, cans of food, cooking pots, plastic buckets, and other necessities for a two-month trip into the rainforest. Our caravan of car and trishaw turned left onto the other main street in town, which ended at the small, English bungalow-style train station, an architectural legacy of British colonial days.

When the 6:30 AM train arrived from the coast, we loaded our gear into the baggage car, farewelled Halimah, and hopped in. We made ourselves

1

comfortable among the baskets of fresh fish, fruits, and other goods that traders sold out of the baggage car door at the numerous tiny villages where the
train stopped on its morning run into the interior. After a forty-five-minute
ride looking out over rubber plantations, we crossed a high bridge over the
Lebir River, a major tributary of the Kelantan River, and got off at the village
of Manek Urai. We were greeted by Halimah's husband, Nordin, the head-
master at the Manek Urai elementary school, who had brought a group of
student volunteers to help us carry our gear to the river. We walked single-file
down the paved main path through the village. On our left a few goats grazed
in the village pasture, and on the right we passed a row of small wooden
houses inside tidy fenced yards, surrounded by fruit trees and ornamental
plants. Descending a winding dirt path to the riverbank, we saw several large
bamboo rafts surmounted by small bamboo and thatch houses. Beyond the
rafts the yellow-brown waters of the Lebir, about 200 feet wide, ran power-
fully toward the sea. The river formed the only "road" to the Batek.

Nordin introduced us to Mat Kibat, the forest produce trader he had
engaged to take us up the river in his boat.

"How does the river look?" we asked.

"Good," he said. "Not too high or too low."

We breathed silent sighs of relief. If the water were low, we would have to
drag the boat up the numerous rapids on the upper river.

While Mat Kibat prepared the outboard motor, we stowed our belongings. Despite keeping our gear to a minimum, our baggage filled the long,
narrow boat. We said our good-byes to Nordin and gave bags of hard candies
to the students. With a throaty roar, the boat pulled away from its mooring
and knifed out into the middle of the river's main channel. A poleman sat
cross-legged on the bow with an eight-foot wooden pole balanced across his
lap. The relative coolness of the early morning was giving way to the heat and
humidity of the tropical day. We pulled on long-sleeved shirts and wide-
brimmed hats to protect us against the sun, and then settled atop our bundles
for the slow ride upstream.

On the high bluffs on both sides of the river, coconut palms marked a
series of Malay villages. Long stairways, which could disappear from view
when floodwaters rose in the December monsoons, climbed from the river to
the villages. Some of the sarong-clad women and young children who were
bathing or washing clothes looked up as our boat droned past. A few people
waved. Beyond Lalok village and the "Long Rapids," once a formidable bar-
rier to river traffic, the human population abruptly thinned out. Miles of
scrubby vegetation and thick patches of tall, razor-sharp *lalang* grass, which
overran abandoned gardens, were punctuated by occasional clusters of two or
three thatched houses, dwarfed by fruit trees and surrounded by fields of
manioc (tapioca root), corn, and hill rice. The forest, kept at bay by the clearings, rose in the background. Most Malays disliked the forest, which they
believed contained evil spirits called *hantu*. They had built their houses close
to the riverbanks, as far from the forest edge as they could get.

About midday we reached Post Lebir, a village and medical post established by the JHEOA (Department of Orang Asli Affairs) in the 1960s as part of an effort to induce the Batek to abandon nomadic hunting and gathering for a settled life of agriculture. Kirk already knew Post Lebir well. It was where he had begun his previous fieldwork in 1971. We climbed the steep dirt bank to the village, where several small wooden houses, a medical hut, and a one-roomed school occupied a flat, hot clearing. Kirk talked with some Batek who had been living there for a few years growing crops. We also met Penghulu Peng (Headman Peng), a man from another indigenous group, the Semaq Beri, who was visiting Post Lebir. He lived on the upper Lebir with his Batek wife. People told us we would have to continue upriver if we wanted to link up with Batek practicing hunting and gathering. Peng invited us to stay on the upper Lebir with him and the ten or so other families who were clearing some gardens but also spending considerable time in the forest foraging and collecting rattan, long vine-like stems of several palm species, to trade. We were glad to accept his invitation, especially as this group was one Kirk had not stayed with before. We returned to the boat, with Peng joining us as our guide and host.

As we continued upstream, the scrubby secondary growth on the riverbanks gave way to dense rainforest broken only by the river. Limbs overhung the water as trees vied for sunlight. Peng pointed to movements in the treetops. "Leaf monkeys," he shouted over the roar of the motor. He also pointed out swathes of flattened vegetation along the riverbanks made by elephants coming down for water. We heard and then saw a rhinoceros hornbill flying slowly overhead, its great wings noisily "chuff-chuffing" through the air. Now and then the river gushed through narrow channels, the poleman on the bow skillfully guiding the boat between the boulders by pushing away from them with his long wooden pole. We arrived at the Batek clearing in the late afternoon.

Our boat drew up to a steep path that led from the river to the top of a bluff. Children bounded down the slope, and a few men and women followed at a leisurely pace. Peng introduced us and explained that we wanted to stay with them and learn about how they lived. They had heard of Kirk from his earlier fieldwork with the Batek of the nearby Aring River and the Batek Teh of the lower Lebir, and one young man had met Kirk while attending school at Post Lebir. People seemed happy to have us and willingly helped us carry our gear up from the river.

Their settlement consisted of nine small Malay-style houses—raised rectangular structures with split bamboo floors and walls and palm thatch roofs—and two traditional lean-to shelters of palm thatch. The dwellings were scattered about a cleared area shaded by small trees. At the behest of the JHEOA, this group was attempting to grow crops. On the riverbank some corn and cucumbers had sprouted. Behind the settlement several acres of trees had been chopped down and lay drying in the sun. Across the river unbroken rainforest stretched from the riverbank to the tops of the hills in the distance. As we soon found out, many of the settlement's ostensible residents were actually living in the forest across the river, collecting rattan, hunting, and gathering wild foods.

Hastened by the darkening sky across the river, which often portends a thunderstorm, we quickly pitched our tent near the center of the settlement. We gave out gifts of rice, flour, sugar, tea, and tobacco. One man helped us build a fire, and we cooked a meal of rice and tinned curry. As darkness fell about 7:30—as it does year-round in Malaysia—cicadas and myriad other insects took up their nightly chorus. Families chatted in their shelters. Lying in our cozy tent as the rain pelted down, we excitedly anticipated the start of our research.

Some Surprises

We had come to the Batek to study several things. Kirk wanted to gather more data on their foraging economy. The groups he had stayed with in 1971–73 had been participating in government-sponsored agricultural projects, so their hunting and gathering activities were sporadic and supplementary (K.M. Endicott 1974). Most of their carbohydrates during that period came from government-supplied rations, self-grown crops, and trade. Kirk was eager to see how the hunting and gathering economy worked when it was their primary source of support. He also wanted more information on Batek social organization and religion, which he had begun to study in his previous research. Karen intended to focus on gender relations and on how children were socialized into adult roles, areas of inquiry Kirk hadn't focused on previously. We knew from the beginning that our investigations would overlap and complement each other.

When we began our research, we expected to find a fairly clear-cut division of labor and of social roles along gender lines. The stereotype of hunter-gatherers at the time was: men hunted, women gathered (and took care of children), hunting was more prestigious than gathering, therefore men were more important and influential than women. We would not have been surprised to find a similar pattern to Batek life. Our first month of fieldwork, however, forced us to rethink everything.

After a few days of living at the clearing, we realized that we had arrived just as the Batek were preparing to move. A few families had already established a camp in the forest across the river, and several others soon joined them. They said they wanted to move closer to the sources of wild foods and rattan, which they could collect and trade to Malays for rice and other foods. Soon we, too, moved to the camp in the forest.

The camp consisted of twelve lean-to shelters, scattered across a forested slope with a shallow stream at the bottom. (We will describe camps in more detail in chapter 3.) Advanced secondary forest shaded the camp from the sun. In a space between the shelters some boys had placed a sheet of flattened tree bark on the ground, and they were spinning homemade wooden tops on it. Most adults were out in the forest working.

After consulting our Batek companions, we chose a site for our tent and arranged for several young men to build a wood and bamboo platform as a base to keep the tent above the wet and sloping ground. We spent the rest of the day making a sketch map of the camp, recording who lived in each shelter, and chatting with people as they returned from the forest. We were happy to see that they were seriously foraging for wild foods as well as collecting rattan. Baskets of wild tubers lay in front of most shelters, and some families were about to process *pɘnaceʔ* (Malay *kepayang kayu*), which are large nuts that had to be boiled, sliced up, and leached in a stream to remove a poison before they could be eaten.

A few days later our education on the Batek division of labor began. We arranged to accompany a group of people who were planning to dig for tubers. To our surprise, the work-group included members of both sexes and various ages: Tanyogn, a woman about forty-seven; her daughter-in-law Chingchong; her son-in-law Daun; Penghulu Peng, Chingchong's father; and two young boys. The digging parties Kirk had observed previously had consisted only of women and children. The group followed Tanyogn to a particular spot. "I saw some young tuber vines here a few years ago," she explained to us. Peng did not do much digging because he had a sore shoulder, but the other adults each got between thirteen and eighteen pounds of tubers. The only person who did any hunting was Tanyogn's nine-year-old son, Pikas. He blowpiped one small bird, which he and his friend soon cooked along with a few of Tanyogn's tubers.

Back in camp, we witnessed other activities that defied the stereotype about the division of labor. We saw mixed groups of men and women gathering and processing *pɘnaceʔ* nuts and *gadoŋ*, a poisonous tuber that also must be boiled and leached before being eaten. The only gender-specialized part of the process seemed to be climbing the trees to cut down the nuts, a job generally performed by men or boys. Most surprising of all, one morning we saw two young women—Tanyogn's fifteen-year-old daughter Lesoh and her recently married friend Chinloy—poisoning blowpipe darts over a fire. Later that morning they left camp together with their blowpipes slung over their shoulders. In the afternoon they returned, having had no luck but smiling broadly. Chinloy strolled back to her shelter where her husband, Kawun, lay on his side casually roasting tubers over their cooking fire. So much for man the hunter and woman the gatherer! That night Karen worried aloud about whether there were any "sex roles" at all for her to write about.

We also found no support for the expectation that men would have greater influence than women in family and camp-wide decision making. Family decisions seemed to be made by husbands and wives together, and leadership beyond the family was not restricted to men. Because we initially assumed that the leaders of the upper-Lebir population were the JHEOA-designated headmen, Penghulu Peng and Penghulu Keladi, it had not fully registered on us when Daun, back at the clearing, had told us that his mother-in-law, Tanyogn, was the *pəŋhuluˀ* (headman) of the group then camping across the river. We later discovered that her name was included in a list of Batek headmen in the JHEOA office in Kuala Krai as Tanjong bin Keboh—"Tanjong son of Keboh"—suggesting that whoever prepared the chart assumed she was a man. Indeed it was Tanyogn who organized the first foraging expedition we went on, while Penghulu Peng merely tagged along. As we learned more about the nature of Batek leadership, we came to understand why Daun and others—including the Malay traders—called Tanyogn *pəŋhuluˀ* as well.

Tanyogn was a middle-aged woman, lean and muscular, with a wide grin and a loud, hoarse voice. She was a person who was always busy. On one typical day she spent the morning plaiting rattan waistbands, then cut down an incense-bearing tree and chopped out the fragrant wood inside the trunk, and later dug five pounds of tubers for dinner. Whenever there was a discussion in camp, she would be in it, arguing with great animation and at breakneck speed. People often came to her for advice and help. She seemed to look out for everyone in camp, including two orphaned teenaged boys, in addition to her own family. We did not understand at first that she was looking out for us, too. One day we were camped on the main Lebir River, which was swollen from heavy rain upstream. We went to bathe on the steep riverbank, gingerly lowering ourselves into the rushing water while clinging to some shrubs. Suddenly a breathless Tanyogn appeared on the path above. "I was afraid you had drowned," she shouted. Then she laughed in relief. It was then that we realized she had taken us under her commodious wing.

As the first month wore on, we also saw that child rearing was not the realm of women alone. We were repeatedly struck by how much time fathers and older boys spent carrying children of both sexes, playing with them, and helping them do things. Tebu—who was probably older than fifty, quite advanced for a Batek man—often carried his four-year-old son Toney, who was crippled by spinal tuberculosis. It was common to see fathers sitting in their shelters with children on their laps, while their wives got on with their work. One day we found Penghulu Peng sitting in his shelter slicing *gadoŋ* tubers with his three-year-old son clinging to his back. We asked him where his wife was. "She's out in the forest looking for tubers," he said. "She got tired of processing *gadoŋ* in camp."

Our research on Batek gender relations, then, began with our having to set expectations and stereotypes aside. Over the next several months, as we followed Batek from camp to camp, we came to realize that we were observing something remarkable: a society in which neither males nor females, as groups, controlled the actions of the opposite sex or the terms by which their actions and characteristics were judged. We were observing a gender egalitarian society.

Tanyogn was an expert on herbal medicines. Here she wipes a mixture of water and medicinal leaves on a man's back.

The Idea of Gender Egalitarian Societies

The concept of social equality has a long history in Western political philosophy (e.g., Rousseau 1992 [original 1753]; Tocqueville 1998–2001 [original 1856]; Marx 1896 [original 1867]). It is usually presented as an ideal or goal to be pursued, not as reality. The goal of societies that value social equality is to ensure that all members are treated the same by the government and under the law, not to make everyone the same. Of course no two people in any society—not even identical twins—are exactly the same in all their personal qualities and circumstances. But social equality can be said to exist when everyone in a society has the same rights and perceived social value.

Anthropologists have long classified some societies as egalitarian, but not necessarily gender egalitarian (see, e.g., Fried 1967; Woodburn 1982; R.C. Kelly 1993; R.L. Kelly 1995; Boehm 1999; Salzman 1999). The general idea is that egalitarian societies positively value social equality and maintain some practices that favor it (Widlock 2005). There may be some differences between individuals and groups in wealth, power, and prestige, but these differences are not passed on and reinforced in succeeding generations and therefore do not lead to the kinds of permanent structures of inequality that exist in hierarchical societies. Interestingly, scholars often specifically exclude relations between males and females and young and old when categorizing societies as egalitarian (e.g., Woodburn 1982; R.L. Kelly 1995). This leaves open the question of whether there is gender equality even in societies that are commonly classified as egalitarian.

Egalitarian societies can be divided into two types: competitive egalitarian and noncompetitive egalitarian (Woodburn 1982; Fardon 1990; Helliwell 1994, 1995). Competitive egalitarian societies emphasize equality of opportunity but still value certain human qualities differently and encourage people to try to excel in valued ways. Such societies reject hereditary or other ascribed differences that would give some people advantages over others. But—because people vary in talent, personality, and circumstances—competition leads to differences in actual wealth, power, and prestige. The wealth, power, and prestige that individuals acquire cannot be passed on to their children, however, so members of each generation must achieve success through their own efforts, and every individual has, in theory, an equal chance to do so. Good examples of competitive egalitarian societies are the Melanesian peoples who have "Big Man" forms of political leadership, in which ambitious individuals (usually men) compete to excel in valued activities such as sponsoring feasts (R.C. Kelly 1993).

Noncompetitive egalitarian societies, on the other hand, emphasize equality of condition or outcome. Although they may value certain social qualities differently, their ideologies emphasize the right of everyone to equal amounts of wealth, power, and prestige, and they maintain practices—commonly termed "leveling mechanisms"—that promote this. Leveling mechanisms induce people to share wealth, undermine the ability of people to exercise power over others, or limit the prestige of the successful. For example, food-sharing obligations commonly found in nomadic hunting and gathering societies are often interpreted as means of evening out the wealth by taking food from the successful providers and giving it to less successful ones.

The notion of gender egalitarian societies has been more controversial in anthropology, with some scholars even denying that they exist or can exist. Whether gender egalitarian societies exist depends in part on one's definition of the term. If by "gender egalitarian" we mean that males and females do exactly the same things in exactly the same frequencies, then of course no such societies exist. But if we mean that neither males nor females are prevented from doing whatever they want to do (short of things that are biologically impossible), then at least the possibility of equality exists.

We define gender egalitarian societies as those in which neither males nor females *as groups* have control over the other sex and neither sex is accorded greater value than the other by society as a whole (cf. Schlegel 1977). This definition combines a behavioral criterion, control, with an ideological one, the people's evaluation of the sexes and their actions. This does not mean that there are no biological, social, or cultural differences between the sexes in a gender egalitarian society, only that those differences do not allow one sex to control or devalue the other. We argue in this book that the Batek were gender egalitarian by this definition because neither men nor women controlled the actions of the opposite sex or the terms in which their actions and characteristics were judged.

Anthropological opinions about the existence of gender egalitarian societies have changed over time. In the early 1970s, many feminist anthropologists maintained that all societies are male-dominated and attempted to explain why. For example, Rosaldo (1974) argued that sexual asymmetry is universal because all societies have separate domestic and public spheres of activity with women being confined to the domestic sphere, where they are isolated and devalued, while men are free to participate in public life, which affords them opportunities to acquire wide powers and prestige. Ortner (1974) argued that all societies associate women with nature—because they bear and nurse children—and men with culture, which is universally regarded as superior to nature. Friedl (1975) attributed male dominance in hunting and gathering societies to men's monopoly on providing meat in the form of big game, meat supposedly being the most valued food and the distribution of meat being a source of power and prestige not available to women. Other anthropologists explained universal male dominance in terms of men's innately higher levels of aggressiveness, greater male strength, male bonding for hunting purposes, and psychological and developmental differences (see, e.g., Tiger 1969; Collins 1971; Chodorow 1974; Schlegel 1977; Mukhopadhyay and Higgins 1988).

Some anthropologists, however, claimed that gender egalitarian societies are possible and did exist. Leacock, following Engels, argued that prior to the existence of private ownership, which places productive property in the hands of men, and before the rise of the independent conjugal family, in which the wife and children are dependent upon the husband for their livelihood (Leacock 1972:29–43; see also Sacks 1974), women were "autonomous" in groups everywhere and had "decision-making power over their own lives and activities to the same extent that men did over theirs" (Leacock 1978:247). A number of other writers (e.g., Sanday 1974; Draper 1975a; Slocum 1975; Schlegel 1977; and Begler 1978) argued that gender relations in societies vary from total male domination at one extreme to egalitarianism at the other, depending on specific economic, social, and ideological circumstances. Evidence for this point of view mounted as ethnographers reported cases of societies that are gender egalitarian or nearly so—and most of them are hunting and gathering peoples. Turnbull, for example, wrote of the Mbuti Pygmies of Zaire that "a woman is in no way the social inferior of a man, and there is little absolute division of labor along sex lines" (1965:270). Draper reported that "most members of the Harvard !Kung Bushman Study Project who have thought about the subject of !Kung women's status agree that !Kung society may be the least sexist of any we have experienced" (1975a:77). Estioko-Griffin and Griffin, who documented how Agta women of Northern Luzon hunt large game, concluded that "Agta women are equal to men" (1981:140).

The question of whether male dominance is universal or not retreated into the background during the 1980s and afterward as researchers focused on the specific meanings, powers, and roles of males and females in particular societies. As Mukhopadhyay and Higgins put it, scholars "shifted away from universalistic theories and grand designs, from key determinants with global applications, to theories more restricted in scope, proposed for particular sets of societies or regions, or applicable to a narrower range of lower-level phenomena" (1988:486; see also Morgen 1989; Flanagan 1989; Errington 1990). This trend arose as researchers realized that certain key concepts in the discussion—such as "women's status," "male dominance," and "gender asymmetry"—were too vague or ambiguous to be useful in cross-cultural analysis (Moore 1988:7; Burbank 1989:121; Meigs 1990:102; Sanday 1990:15). Proliferating ethnographic studies of male–female relations in specific societies revealed that gender relations are too complex to be classified according to such simplistic concepts. These studies also showed that associations such as those between women and the domestic sphere and between women and nature are not found in all societies and cannot, therefore, be evidence of or causes of universal female subordination (Moore 1988).

Significantly, studies of gender in non-Western societies challenged the Western assumption that all differences between males and females—in roles, rights, duties, conceptions, and so forth—are inequalities (see, e.g., Sacks 1976, 1979; Moore 1988; Strathern 1987; Kent 1995). Studies of gender in non-Western societies show that the differences between the biological sexes are conceptualized in various ways, many of which do not imply superiority of one or the other. For example, Meigs found that Hua men of Papua New Guinea "have three separate and contradictory gender ideologies. One is brutally chauvinistic, the second frankly envious of female reproductive powers, and the third egalitarian" (1990:102). Gender differences, then, may be evaluated in different ways, and we cannot assume a priori that differences are seen as inequalities in particular societies.

Most cultural anthropologists now accept that some gender egalitarian societies exist, but consider such societies very rare. Most, but not all, are nomadic hunting and gathering peoples, including the Ju/'hoansi (formerly called "!Kung"), Mbuti, and Hadza of Africa; the Malapantaram and Paliyan of India; and the Agta of Luzon in the Philippines. Perhaps other existing or recent foraging societies should be added to the list. Some horticultural societies, such as the Semai of Malaysia (Dentan 1968; Gilmore 1990) and the Vanatinai Islanders of Papua New Guinea (Lepowsky 1990, 1993) appear to be gender egalitarian as well. But gender equality is not necessarily produced the same way in all gender egalitarian societies. In this book we focus on the Batek and attempt to determine what conditions produce their gender equality.

The Batek

The Batek, numbering about 800 people, are one of the smallest linguistically distinct ethnic groups in Peninsular Malaysia. They are one of nineteen or so groups that comprise the aboriginal peoples of Peninsular Malaysia, the *Orang Asli* (Malay for "original people"). The Orang Asli as a whole, who numbered about 147,000 in 2003, make up only a tiny fraction of Malaysia's population of twenty-four million. More than half of the inhabitants of Peninsular Malaysia (which excludes Sabah and Sarawak, the two Malaysian states on the island of Borneo) are Malays. When the British began to colonize the Malay Peninsula in the nineteenth century, most Malays were farmers or fishermen living in rural areas near the coasts and along the major rivers. The British incorporated the traditional Malay sultanates into the colonial government, and Malays have dominated the postindependence governments and bureaucracy. Second in population are Malaysia's mainly town-dwelling Chinese, who have long been dominant in business. Indians, originally brought to colonial Malaya (as Peninsular Malaysia was then known) by the British to work on rubber plantations and build railroads, comprise the smallest of the major ethnic groups in the peninsula.

The Batek are one of several ethnic groups conventionally classified in the Semang or Negrito division of the Orang Asli. The Semang, who total about 3,500 persons, share a cluster of physical, linguistic, and cultural characteristics that set them off from other Orang Asli. The term *Semang* (which probably comes from *səma?*, the word for "human being" in several Orang Asli languages) was used by early scholars primarily as a racial designation (e.g., Skeat and Blagden 1906a and 1906b). Physical anthropologists classified the Semang as "Negritos" because, like the Negritos of the Philippines, they are typically short, dark-skinned, and have such "Negroid" features as woolly hair and broad, flat noses. These features set Semang off from the brown-skinned, straight- or wavy-haired Malays and—though less clearly—from other Orang Asli.

The Semang languages and dialects, except the language of the Lanoh Semang, are distinctive enough that linguists group them together as the "Northern Aslian" (or "Jahaic") subgroup of the "Aslian" languages spoken by many Orang Asli peoples. The Aslian languages are part of the Austroasiatic language stock, which includes the Mon-Khmer languages spoken by various groups in mainland Southeast Asia, India, and China. By contrast, Malay, the language of the numerically and politically dominant Malays, is an Austronesian language related to the languages of island Southeast Asia and the Pacific. But because Malay is the lingua franca of the Malaysia, Batek and the other Northern Aslian languages have absorbed a large number of Malay words, probably mostly in the last few centuries.

Culturally the Semang have long been identified with the nomadic hunting and gathering (foraging) way of life, although in the twentieth century some Semang groups (e.g., the Lanoh and Batek Nong) took up farming. The Semang may be direct descendants of the Hoabinhian peoples who occupied the coasts and interior of the Malay Peninsula from about 10,000 to 1000 BC, leaving their traces—simple stone tools, animal bones, and some of their own skeletons—in scattered caves, rock shelters, and shell heaps (middens) (Bellwood 1997). The Hoabinhians, like the Batek today, ate a wide variety of wild plants and animals (Bulbeck 1985). The Semang, like many other tropical forest-dwelling foragers of the world (e.g., the Agta and the Pygmies of Africa) engage in some trade with agricultural peoples in addition to foraging for wild foods, a practice that may go back thousands of years (Dunn 1975). These peoples are sometimes called "forager-traders" (Morrison and Junker 2002).

In the 1970s, the Batek subgroup of Semang lived in the upper watersheds of the Lebir, Aring, and Relai rivers in the state of Kelantan and along some of the northern tributaries of the Tembeling River in neighboring Pahang (see the map). At that time, Batek were the only permanent occupants of an area, roughly rectangular in shape, stretching from near Lalok village in the north to the Tembeling River in the south and from the Terengganu border in the east to the Chiku River in the west, giving them a population density of less than one person per three square miles. (Land at higher elevations was uninhabited most of the time.) They lived in nomadic groups of twenty to forty persons and usually camped deep in the interior of the forest, at least a day's travel by motorboat from the nearest Malay village. In 1975–76, there were two "river valley groups" of Batek in Kelantan: the Aring River people and the Lebir River people. The group of Batek we stayed with on the upper Lebir numbered ninety persons, thirty-seven females and fifty-three males.[1] They usually formed three or four separate camp-groups. Minor cultural differences existed between Batek living in the various river valleys—including those in Pahang state—but constant visiting back and forth and intermarriage between groups prevented major, enduring cultural differences from developing.

The Batek Environment

The Rainforest

In the 1970s tropical rainforest covered the Batek home area.[2] It was broken only by the larger rivers and occasional limestone buttes, which rose like thick columns through the forest canopy in the headwaters of the Relai, Chiku, and Keniyam rivers. Just south of the Pahang border, Mount Tahan rose 7,186 feet above sea level, crowning the jagged, bare escarpments of the Tahan mountain range. Beneath the forest canopy, a fine network of rivers and streams cut through the hills, creating a pattern of ridges separated by ravines. Ridgetops and alluvial terraces found here and there along the larger streams offered the only level stretches of land.

Most of the rainforest in the Batek area in the 1970s was primary forest, forest that had never been cleared. Primary lowland rainforest is dominated by towering trees of numerous species whose smooth gray trunks stretch a hundred feet up before branching out like open umbrellas to form the top story of the forest canopy. Flange-like buttresses brace the trunks of the larger trees. The forest's woody framework supports a vast community of aerial plants: orchids, ferns, fungi, and vines, including the economically valuable rattans. Small trees, stemless palms, and shade-tolerant herbs and ferns form a thick but not impenetrable undergrowth. Between these plants the ground is almost bare, except for rotting leaves and branches, as the scattered shafts of sunlight that penetrate the leafy canopy are too feeble to support most grasses. But where trees have fallen and let in the sunlight, dense stands of new trees, shrubs, herbs, and grasses spring up, as in the early stages of recovery after forest has been cleared for farming.

In 1975 patches of advanced secondary forest grew along the Lebir and Aring rivers and for a half-mile or so up the major tributaries of the Lebir, where Malay farmers had cleared fields earlier in the century. In secondary forest, trees are smaller and more uniform in size than in primary forest, and the canopy is thinner and less burdened with vines and epiphytes. By 1975 only a few domesticated fruit trees, such as durians and rambutans, marked where Malay villages had once stood.

The rainforest of the Lebir valley abounded with animal life. Rivers and streams were home to numerous species of fish, turtles, mollusks, and crustaceans as well as otters and water monitor lizards. Countless insects and other invertebrates inhabited the trees, earth, and air. Most of the vertebrates lived in the forest canopy. Birds, bats, squirrels, monkeys, and gibbons were among the animals that fed on the fruit, leaves, and insects in the tree-tops. They in turn became prey to such arboreal predators as civets, bearcats, and leopards. Snakes and various species of lizards, some up to three feet in length, lived in the trees and on the ground. Ground-dwelling herbivores, including elephants, Sambhur deer, barking-deer, mouse-deer, and tapirs, were scattered thinly, reflecting the scarcity of edible plants on the forest floor. Specialized feeders, such as porcupines and scaly anteaters, appeared here and there. Wild pigs, the most numerous of the larger mammals, fed mainly on roots, tubers, and fallen fruit. They moved about the forest in small herds. Bamboo rats—burrowing rodents roughly the size and shape of guinea pigs—were abundant enough along some streams to be a frequent food source for Batek. Tigers, once numerous enough that Batek sometimes lived in tree houses or fortified campsites for protection, were quite rare by the 1970s, but Batek still regarded them as a real danger to the lone hunter or forager.

The climate in lowland Malaysia is hot and humid year round. Seasons are marked not by changes in temperature but by changes in the amount of rainfall, although there is no true dry season in the Peninsula. The northeast monsoon usually strikes Kelantan in November and lasts into January. It brings heavy and continuous rain, as much as fifteen inches per month, and quickly leads to flooding in all the major rivers of the state. This is followed by a relatively dry period in February, March, and April, during which there may be periods of days or occasionally even weeks without precipitation. During the rest of the year, rain is almost a daily occurrence, usually taking the form of localized thunderstorms that strike in the afternoon or early evening. The total rainfall in the Batek area is about 100 inches per year.

The annual pattern of rainfall affected Batek activities both directly and indirectly through its influence on the food supply (K.M. Endicott 1984;

Endicott and Bellwood 1991). The heavy rain and flooding that occur between November and January restricted Batek mobility to a radius of a mile or so from camp, as the forest floor became muddy and slippery and streams were too high and swift to ford or navigate by raft. All methods of fishing became virtually impossible, and supplies of rice and flour were unavailable as traders avoided traveling up the swollen rivers. During the rainy season in the 1970s Kelantan Batek generally split up into small camps and stayed in the headwaters of side-streams, where they subsisted on game, wild tubers, and palm cabbage and pith. Although the staples of the foraging diet, game and wild yams, were available year round, two important food sources, honey and fruit, were seasonal, controlled ultimately by the pattern of rainfall. The relatively dry period following the floods sets off the flowering cycle of the major forest trees, and this in turn determines when the bees make honey and when the fruit trees bear fruit. The honey season normally extends from April to early July. Most of the important fruits ripen between June and September, but some, such as *baŋkoŋ* (*Artocarpus integer;* a relative of the breadfruit), ripen as late as December, and others, such as the durian and its wild relatives (*Durio* spp.), bear fruit twice a year.

According to Batek beliefs, superhuman beings created the rainforest for the Batek to use and will destroy the world if the Batek were ever to leave the forest (K.M. Endicott 1979a; Lye 2004). Batek said that superhuman beings created certain plants for them to eat, others to thatch their shelters, and still others to provide equipment and decorations for their rituals. Batek preferred to stay in the "cool" forest, and they regarded the heat of the outside world as unhealthy. They moved seriously ill people to forest camps and performed curing rituals at night to ensure that conditions were as cool as possible (K.M. Endicott 1979a). Batek associated so closely with the rainforest that they sometimes referred to themselves as *batɛk hɔp,* "forest people."

The Social Environment

In the 1970s the Batek were the only people living permanently in the entire Lebir-Aring river system upstream from the Malay village of Lalok. But the region had not always been so isolated. Since at least as early as the Mon kingdom of Tambralingga (sixth to thirteenth centuries A.D.), centered at Ligor in what is now southern Thailand, the Lebir River formed a trade route between the north and the goldfields of the Tembeling River valley in Pahang (Linehan 1936; Benjamin 1987). Benjamin points out (1987:124) that the term *lebir* means "sea" or "river" in old Mon, and Linehan argues (1936:10) that "Tembeling" is a local rendering of "Tambralingga." Possibly the Thais who conquered Tambralingga in 1280 continued to use the Lebir-Tembeling trade route until the gold deposits gave out.

In the late nineteenth century the Lebir valley became a major refuge for Malays fleeing wars and political upheavals in the state of Pahang (Linehan 1936; Clifford 1961). Clifford estimated that nearly 3,000 Malays, mostly from Pahang, lived on the Lebir in 1895 (1961). The Malays built villages—many consisting of only a few houses—at the mouths of the major tributaries of the Lebir. In the late nineteenth and early twentieth centuries Batek relations with the Malay villagers were ambivalent and changeable. Apparently Batek traded with the Malays when relations were good, but fled from them during periods when local villagers or Malays from outside the area attempted to capture Batek women and children to sell as slaves, killing the men in the process (K.M. Endicott 1983). The Russian explorer Mikluho-Maclay records that in 1875 there were two kinds of Batek: "tame" ones who would camp near the Malays and trade with them and "wild" ones who avoided the villagers entirely (1878b:211–212). After the British abolished slavery in the western states in the 1890s, the threat of slave raiding slowly faded away, and Batek carried on regular trade with Malay villagers. After the completion of the railway between Pahang and the Kelantan coast in 1931 (see the map), Batek periodically traveled to villages along the railway to trade or to seek wage-paying work.

In December 1941 the Japanese army landed on the Kelantan coast and marched down the railway line, eventually capturing the entire peninsula and the island of Singapore. The Batek went into hiding in the depths of the forest. After the war the British colonial government returned but was challenged by Communist guerrillas, mostly from Malaya's Chinese community. The guerrillas operated from forest sanctuaries, some in the limestone hills near the town of Gua Musang on the western border of the Batek area. This insurrection, known as the Emergency, lasted from 1948 to 1960. In order to prevent Malay villagers on the Lebir and Aring rivers from providing food and aid to the Communist terrorists, either willingly or through coercion, the government resettled all Malays in new villages below Lalok village in 1949. This allowed Batek to move into the vacated Aring and upper Lebir rivers, some going as far as the Keniyam and Sat rivers in Pahang, where there were still Malay villagers with whom they could trade forest products for tobacco, cloth, tools, and various foods. These Batek seldom saw Communists and were not bothered by them.

In 1952 the government established the JHEOA to try to win the Orang Asli over to the side of the government in the conflict with the Communists. One of the JHEOA's first acts in Kelantan was to attempt to get the Batek and some neighboring Semaq Beri Orang Asli to settle together at a site above Lalok village and take up agriculture. The Batek stayed for eighteen months, until the government-supplied food ran out, and then immediately returned to the vacant upper reaches of the Lebir, Aring, and Relai rivers to resume mobile foraging (Carey 1976). In the mid-1960s the JHEOA, shifting to a post-Emergency role, established medical posts on the Lebir and Aring and continued sporadically trying to get the Batek to settle down and grow crops.

In the 1970s the only other Orang Asli peoples with whom the Batek had regular contact were the Batek Teh and the Semaq Beri. The Batek Teh are a small splinter group of Mendriq, most of whom live in the Nenggiri River valley to the west. The Batek call them Batek Teh because they use the term *tɘh* to mean "this." They had moved up the Lebir in the early twentieth century and settled at Post Lebir in the late 1960s. The Batek Teh were more experienced at horticulture than the Batek and were much more inclined to cooperate with the JHEOA's plan to settle the Semang and turn them into subsistence and cash crop farmers. The Batek Teh differ from the Batek in language, beliefs and rituals, and in various social practices. Though the two groups interacted at Post Lebir and their children attended school together there, they tended to camp apart and to regard each other with some suspicion. Batek claimed, for example, that some Batek Teh poisoned people they did not like. Nevertheless, a number of marriages took place between the two groups, especially between youngsters who had gone to school together.

The Semaq Beri (which means "forest people" in their language) are a Southern Aslian-speaking, non-Negrito people who, in the twentieth century, inhabited the area south and east of the Tembeling River, in Pahang and Terengganu. They differ greatly from the Batek in language, religion, and social practices, but relations between the two groups are generally cordial. In the 1970s the Semaq Beri economy ranged from swidden farming to hunting and gathering, both supplemented by trade of forest produce (Kuchikura 1987). The Semaq Beri living adjacent to the Batek in the Kelantan–Pahang border area were the most committed to the nomadic foraging way of life. Batek and Semaq Beri freely intermarried—one Semaq Beri man (Peng) and two women had married into the upper Lebir Batek group that we studied in 1975–76.

Of nonaboriginal peoples, Malays were the people with whom Batek had the most extensive contact. Although Malay farmers had been removed from the region in 1949, Batek still had regular interactions with the Malay traders from the villages of Manek Urai and Lalok who made frequent trips up the Lebir by motorboat. Malay officials and employees of the JHEOA also traveled upriver to the Batek, but only sporadically. The cultural gap between Batek and Malays is wide. Malays differ from Batek in physical appearance, language, culture, and, most significantly, in religion: Malays are Muslims, while Batek have their own distinctive religion (K.M. Endicott 1979a). Malays generally look down on Orang Asli, especially Semang, whom they refer to as "savages" (Malay *sakai, pangan*). Many Malays were openly contemptuous of Batek and did not hesitate to ridicule them. Some Malays treated Batek more kindly, but still carried an air of cultural superiority. Batek—and other Orang Asli—called Malays *gob* (outsiders) and generally viewed them with a mixture of resentment, anger, and fear, the last reinforced by the cultural memory of slave raiding. They tried to keep their contacts with Malays as limited in duration and scope as possible. We heard that a few marriages between Malays and Batek had existed in the past, but these seem to have been very rare even when Malay farmers still lived in the area.

Batek were most tolerant of the Malay traders who supplied them with goods and food and sometimes helped them in other ways, for example, by giving them rides in their boats. In the 1970s several groups of traders were vying for "contracts" with the Batek at any given moment, so they tried to be as agreeable to the Batek as possible. This competition also minimized the element of exploitation that had existed in earlier days, when powerful Malay villagers had exercised some degree of monopoly control over Batek trade. Although the relationship between Batek and traders was basically limited to the economic sphere and continued only as long as it was mutually advantageous, Batek seemed to like and trust some of the traders.

Batek were generally less well-disposed toward Malay government officials and employees, whom they saw as meddlers trying to force them to change their way of life. As early as the 1950s the JHEOA had begun trying to convert them to sedentary farming, a way of life the Batek did not enjoy or see as advantageous. Later JHEOA employees began to pressure them to adopt Malay customs and convert to Islam, in short, to cease being Batek. The most persistent agents for change were the school teachers stationed at the one-room school at Post Lebir. Batek spoke affectionately of several of the teachers, but described others as contemptuous and uncaring. Most of the teachers were poorly qualified and resented being posted so far from "civilization." Tensions between Batek and teachers rose and fell, depending on the personalities of the individual teachers, and Batek parents removed their offspring from school whenever they disapproved of the treatment the children were getting.

Despite the social distance between Malays and Batek, a few Malay influences were evident in Batek religion, folklore, and especially in the Batek language, which has absorbed numerous Malay words. Malay gender roles, however, seem to have had little effect on the Batek. Many observers have remarked on the high degree of freedom and independence that marks the lives of Kelantanese Malay women, as shown in their control over the marketing of fish and farm produce, but Kessler (1977) argues that husbands traditionally exerted control over their wives in numerous ways. Certainly the highest prestige sphere of Malay life—religion—was dominated by men (cf. Errington 1990), and the Islamic revival in Malaysia since 1970 eroded women's autonomy in Kelantan and elsewhere (Nagata 1984). Batek in the 1970s knew little of these matters because they had few opportunities to observe the interactions of Malay men and women. However, one thing Batek did know about Malay gender relations was that Malay men could marry more than one wife. We knew of one Batek man who tried to emulate this Malay practice, and the outcome was quite revealing: after a short period of reluctantly sharing her husband with his new wife, the first wife threatened to leave him and get another husband; the man soon caved in and separated from his second wife.

In the 1970s Batek in Kelantan had little direct contact with Malaysia's citizens of Chinese descent, who mostly lived in towns and engaged in business, or with the Indians employed on rubber plantations on the coastal plain. Batek considered Chinese to be slightly more like themselves than

Malays because Chinese were willing to eat pork and monkeys. We knew one old woman who had once been married to a Chinese wood-cutter, and in 1990 one Chinese logger had a Batek wife and another was trying to persuade a Batek woman to marry him. Nonetheless, in the 1970s Chinese and Indians had virtually no cultural influence on the Batek.

Earlier Reports on the Batek

Although scholars had been interested in the Semang since the late nineteenth century (see, e.g., Skeat and Blagden 1906a, 1906b; Schebesta 1928; Evans 1937), the Batek were almost unknown to the scientific community (and even to most other residents of Kelantan) until recently. The first European to encounter Batek was the Russian naturalist-explorer Nikolas Mikluho-Maclay, who went in search of the "aboriginal Melanesian inhabitants" of the Malay Peninsula (i.e., the Semang), then known to Europeans only through the often fabulous reports of Malays. In 1875 he journeyed by boat up the Pahang and Tembeling rivers, crossed over the divide to Kelantan on foot, and rafted down the Lebir River to Kota Bharu on the coast. He encountered Batek on both the Lebir and Aring rivers. The journal of his trip has been lost, but two published articles (Mikluho-Maclay 1878a and 1878b) contain valuable word lists and observations on the Batek way of life at that time. In 1899 W. W. Skeat's "Cambridge University Expedition to the North-Eastern Malay States, and to Upper Perak" traveled up the Lebir and on to the upper Aring River, where they spent several days in contact with some Batek, whom Skeat called "Pangan." He incorporated his rather scanty findings, which are mostly on Batek religious beliefs and practices, and his list of Batek words in his monumental book *Pagan Races of the Malay Peninsula* (Skeat and Blagden 1906a, 1906b).

In 1901 a zoological collector, John Waterstradt, followed Skeat's route to the upper Aring while seeking a way to Mount Tahan, the Peninsula's tallest mountain. He hired some Batek as bearers and guides, but recorded no information about them except that they were strong and healthy looking and not troubled by skin diseases (Waterstradt 1902:5).

There are no records of further contact between outsiders and Batek until the 1950s when the JHEOA tried to settle them at Post Lebir. Although the threat of slave raiding diminished in the early twentieth century, Batek seem to have avoided contact with outsiders whenever possible, fleeing and hiding at their approach (Needham 1976; Lye 2004:103, 107). Then, in 1970, Geoffrey Benjamin, a linguistically-trained anthropologist who had done extensive fieldwork with the Temiar Senoi, spent a week with Batek then living on the Aring River. Benjamin gathered preliminary information on a wide range of sociological and cultural topics, compiled a long Batek word list, and worked out a basic grammar of the Batek language.[3]

Our Fieldwork

Our acquaintance with the Batek spans more than three decades. Between January 1971 and May 1973, Kirk spent twelve months living with Batek and Batek Teh on the middle Lebir, Aring, and Relai rivers and visiting Mendriq at Sungai Lah (Kelantan) and Batek, Batek Nong, and Semaq Beri in Pahang. His research focused on the economic systems and social organization of the groups, but he also gathered some information on their religions. Between September 1975 and June 1976 we both lived for five months with the Batek of the upper Lebir River, with Karen focusing her research on gender relations and child rearing. That period of fieldwork forms the main basis for this book. Kirk returned alone for a month in 1981 to investigate the Batek's responses to extensive logging in the Lebir River valley. Kirk also spent five months with the upper Aring Batek in 1990, joined by Karen at the beginning and end of the study, looking at social changes, including changes in gender concepts and male–female relations. In July and August 2004, Kirk made brief visits to several groups of Batek in Kelantan and Pahang.

Our research procedure in 1975–76 was to camp with Batek, moving with them whenever they moved, and to collect as much information as we could by talking with people, observing, and participating in everyday life. There were no roads into the Lebir area until the late 1970s. We made three trips in by boat, each time bringing enough supplies—including food, medicines, films, audiotapes, notebooks, etc.—to last for the planned duration, after which we caught a prearranged boat ride out or had some Batek bring us out on a bamboo raft.

We lived in a small nylon tent with a rain fly and a zip-in screen, which offered a cozy refuge from insects and the elements, but not always from water that sometimes made its way in through the bottom seams of the tent during heavy rainstorms. We usually hired a few people to build us a low platform to give the tent a level base and raise it above the damp forest floor. The front edge of the platform formed a convenient seat. We slept on a thin foam pad with a few cotton blankets. Our packsacks, food, medicines, and equipment lined the sides of the tent. A campfire, a clothesline, two plastic buckets, some cooking and eating utensils, and a simple latrine back in the bushes completed our household furnishings.

Despite keeping our equipment to a minimum, we were greatly overburdened compared to Batek, who could pack their belongings in minutes and did not hesitate to move camp on what seemed to us the merest whim. To us the most dreaded words in the Batek language were *simpεn pəkakas; hεm jok*, "pack your things; we're moving." It took at least an hour for us to pack, and even though we carried large packs ourselves, we had to hire others to carry our excess belongings. Occasionally, we suspect, Batek shortened a planned move because of the extra burden of lugging our things.

We lived as an independent household, much like a childless Batek couple, but we were an unusually inept couple by Batek standards. Although both of us were experienced campers, Batek regarded our outdoor skills as laughable. We quickly fell into the role of camp buffoons; our attempts to chop down trees, for example, became merry social events. Probably some Batek tolerated us only because of our amusement value. A Batek friend once jokingly called us their "toy" (*?ɔt*). We learned to use our ineptitude to our advantage, however. For instance, when we had trouble lighting our fire on damp mornings, we would simply fumble with the firewood and embers for a few minutes until a child would come over and build it for us, usually tossing off a remark like, "Let me do that. I'm a Batek." We cooked our own food, usually having three meals per day: crackers with jam and tea in the morning, crackers at midday, and rice with canned fish or curry in the evening. Batek, by contrast, usually had only two meals each day: leftovers in the morning and a major hot meal in the late afternoon.

We dressed in shorts, tee-shirts, and rubber thong-sandals in camp. When trekking into the surrounding forest, we put on long pants and high canvas "jungle boots," which are meant to protect the feet from thorns and leeches. Like Batek, we bathed in the stream every afternoon, and we washed our clothes every few days, sometimes having to dry them over the fire because there were so few sunny spots in the forest. The main difference between our routine and that of the Batek was that we did not spend time gathering or hunting food. Our work, as one Batek friend said, was writing, and indeed writing was what we did most of the time.

In one major respect we not only departed from Batek custom but violated a basic tenet of their moral code: we did not share our food on a daily basis. Kirk had experimented with various living arrangements in his earlier fieldwork and had decided that for our purposes it was best to bring in our own food and keep it separate from the Batek food supply. We did not want to distort the Batek economy, which we were studying, by drawing on the already limited Batek food supply. (We did sample the various foods they brought in, however.) Knowing that to withhold food when others are hungry is a serious offense among the Batek, we discussed our planned procedure at length with the people in the first camp before embarking on it. They understood that we were incapable of collecting our own food and accepted our general rationale. To compensate for our stinginess, we gave food to everyone at the beginning and end of each stint of fieldwork, being careful not to begin collecting economic data until the gift food had been used up, and we gave small amounts in emergencies, as when everyone in camp was sick. Fortunately their food-getting efforts were quite successful during the period of our research, and they seldom asked us for food.

In addition, we gave people nonfood gifts such as tobacco, medicines, cloth, and flashlight batteries, and we paid them in cash for helping us move and for building our platforms. We felt guilty about giving tobacco, but it was the item people desired above all else. In 1990, Kirk tried substituting toothbrushes, toothpaste, and soap, but was chided by a Batek friend. "You should keep bringing us tobacco," he said. "We can buy toothbrushes ourselves." We also hired a youngster to bring us firewood and water every day, rotating the job among the whole group to spread the money around. We helped them in any other small way we could, for example, by conveying their wishes and complaints to the JHEOA. It is impossible to live and do research in a small group without affecting their economy in some way, but we think the distortions we introduced were small and obvious enough that we could take account of them.

We communicated with Batek in a mixture of Batek and Malay. Both of us had learned simple "bazaar" Malay, and Kirk already had a beginning knowledge of Batek from his previous fieldwork. We studied Batek intensively as we went along and achieved a basic working facility in speaking and understanding.

Like the Batek economy, our method of data collection was opportunistic. Batek activities varied daily, and we followed up whatever looked most interesting or filled a gap in our findings. If nothing special was happening, we would hang around camp and watch the children, observe any work or crafts people were doing, ask questions, and work on the language. We paid special attention to interactions between men and women, trying to discern whether anyone was controlling or exploiting anyone else.

Every few days one or both of us would follow a work party on an expedition of tuber digging, fishing, hunting, honey gathering, rattan collecting, or the like. On such outings we took photographs and made detailed notes on how the work process was done and how long the different phases of the activity took. The most systematic data collection we did was to compile daily work diaries of all adult (over age fourteen) members of each camp we lived in. These records included what each person had done that day; the names of their companions; the amounts of any food or other materials obtained; what foods they and their children had consumed, including snacks eaten outside camp; and who they got their food from if they didn't get it themselves. We tried to get this data every day, except when the group was living on rations supplied by us or by the JHEOA. But sometimes this was not practical, as on days when we made a long move. As far as possible, we noted when people went out in the morning and when they returned in the afternoon or evening, thus getting a measure of time expended, and we questioned them about everything they had done.

Getting the data when people returned was sometimes difficult, for the daily rainstorm often struck about the time they got back, and occasionally someone—usually a hunter—would return after dark. It was an advantage that there were two of us, so one could write (and hold the umbrella or flashlight) while the other weighed the food and asked the questions. Despite the highly intrusive nature of this routine, Batek got into the spirit of it. Sometimes people would actually yell across the camp for us to come weigh something, as they were hungry and eager to eat it. On the other hand, Pales once teased Kirk for being rude when he rushed up to weigh a bundle of monkey meat. "Can't you give me a chance to have a cigarette before you ask me questions?" he asked. People were keenly interested in the weight of the foods they brought in, but seemed satisfied with the knowledge for its own sake; we never heard the kind of "I got more than you did" comparisons that we would have expected in American society.

We cannot overstate the value of this systematic snooping into people's lives. Compiling work diaries forced us to find out what everyone was doing every day and thus gave us a more balanced picture than if we had just recorded whatever caught our attention.

Batek generally thought of us as friends despite our intrusions into their lives. During our first few months with the upper Lebir group, people treated us with some formality, perhaps thinking we were some kind of officials. They called Kirk *tuan* (Malay for "sir," "mister") and Karen *keneh tuan* ("sir's wife"). But after they realized that we had no authority or official connection with Malaysian governmental agencies, they began calling us by our first names, which is appropriate for adults without children. They referred to us as "friends/relatives" (*kabɛn*), but did not adopt us into their kinship system, as tribal peoples often do with anthropologists. Socially we were treated as a young married couple. The main incongruity by Batek standards was that Karen was already in her twenties and had not yet had a baby, which caused some puzzlement. Since she was also asking a lot to questions about reproduction, some women began to wonder whether we even knew how to make babies. One day Tanyogn took Kirk aside. "Has Karen started to menstruate yet?" she asked.

We cannot know how the Batek really felt about us, but can only say that they treated us with great kindness, respect, and understanding, and they professed to miss us enormously when we were away. Some individuals seemed to regard us with genuine affection, which we reciprocated. Most people were kind enough not to treat us as the idiots we no doubt appeared to be. Some people simply tolerated us, and a few seemed to avoid us, for reasons we never found out. But many people—especially Tanyogn and her husband, Langsat—took an interest in us, took us with them when they moved, and generally looked after us. We always felt safe when living with the Batek. Once when we were camped on a tributary of the upper Lebir, we heard a tiger growling nearby. We hurriedly asked our friend Pales what we should do if the tiger came into camp. "You should climb a tree," he said. "But we aren't good at climbing trees like you are," Kirk responded. "In that case, you should just go inside your tent and sit," he said. "There are people here who know spells that will keep the tiger out of camp." We heard nothing more from the tiger.

We felt, and still feel, great affection for the Batek and admiration for their ability to live in conditions we found to be trying. Of course, personalities spanned a broad spectrum (see Schebesta 1928 for lively descriptions of some Jahai Semang individuals), and we liked some people better than others. We never felt there was a gulf between us, however, despite our language limitations, and we did not think of them as "primitives" or as the exotic "other." We thought of them as our friends.

In this book we present some of our findings, focusing on male–female relations. We explore Batek ideas about the sexes and examine how these ideas were acted out in everyday interactions between males and females of all ages. We look especially closely at the social and economic activities—including marriage, work, and child rearing—that supported, reproduced, and expressed relations between the sexes. And finally, in the last chapter, we attempt to explain why Batek gender relations took the form they did.

Notes

[1] The large imbalance in the ratio of males to females—1.43 to 1—was most likely a random sampling effect due to the small overall population size. According to statistical tests, in a group this small this ratio could occur by chance alone at least 95 percent of the time. Sex ratios fluctuated continuously in the populations of the different river valleys between 1971 and 1990. Sometimes the sex ratios were balanced, and sometimes females were in the majority (cf. Gomes 1982 on the demography of the Jahai Semang).

[2] For a detailed study of the Batek natural environment and their views of it, see Lye 1997:143–73; 2004.

[3] Benjamin encouraged Kirk to do his doctoral research on the Batek and generously made his findings available to him, even going so far as to drill him on the pronunciation and transcription of Batek words.

Chapter 2

Batek Views of the Sexes

Anthropologists generally use the term *gender* to refer to the culturally defined categories, meanings, and behavioral expectations that particular groups impose on the biological sexes.[1] Although most people regard their own society's gender concepts as "natural" and thus universal, ethnographic studies show that different cultures have different ideas about the nature of males and females, the kinds of behaviors that are appropriate to each sex, and even the number and kinds of gender identities that exist. Some societies recognize more that two genders. For example, some Native Americans distinguished a category of biological males who dressed and behaved in some respects like women—usually termed *berdache* in the literature—as a separate gender alongside males and females (see, e.g., Williams 1986). When confronted with another culture's very different views of the sexes, we see how arbitrary and culture-bound such notions of "human nature" are.

Many different gender concepts are found among Southeast Asian peoples. Errington points out that in Island Southeast Asia there are at least two major ways of conceptualizing the differences between males and females. One emphasizes the similarities between the sexes, viewing the differences as trivial. The other pictures the sexes as complementary opposites, part of a dualistic cosmology in which the well-being of people and the world depends on a harmonious balance between opposites (right-left, sky-earth, sun-moon, male-female, etc.), neither of which is regarded as inferior to the other (1990:39–40, 54–56; see also Reid 1988). A third pattern is also widespread. Malays and other Islamic peoples of Southeast Asia generally view men as more rational and more in control of their emotions than women, which is seen as a justification for men exercising control over women to prevent them from succumbing to their passions (see, e.g., Siegel 1969; Ong 1987; Peletz 1996).

The Batek had another view of gender. They saw men and women as being different in various ways, but did not regard these differences as making either sex superior to the other.

25

Gender was not a frequent topic of conversation among Batek. They, like most other peoples, took their views of the sexes for granted—as obvious and not needing discussion. They did not have beliefs, such as menstrual blood is polluting to men (a common idea in Melanesia, for example), that required them to pay continual attention to the sexes of their companions. Nor did they have adolescent initiation rituals, as many societies do, that explicitly articulate their cultural concepts of the nature of the sexes and the roles they should play in society. We did not hear derogatory stereotypes of either sex. Batek gender concepts revolved mainly around their ideas about the physiological differences between the sexes. To Batek, gender was just one of many qualities of people—including personality, position in the kinship system, age, and ethnic identity—that might be relevant in particular situations. Gender was a focus of *our* interest rather than theirs.

Because Batek did not spontaneously articulate a set of gender concepts, we had to assemble their views of the sexes from diverse cultural domains, ranging from myths to body decoration. In so doing, we realize that we risked imputing a degree of coherence to those ideas that is alien to Batek thinking. Also, by asking questions about what men and women do, about the sex of mythological beings, and so on, we may have led people to focus more on differences between the sexes than on similarities. Therefore, as you read what follows, bear in mind that "Batek views of the sexes" did not form a single topic for the Batek and that notions of differences between men and women were only minor features of their thinking about people in general.

Gender in Social Classifications

Batek recognized just two genders, male (*təmkal*) and female (*yalʉw*). (*Təmkal* also means "man" and *yalʉw* means "woman.") They applied these categories to humans, animals, some superhuman beings, and occasionally to other things, such as plants. The Batek, unlike the Malays, did not have a named gender category for homosexuals. Batek knew about homosexuality among outsiders, but said they knew of no homosexual Batek.

The major social classifications used by the Batek—age categories, names, and kinship terms—made only minimal distinctions by gender. Before puberty both boys and girls were called simply "children" (*kɛn* or *ʔawã*). There were no words for "boy" or "girl" as such. If gender distinctions were necessary, people said "male-child" (*ʔawã* *təmkal*) or "female-child" (*ʔawã* *yalʉw*). When youngsters begin to show physical signs of puberty, they became known as "young men" (*jəmagaʔ*) or "young women" (*kədah*). The change in terminology was, in fact, the only cultural marker of the onset of puberty. There were no puberty ceremonies or initiation rites for either sex. The terms *jəmagaʔ* and *kədah* applied until a person had a child, when he or she became known as *mabɛr*. Spouses who never had children were usually known throughout adulthood as *jɛmagaʔ* and *kədah*. Elderly men and women alike were known by a single term, "old person" (*bakɛs*).

Personal names of men and women showed some degree of gender distinction. Everyone received or took several different names during their lives (see also Lye 1997). Approximately a month after birth, the midwife or parents gave the baby a "true name" (*kənmɔ̃h bətɔl*) or "flesh name" (*kənmɔ̃h sec*), usually the name of the side-stream near which the baby was born, an animal or plant seen near the birth site, or even the name of some food eaten by the mother around the time of the birth. Although many such names were not associated exclusively with one gender, a few, such as the name "Flower" (*Bungaʔ*) and names referring to specific species of flowers, were used only for girls. At adolescence Batek often took "outsider names" (*kənmɔ̃h gob*), which they used in discourse with outsiders, to avoid revealing their "true" names, and to some extent in discourse with other Batek. These outsider names, which were usually Malay words for common things in the environment (e.g., *Batu*, "Stone," and *Dusun*, "Orchard") did not fall into clear-cut gender categories. Parents were called by teknonyms: father (*ʔɛy*) or mother (*naʔ*) of a particular child. The teknonym usually included the name of the oldest living child, regardless of the child's sex. For example, the father and mother of Tekoy, a girl, were normally called *ʔɛy* Tekoy and *naʔ* Tekoy.

Gender was of limited scope and importance in Batek kinship terminology. Only eight of twenty terms of reference specified gender, and all of these referred to married couples: mother (*naʔ*) and father (*paʔ*), grandmother (*yaʔ*) and grandfather (*taʔ*), aunt (*bəʔ*) and uncle (*bah*), wife (*kəneh*) and husband (*kəsuy*) (see the Appendix for all the kinship terms). The terms for siblings and cousins distinguished relative age rather than gender. Older siblings and cousins were called *toʔ*, while younger siblings and cousins were called *bɛr*. Similarly terms for in-laws made no gender distinctions.

Batek kinship terminology was cognatic or bilateral, using the same terms for maternal and paternal relatives. Cognatic terminologies suggest that social ties through one's mother and father are equally important. Significantly, throughout Southeast Asia there appears to be an association between cognatic kinship terminologies and gender equality (Errington 1990).

Gender in Origin Stories

Societies with substantial inequality between the sexes commonly have myths explaining why this is so and why, at least from the point of view of men, it is right and good (e.g., Murphy and Murphy 1974; White 1974; Brown and Buchbinder 1976; Gregor 1977).

Batek did not have a myth that overtly discusses gender. But their story of the origin of humans subtly reveals some aspects of their concept of males and females. Different Batek informants gave us slightly differing versions of

the story, but all were consistent in their basic features. The following ver-
sion—the most coherent we obtained—came from an Aring River man.

> Once two superhuman brothers, Allah (the elder) and Ta' Allah (the
> younger), came to earth. Each took some soil and molded it into the
> shape of a human body. They called out the names of the body parts as
> they made them. The older brother created a man with soil from the place
> where the sun comes up, and the younger brother produced a woman
> with soil from where the sun goes down. But the bodies were not alive
> and could not stand up. So Allah went to see Tohan [Malay *Tuhan*,
> "God"], who lived where the sun goes down, while Ta' Allah stayed to
> guard the lifeless bodies. Allah asked Tohan to give him some life-soul,
> and after much persuasion, Tohan agreed. He gave Allah some water life-
> soul, which was immortal. Allah took the water life-soul in his hands, but
> on the way back he tripped and spilled it. Tohan quickly spat on the place
> where the water life-soul fell, drew it back to himself, and hid it under his
> seat. After looking for the water life-soul for seven days, Allah went back
> to Tohan and asked for more, but Tohan refused. So Allah borrowed
> some wind life-soul from a banana plant. He took it in a bottle back to the
> inert bodies and blew some of it on their heads and some on their chests,
> over the heart. The bodies came to life. But the wind life-soul was mortal,
> so now humans, like banana plants, die and are replaced by their children.
>
> Later these first humans married, following the instructions of Tohan,
> in order to have children. The children married each other and likewise
> produced children until another superhuman being came down and told
> them that it was forbidden for brothers and sisters to marry. After that
> people did not marry relatives closer than first cousin.[2]

This story suggests that men and women are distinct in shape but essentially the same in composition, having been formed of the same material and
animated by the same kind of soul. It is tempting to see the story's associations
of male with east and female with west in terms of symbolic analyses of cultures that systematically link male with east, life, and goodness while linking
female with west, death, and evil (see Hertz 1960). But not all versions of the
Batek creation story made those connections. Moreover, Batek did not imbue
east and west with strong positive and negative connotations, although some
people said that the land of the dead is located in the west. The division of labor
in the origin story—the older brother forming the man and the younger brother
forming the woman—was a more consistent feature of different versions of the
story. In Batek stories, the younger of two siblings is usually considered smarter
and more capable than the older. The origin story may not be suggesting that
women are superior to men, but neither is it suggesting that women are inferior.

Physiology of Gender

Batek considered the souls of males and females to be the same. In addition to having a wind life-soul (*ŋawaʔ*), both men and women have a shadow-

soul (*bayaŋ*), which is associated with individual consciousness and leaves the body temporarily in dreams and trance and permanently at death. But Batek believed that men and women are physically different in several ways, beyond the obvious dimorphism of their bodies.

According to the Batek, men's breath (*napas*) is stronger than women's, a difference mentioned primarily in explaining why men are better blowpipe hunters than women (see chapter 4). Both men and women said that men can blow darts harder and further because they have stronger breath than women. The distinction between male and female breath strength was not elaborated into an evaluative statement about men and women, however. It was regarded as just another physiological difference. Lebir River Batek did not prohibit women from blowpipe hunting, and some women did hunt for fun. But they were said to be able to hit only squirrels and birds, not monkeys, which live higher in the trees.

Similarly, Batek sometimes said that men are stronger than women, especially in the arms, to explain why men are better at climbing tall trees. As one woman expressed it, "women cannot arrive at the top." This did not prevent them from climbing smaller trees and vines, however, which young women did with ease. Once, while on a fishing trip, a young mother, Dusun, climbed about twenty feet up a vine and swung on to a limb of a tree just to get some red flowers. Such feats were commonplace, and even young girls and boys were good climbers. Greater upper-body strength of men was also given as the reason why men rather than women took on the job of chopping down large trees. But women did not hesitate to cut down small trees. By Western standards, Batek women were amazingly strong and agile.

Batek also believed that the blood of men and women smells different— though not better or worse than each other. The reason for the difference in smells, according to informants, was that women do not eat meat or salt during their menstrual periods. Menstrual blood, they said, has yet a different smell from ordinary female blood. They said it smells bad, like raw meat. Therefore some Batek treated menstrual (and postpartum) blood in the same way they treated the blood of certain animals (e.g., pig-tailed macaques, long-tailed macaques, tortoises): they prohibited the blood from going into streams. They worried that the thunder-god, Gobar, and the underworld deity, Ya', would be offended by the odor of such blood and would cause a thunderstorm or flood to punish the offenders. Lebir River Batek women did not observe this prohibition, although they were well aware that some other peoples, such as the Batek Teh, were very strict about keeping menstrual blood out of streams.

None of the Batek groups, however, considered menstrual blood to be polluting to humans, and menstruating women were not feared, isolated, or shunned. Menstruating women went about their normal activities and were also free to perform the blood sacrifice and other rituals (see below). They continued to sleep in their houses with their husbands and children. Some people said sexual intercourse was prohibited during menstruation but did not seem to regard it as a serious offense. The clothes women wore during menstruation could also be worn at any other time; they were not polluted by their contact with menstrual blood. Women used old loincloths to absorb menstrual blood, then washed them for re-use; where women observed restrictions about menstrual blood entering rivers, the washing was done on dry land.

All Batek women observed a number of food taboos during their menstrual periods and for a month or two after giving birth. Menstruating women ate only foods classified as bland, including wild tubers, fruits, leafy vegetables, palm cabbage, rice, flour, and medicines. They abstained from eating foods classified as sweet or flavorful, including meat, fish, *pɔnaceʔ*, bee larvae, honey, cassava, salt, sugar, chili, peppers, curry, oil, bread, milk, and tea. According to Batek, if a woman ate any of the prohibited foods during her menstrual period, she would suffer dizziness.

Despite the food restrictions, menstruating women did not go hungry, as they were free to eat the staples of the Batek diet. Some menstruating women occasionally grumbled when there was plenty of meat in camp at a time when they were avoiding it. But, the menstrual prohibition against eating meat cannot be interpreted as a way for men to reserve the greater share of protein foods for themselves. People explicitly stated that when women were not menstruating, they ate larger portions of meat than men in order to make up for the times when they couldn't eat it. We once noticed that a man, Daun, was preparing to go hunting unusually early in the morning. He explained that his wife had just finished having her period, and she was hungry for meat.

Batek seemed to regard both menarche—the onset of menstruation—and the passage into menopause pragmatically. They said that spells and wild plant medicines could bring on the start of menstruation. One fourteen-year-old girl was said to have taken a medicine, prepared from a root, to induce menstruation, and within two months she had begun to menstruate. Menarche was not marked with ceremonies or puberty rites, but it did signal a change in a girl's classification from the category of prepubescent *awãʔ* (child) to the category of *kədah* (young woman)—although other signs of physical maturation might have already qualified her as *kədah*. The passage into menopause was equally simple: Batek reported that as women age, they stop menstruating and can no longer bear children. Menopause was not thought to otherwise affect women physically or transform them socially, as is the case in many other societies. The Batek term for an old person, *bakɛs*, was not tied to menopause; rather women and men became known as *bakɛs* whenever their health, appearance, and behavior made the term seem appropriate.

Expressions of Gender in Clothing and Body Decoration

Batek clothing, while minimal, differed slightly for men and women. In the 1970s, the usual outfit for men was a loincloth made from a piece of sarong material or, the modern equivalent, swimming trunks, both of which they obtained from Malay traders. Before they had access to woven cloth, people made loincloths from barkcloth, which they still knew how to make in 1975–76, although they seldom did it by then. Batek did not wear animal skins or other animal parts, except occasionally monkey bones as hunting charms. People said that Batek once wore animal skins, but a superhuman being came and told them not to, because the smell would drive game away. Men also wore a single-strand rattan waistband, from which they hung their bush-knives and quivers of hunting darts. They sometimes wore plaited arm-bands, made from rattan or black fungus rhizomes, and inserted flowers or fragrant leaves into them. Some men had bought shoes, shirts, and trousers, which they usually reserved for wearing on trading trips to Malay villages. (By 2004, shirts and trousers had become the most common form of dress for men, even in the forest.) Men kept their hair short, sometimes shaving it completely off to rid themselves of lice. Most Batek men did not have much facial hair, although a few grew mustaches or sparse beards.

In the 1970s, women wore loincloths held up by long plaited rattan belts, *nεm*, which they wrapped around their hips ten to twenty times. (When women plaited new belts, they gave their husbands or children pieces of their old belts to wear.) Women often wore sarongs as skirts over their loincloths. Tanyogn said that Tohan wanted Batek women to wear *nεm* under their sarongs even when they were in towns. In the presence of Malays most women pulled their sarongs up to cover their otherwise bare breasts. (In recent years, women living where they had frequent contact with outsiders normally kept their breasts covered at all times.) Women often wore bracelets of woven pandanus leaves or fungus rhizomes. They also made a variety of necklaces, belts, and bracelets for medicinal or purely decorative purposes. Women left their hair a bit longer than men, and some cut a short fringe across the forehead. Unlike men, women seldom shaved their heads even when plagued by lice, preferring instead to help each other remove them by hand.

Batek beautified themselves in several ways. Some women tattooed lines across their foreheads or across their wrists by pricking charcoal paste into the skin with a thorn. Women—and occasionally men—painted lines and dots on their foreheads with white lime paste and charcoal. Following a Malay custom, some women and a few men filed their teeth down to a uniform line, though most people did not consider this worth the trouble or pain. All women, but not men, had their ears pierced so they could wear flowers, rolled-up fragrant leaves, or even cigarettes in the holes. Even though all women underwent ear piercing, it was not considered a puberty rite or marker. Girls decided for themselves when they were ready to have it done, usually in late childhood. Either a man or a woman could do the piercing, using a porcupine quill and reciting magical spells to prevent infection. Many women and a few men also pierced their nasal septums to sport leaves or quills. Women frequently and men occasionally wore decorated bamboo combs in their hair at the back of the head. Both women and men made the

Batek often dressed up just for fun when the forest trees were in full flower. Here Chinloy and her husband Kawun wear identical headdresses of flowers on a bark band, and both have porcupine quills inserted through their nasal septums. Chinloy has a typical design painted on her forehead with charcoal and lime paste.

combs, which they often gave to each other as gifts. Carved designs on the combs represented leaves, fruits, stems, and other forms inspired by the plant world around them. During the flower season most Batek—women and men alike—adorned themselves with colorful forest flowers, sometimes making elaborate headdresses that covered the entire head. Both women and men wore necklaces and bracelets obtained through trade.

Body decorations worn in ritual were similar for both sexes. During all-night singing sessions, which might culminate in trancing and communication with the superhuman beings, both men and women donned bandoliers of fragrant leaves, mainly wild gingers, and wore flowers or fragrant leaves in their waistbands and hair. People said these decorations were pleasing to the superhuman beings because they are what the superhumans themselves wear. The good smells of the flowers and leaves were also thought to attract the superhuman beings to come down and listen to the singing.

Batek believed that the superhuman beings prescribed particular decorations for each sex. The rule was that only women could wear bunches of flowers in their ears, and only men could wear flowers in their armbands. These flowers were considered markers of the wearer's gender. These gender-distinguishing decorations could be worn at any time, depending on a person's own wishes, but they had to be worn by the dead. The Batek said that if a corpse wore an inappropriate gender marker, when the shadow-soul (*bayaŋ*) of the deceased went to the afterworld, Tohan would be angry. Corpses were "buried"—usually on a platform in a tree—together with personal possessions: usually blowpipes and dart quivers for men and bamboo combs and flutes for women.

Infants and young children did not usually wear clothes or adornments. However, some parents enjoyed dressing their young children in waistbands or beaded belts, the beads for which were obtained through trade. Older children and adults always covered their genitals, even while bathing or swimming. People said that children begin to wear clothes when they acquire a sense of modesty, usually at about four or five years of age.

Gender in Religion

Batek religion was an all-encompassing set of beliefs, rituals, and behavioral regulations enforced by superhuman beings (*hala? ?asal*) (K.M. Endicott 1979a, 1979c; Lye 2004). According to Batek beliefs, the *hala? ?asal* populate the three linked realms of the universe: the earth, the upperworld, and the underworld. The earth is a disk of land surrounded by sea. The underworld is a sea. The upperworld is a solid layer above the sky. Stone pillars—probably modeled on the limestone buttes that rise dramatically from the forest floor at various places—connect the earth and upperworld. The sun and moon circle the earth, passing through the underworld and upperworld. In some stories, the moon is described as male, married to a large star, and the unmarried sun is female.

Hala? ?asal control natural processes, such as weather and fruit seasons, and enforce various prohibitions. Humans communicate with the superhuman beings through dreams, trance, songs, and rituals. Batek believed that their well-being depended on their performing certain rituals and following the patterns of behavior laid down for them by the superhuman beings.

Batek conceptualized some *hala? ?asal* as males, some as females, some as both, and some as unspecified in gender. Several superhuman beings were named and individualized enough in Batek stories to be termed deities, but even in these cases gender was not always indicated. (Batek third-person pronouns do not distinguish gender, so people could talk about people and beings without specifying their gender.) The creative roles of superhumans were not tied exclusively to one gender or the other. For example, there were numerous versions of the story of how solid matter and water from the primordial sea became separated to form the first land (K.M. Endicott 1979a; Lye 2004). In some versions the creator being took the form of a huge turtle, Labi?, who rose from beneath the primordial sea, and in others it was a sandpiper bird, Kawaw Kədidi?, who came down from the upperworld. Labi? was said to be female (Lye 2004), but the sex of Kawaw Kedidi? was unspecified. However, Allah and Ta' Allah, the superhumans who created the first humans, were both pictured as male.

Tohan, the creator being who sends and retrieves life-souls, was usually described as male. But displaying a Batek tendency to conceptualize *hala?* *?asal* as married couples, some informants said Tohan has a wife who looks just like him and is also called Tohan.

The genders of the other two important deities—Gobar, the thunder-god, and Ya' or Naga', the underworld deity—varied in different versions of the stories about them. Batek usually talked as though Gobar is a single male, but Gobar was sometimes described as two brothers, a married couple, and a brother and sister pair. One informant said Gobar wears a plaited waistband, which is a woman's garment, as well as a shirt, a man's garment.

Stories of Gobar's time on earth in human form depicted him as a young man (or two brothers) who ate tubers dug for him by his aunt. While Gobar was still on earth, two superhuman sisters built a huge lean-to shelter that turned to stone and became Batu Kenyam, a stone pillar connecting the earth to the upperworld. Gobar climbed Batu Kenyam and made his home in a cave halfway up the pillar. From there he unleashes thunderstorms to punish people who break certain prohibitions and sends diseases to people who commit sexual transgressions. In addition, Gobar is responsible for guarding the fruit flowers on Batu Kenyam and sending them—or ordering other *hala? ?asal* to send them—to earth for the fruit season, an interesting pairing of a male character with themes of fertility. The female characters in the stories—the aunt and the two sisters—carry out tasks that are chiefly, though not exclusively, associated with women in Batek society, such as digging tubers and building lean-tos. Those characters and the work they did in the myths helped to establish and maintain the cosmos: the sisters created one of the major cosmic structures, Batu Kenyam, and, according to some Batek, when Gobar ascended the stone pillar, his aunt descended into the earth to become the underworld deity, who controls floods that well up from the underground sea.

Like Gobar, the underworld deity has more than one image and identity. The Aring River Batek generally pictured the underworld deity as an old woman called Ya', "Grandmother." Some informants identified her as Gobar's aunt, but others said she is his wife. The Lebir River Batek, on the other hand, used the term Ya' in incantations, but described the deity as a giant snake or dragon (*naga?*), a common image in the traditional beliefs of Southeast Asian peoples. (One well-known shaman said the reason Batek do not eat snakes is because Gobar's aunt became one when she became a *naga?*.) Informants sometimes spoke of the *naga?* as a married couple, and some said there were numerous *naga?* of both sexes. Whichever image they held, Batek believed that the underworld deity helps Gobar punish transgressors of prohibitions by unleashing floodwaters around the offenders while Gobar sends thunderstorms to blow trees down on them. As Ya', the deity releases the floods from underground by digging up through the earth with her digging stick. As a *naga?*, the deity opens a fissure to the underground sea by shifting its position beneath the earth.

Ambiguities in the gender of the thunder-god and the underworld deity preclude seeing Batek ideas about Gobar and Ya' as forming a clear symbolic opposition between a superior male sky deity and a subordinate female deity of the underworld, as, for example, Schärer does for the Ngaju Dayaks of Borneo (1963). Such a symbolic opposition does exist among the western Semang (Schebesta 1928, 1957; Sanday 1981), but in Batek cosmology gender connotations of the upperworld and underworld were more varied. Batek thought both the upperworld and the underworld are populated by numerous *hala? ?asal* of both sexes. Batu Kenyam, the stone pillar connecting the earth and upperworld, was associated both with the male Gobar and the female sisters who created it. (The Batek did not make the rather obviously phallic pillar a symbol of masculinity.) Batek did not view the upperworld as better than the underworld. Both were associated with destruction and fertility. Gobar can unleash punitive storms from above; Ya'/Naga' can unleash floods from below. Gobar was associated with fruit blossoms, and the underworld deity was associated with wild tubers. In short, Batek cosmic realms did not divide neatly into male and female, superior and subordinate, good and bad.

Gender in Myths and Stories

Like most nonliterate societies, the Batek had a large body of oral traditions of various types, from myths to folktales (see Lye 2004). The protagonists of the stories included superhuman beings, in human or animal forms, and ordinary men and women. The actions depicted ranged from magical to mundane.

Most Batek stories treated gender and male–female relations only in passing or not at all. For example, a series of stories concerned the origins of the basic elements of Batek culture, such as their knowledge of fire making and cooking. These practices were usually portrayed as having been introduced to the Batek by superhuman beings in the form of forest animals. One brief story tells how the Batek learned to dig tubers, the mainstay of the foraging diet: when the original couple became hungry, they simply dug in the ground for tubers. The Batek story reflected the reality that both men and women do this work. Similarly, women and men appeared in other Batek stories, and the activities of these story characters were consistent with real-life gender roles. Often the protagonists were married couples, although pairs of brothers and pairs of sisters played leading roles in some stories. Taken as a whole, Batek tales suggested that the Batek did not use myth to privilege one gender over the other.

Religious Expertise

Religious expertise could be developed by anyone who was interested in religious matters. Neither men nor women as groups were considered to be the guardians of religious knowledge or the experts on religion. Children learned about Batek religion by hearing songs and stories, participating in rituals, being taught the prohibitions, and asking questions. Dreams were also an important source of religious knowledge, including knowledge of songs and medicines. People considered dreams to be communications from the superhuman beings who guided Batek life, so everyone's dreams were taken seriously. Some people thought more deeply than others about religious matters, and they became the ones to whom others deferred when in doubt about religious questions. But any man or woman was welcome to express his or her understandings. Frequently individuals put forth very different views of the same matter during discussions.

Both men and women could become shamans (*hala?*; that is, like superhuman beings), either by studying with a practicing shaman or by learning from superhuman beings through dreams. People who acquired some religious knowledge, including songs and spells, were considered "a little bit *hala?*." For example, one Batek woman was a *hala? ?angin*, a "wind shaman." When a strong wind hit the camp, she would shout to the superhuman beings above to remember their friends down here and stop the wind. People believed in her power to influence the wind. Fully expert, "true" shamans (*hala? bətɔl*) could go into trance to send their shadow-souls to distant parts of the universe, where they met and consulted with superhuman beings. Male shamans were said to have superhuman wives and female shamans to have superhuman husbands who help them. Shamans might plead with the superhumans to send abundant fruit, ask them for spells or songs, or ask for a magical liquid, *mun*, which can cool and heal the sick.

Most shamans who were able to go into trance came from shamanistic families. Shamans were thought to have cool, clear blood (*yãp mun*) like that of the superhumans, in addition to their normal human blood. All children of shamans inherited some *yãp mun*, but only some had the interest and persistence to learn the songs and techniques necessary to become a practicing shaman. During the 1970s, only five Batek in Kelantan were acknowledged to be able to trance and send their shadow-souls on cosmic journeys. Four of them were siblings, three men and one woman. At least three men living on the upper Lebir were considered to be "assistant shamans" (*gəniŋ*). All three had succeeded their fathers in that role. In 1990 another man and a woman had become known as true shamans. The woman was the daughter of a renowned shaman and the former wife of another.

Gender Roles in Rituals

Both men and women participated fully in Batek rituals. A few times a year people held communal singing sessions to communicate with the superhuman beings who send honey and seasonal fruits. Men and women together constructed a large ritual shelter (*hayã? təbəw*), similar in design to their ordinary living shelters but many times bigger, with a bark floor for dancing. Usually men brought in the thatch and other building materials and constructed the dancing platform and the log drum, which they suspended from rattan cords. Women thatched the roof and gathered sweet-smelling leaves to adorn the *hayã? təbəw* and to make body decorations for the singers and dancers. They also made finely patterned pandanus mats, which they saved specifically to sit on during singing sessions. Tanyogn said that Tohan had determined which sex does which job in the *hayã? təbəw*. She added that although women actually knew how to get the bark and log drum, they were not strong enough to do it, while men, on the other hand, did not know how to make the necessary mats and body decorations.

The singing sessions involved everyone in camp. Usually true shamans planned the ritual. Women—and occasionally men—played the log drum and bamboo flutes; men played nose flutes and bamboo zithers; and both sexes played Jew's harps, sang, and danced in time to the drum with a shuffling step in a circle around the platform. A *gəniŋ* led the singing. The true shamans went into trance and sent their shadow-souls to visit the superhuman beings.

Batek had spells and incantations for almost all aspects of life, and throughout the year these were recited on behalf of the group by any man or woman who knew them and who was thought by others to get results. Most adults knew a few spells, and some had a large repertoire. They recited spells for such diverse purposes as keeping tigers and other dangerous animals away, keeping bees from stinging people while collecting honey, and curing minor illnesses.

The blood sacrifice, the most famous Semang ritual in the anthropological literature (e.g., Needham 1964; Freeman 1968), was performed to stop the thunderstorms sent by Gobar as punishment for someone breaking a set of prohibitions (*lawac*), which include a wide range of acts, from incest to laughing at butterflies. If a thunderstorm occurred dangerously close to camp, people usually assumed that someone there had broken a prohibition, although they sometimes claimed that Gobar was mistaken. Anyone who thought he or she might be guilty had to perform the blood sacrifice to induce the thunder-god to stop the storm. To perform the blood sacrifice, a person cut the calf of either leg by tapping the blade of a knife against the skin. Only a few scratches, enough to draw a small amount of blood, were needed. The blood was scraped onto the knife blade and then mixed with water in a bowl or bamboo container. The person then threw the blood and water mixture upward toward the sky and downward to the earth while beseeching Gobar and Ya', who might assist Gobar in punishing the offender by causing an upwelling flood, to acknowledge the blood and stop the storm.

If none of the adults felt guilty, a mother, or occasionally a father, might perform the blood sacrifice on behalf of any child who might have committed a *lawac* act. Children sometimes broke prohibitions even after being told not to, as if to see what would happen. The next thunderstorm was then blamed on them. Although people said that Gobar does not hold children responsible for breaking the prohibitions because they do not yet know any better, parents performed the ritual anyway, just to be on the safe side. If a mother was performing the ritual on behalf of a child, she wiped the blood on the child's leg to pick up the child's smell before mixing it with water and throwing it to the deities.

Although men sometimes performed the blood sacrifice, for their own transgressions or those of their children, women said that men were not brave enough to do it unless they got really scared. Thus, women were more likely to do it than men. Sometimes, particularly during a severe thunderstorm directly over the camp, several people independently performed the ritual. Anyone who knew how and had enough courage could carry out the blood sacrifice on behalf of the whole camp.

Curing rituals were also performed by anyone who knew how to treat the condition in question. Both men and women could acquire curing skills by learning from others about medicinal forest plants, curing spells, massage, and other treatments or by obtaining the knowledge from superhuman beings through dreams. People normally used spells and herbal medicines as the first steps in treating illnesses. If those were not effective, a shaman might organize a singing session and seek the aid of the superhuman beings. People were allowed to treat members of the opposite sex for most ailments; Batek were willing to make use of any man or woman whose curing techniques had proven successful in the past. Curers were not blamed if the patient died, however, and Batek did not credit curers with the power to inflict diseases on others, in other words, to practice sorcery (K.M. Endicott 1979a).

Conclusion

The symbolic and behavioral expressions of gender reviewed in this chapter show that Batek recognized and accepted the physiological differences between the sexes. In a few limited domains, such as body decoration, they elaborated the distinction between males and females. But in many respects they viewed the sexes as the same or similar. Their gender concepts did not explicitly or symbolically devalue or privilege males or females either in the human or superhuman realm.

Notes

[1] This is not the place to discuss the challenges to the sex–gender distinction that have arisen from performance theory and queer theory (Butler 1990; Morris 1995; Moore 1999; Voss 2000). When we use the term "sex" we are referring to biological sex as understood in Western science. We discuss in this chapter how Batek view the physical differences between the sexes in the context of their own concepts of biology.

[2] This story contains Islamic elements borrowed from the Malays but reconfigured into a distinctively Batek story with Batek meanings.

Chapter 3

Social Life

All human social life has gender dimensions. In this chapter we present a general description of Batek social concepts and practices as the broad context for understanding gender concepts and relations between males and females.

The Camp: The Center of Social Life

Most Batek social interactions took place in camps, the temporary settlements they made and occupied for days or weeks until moving to another location. Although Batek did not physically or symbolically demarcate their camps from the forest, they did so conceptually: they spoke of going to the forest (*həp*) and returning to the camp (*hayã?*; literally "shelters"). Batek camps usually consisted of five to ten thatched lean-to shelters, each of which might be occupied by a separate conjugal family (husband, wife, and their young children), one or more older children, an unmarried adult with or without children, or a small group of adolescents.

There was no ideal camp shape; the layouts of camps varied depending on the terrain and people's whims, but usually most shelters faced roughly toward each other, backs to the forest, forming a communal space somewhere amidst the cluster of shelters. If the camp contained a dancing platform or ritual shelter, it was normally located near the center. There were no separate areas for men's and women's activities. Families chose their shelter sites independently, although children's shelters were often near those of their parents. In unusually large camps, the families that were more closely related sometimes chose to build their shelters near each other.

A shelter consisted of a sloping thatched roof covering a slightly raised bamboo sleeping platform. The roof was made of three or four poles thrust into the ground at a 45-degree angle and covered with wide shingles of palm-leaf thatch. When the thatch on the lean-tos was still fresh and green, camps blended almost invisibly into the undergrowth and shadows. If the weather was especially wet or if people wanted extra privacy, they might add triangular side walls of thatch. Shelters offered a living space roughly seven feet wide, the length of the palm fronds, by five feet deep. During the day, pandanus sleeping mats were rolled up and stored at the back of the platform, along with baskets of personal possessions. At night the occupants (adults and pre-adolescent children) rolled out their sleeping mats, and the platform became their bed. Each shelter had a cooking fire at the front or side, just far enough under the overhang of the roof to protect it from rain. Blowpipes and dart quivers were stuck in the thatch, above the reach of children.

Camp activities took place both in family shelters and in the spaces between them. Because shelters were close together and open to each other, little, if anything, could be done or said in them without other people knowing about it. Each family cooked, ate, and slept separately but shared food, cooperated economically, and socialized with other camp members. When people were in camp, small groups lounged or worked inside their shelters or those of friends. Some groups worked or socialized in open spaces between the shelters, and children played throughout the camp and in the adjacent trees and streams.

The pattern of camp life differed somewhat day to day, but some regularities were evident in forest camps in Kelantan in the 1970s. By about 7 AM most people were awake. The first in a family to rise poked their smoldering fire back to life. Some people went down to the water—all camps were situated near a river or stream—to bathe and fetch water in bamboo containers or plastic pails. Others walked into the forest or downstream to relieve themselves. If a family had any food left over from the previous day, they cooked and ate it. People discussed their plans for the day and formed work parties according to their shared interests. Hunters prepared new darts and cleaned and dried their blowpipes. People intending to dig tubers sharpened the metal blades of their digging sticks. By 8:30 or 9 AM most people had left camp for their various activities, which generally occupied them until mid to late afternoon. Sometimes a few people remained in camp to rest or work on tools, baskets, or other equipment and look after their children.

When workers returned home from the forest, they stirred up their cooking fires and prepared and shared the day's food. From then until dark, about 7 to 7:30 PM, people occupied themselves with a variety of activities: relaxing, chatting, singing, playing flutes or Jew's harps, delousing each other's hair, working on hunting equipment, weaving pandanus mats and baskets, carving bamboo combs, making plans for the following day, and airing thoughts or grievances. Men and women mixed freely. On dry evenings many people continued their activities by the light of resin torches or store-bought kerosene wick-lamps or flashlights, while cross-camp conversations, and sometimes singing, continued long into the night.

Any particular camp was merely a moment in a continual process of residential movement and change. When people abandoned a camp, they often split into two or more groups, some moving together to new locations and some joining other, already existing camps. Each family packed its belong-

When moving to a new camp, people carried most of their belongings in pandanus back baskets, their babies perched on top of the load. Here Tebu and his family prepare to abandon their shelter at a clearing and move into the forest.

ings in pandanus baskets, plastic sacks, or cloth slings. Everyone shouldered a load, even children. Mothers with more than one small child might carry one on her back and another on her hip, while fathers took the heaviest loads of food and household goods. Families set off toward an agreed-upon destination at their own pace. Often the adolescent boys and girls went ahead, looking for food as they walked, and the older people and children came along behind them. Although they had determined a general destination beforehand, they chose the actual location when they reached the area. Sometimes it was a place they had camped before, but usually it was new. They avoided former campsites where people had been ill, on the theory that the diseases had gone into the ground and could re-emerge if people built fires over them. If the campsite proved unsuitable for some reason, they moved on.

The first people to arrive at a new site scanned the treetops in order to avoid dangerous dead trees or branches, and they examined the ground for filth, such as elephant dung. Sometimes the men chopped down trees that looked like they might fall in a storm. The camp gradually took shape as each successive family selected its homesite, cleared some space, and built a fire. There was always a sense of excitement and anticipation in the air when they set up a new camp. Both men and women set about gathering the logs, bamboo, saplings, and thatch needed to build their shelters.

Women constructed the lean-tos and men made the sleeping platforms. Batek considered women the experts at building lean-to shelters, while men took responsibility for constructing Malay-style raised houses at clearings. Adolescent girls often made shelters for the unmarried men. While shelters were being built, some men and older boys would rush off to hunt before the nearby game got scared away. It took only a couple of hours for a new camp to be completed. If there were any tubers or fruits near the campsite, some women might gather them, and others might go fishing. In the late afternoon people cooked their evening meal. The general air of adventure usually carried on into the first evening at a new camp. At one new site people found a large amount of solidified resin and burned it all in one spectacular bonfire.

Camps changed shape daily. At first people cleared only enough undergrowth to accommodate their own shelters. Over a period of several days, they gradually trampled paths between shelters and chopped down more trees, especially those most likely to topple during thunderstorms. Children felled small saplings just for fun. Often other families arrived and set up their shelters. People might move their shelters for various reasons. For example, once a couple of adolescent girls moved their shelter away from the adolescent boys' shelter after the boys got angry at the girls for not saving some food for them. As camps got bigger, some of the original inhabitants might move their shelters to the periphery to get away from the increased bustle and noise. But if people heard or saw tigers or elephants nearby, they usually moved their shelters closer together to increase their feeling of security.

Eventually, after camp members used up the nearby resources of food and rattan, talk would turn to the possibility of moving on. People said that if they had to walk more than an hour to get tubers, it was better to move to a new area, though rattan collectors were willing to roam farther. They also moved if someone died in the camp, if the camp became too messy, or if they learned of a new opportunity, such as ripening fruit, somewhere else. Once some families moved, the rest usually left soon after. Batek did not like to live in a camp with numerous vacant shelters, for they believed that such "dying" camps attract dangerous animals. For Batek, moving was often easier—and certainly more interesting—than staying put. Moving was a burden only for those who were elderly or ill. However, younger and stronger people always helped them, rafting them to new sites if possible or carrying them if necessary.

Ethical Principles of Social Life

Batek behaved in a manner that maximized individual freedom and autonomy yet required people to help each other when needed. We term this behavior pattern "cooperative autonomy," as distinct from the "competitive autonomy" of such peoples as the New Guinea highlanders or from what Americans call "rugged individualism," self-reliance unhampered by obligations to others.

We think of Batek social behavior as having been influenced by—but not absolutely determined by—their ideas about how people *should* behave, a set of ethical principles. These principles were not explicitly articulated as in the Judeo-Christian Ten Commandments, but rather were embedded in their religious beliefs, values, norms, sanctions, and everyday practices. For ease of discussion, we distinguish the following ethical principles: personal autonomy, respecting others, helping others, sharing food, nonviolence, and noncompetition. Batek themselves did not use these categories and labels, and other categories and labels are possible. But we think that the beliefs and values encompassed by these terms did exist in the minds and actions of Batek people. Some components of these principles were conscious, explicit, and named, while others were merely implied by people's statements and behavior. Taken together, Batek ethics gave a distinctive shape and tone to their social life, including relations between men and women.

The principles behind cooperative autonomy may be thought of as ideals that were not always fully achieved in practice. As in all ethical systems, Batek ethics were not entirely consistent with each other. For example, the obligation to help others sometimes conflicted with the value on personal autonomy. Should a man stay near his parents-in-law to help them, or should he exercise his right to move and pursue his personal interests? People tried to balance these conflicting obligations in appropriate ways. Other people's responses helped them gauge whether they had made the right choices. Occasionally people might violate a principle entirely, but in doing so they risked alienating other people or offending the superhuman beings.

Ethical principles were enforced in various ways and to varying degrees. Batek did not have an authority structure that could be used to directly punish wrongdoers. In fact it would have violated the principle of personal autonomy had anyone attempted to sanction anyone else's behavior directly. However, two sets of prohibitions had a law-like character: *lawac* prohibitions (against incest, mixing some categories of foods, mocking some animals, etc.) and *tolah* prohibitions (against disrespectful acts). Significantly, these prohibitions were enforced not by humans, but by superhuman beings—in cases of *lawac*, by Gobar and Ya?, and, in cases of *tolah*, by Tohan. Other principles were enforced by diffuse social pressure, such as gossip and criticism, backed up by the implicit threat of the withdrawal of social support. For example, people said they would abandon anyone who consistently engaged in violent behavior. In addition, the process of enculturation (or socialization) was highly effective at inculcating Batek ethics in children (see chapter 5). Most people felt a strong commitment to Batek ethical principles by the time they were old enough to understand the difference between proper and improper behavior. Our impression is that Batek had strong social consciences, and they generally conformed quite closely to the ideals described here.

Personal Autonomy

What we call personal autonomy is based on the Batek expectation that everyone could do whatever they wanted to do as long as it was consistent with their obligation to help and respect others. This does not mean that Batek did not cooperate with each other in various ways but merely that such cooperation was voluntary. For example, if a group of men went out to collect rattan together, they did so because they wanted to, not because someone forced them to.

A related component of personal autonomy is the idea that no one had the authority to coerce anyone else to do anything that person did not want to do. People could try to persuade others to do something, using every rhetorical device they could muster, but anyone could simply refuse (*ye?*), without any need to explain the refusal. Batek did not accept the authority of anyone else over themselves. A man we knew once organized a group of workers to collect rattan for a Malay trader with whom he had made a contract. After he had distributed the advances of food and goods to his workers, he was unable to get those who had agreed to participate to collect the rattan. He finally gave up in frustration, fulfilling the contract himself and refusing to organize such a project again. He had no way to force the others to do the work. We were struck by how Batek of all ages and both sexes would simply refuse to do what others "ordered" (*pi?or*) them to do if they did not want to. This was a source of great frustration to the staff of the JHEOA, who expected their orders to be carried out and who expected the headmen they appointed to be able to exercise control over other Batek. Even Batek parents could not force their children to obey them and dismissed unruliness in their children by saying they "don't yet understand." As children matured they increasingly considered the wishes of their parents and other elders out of respect.

The principle of personal autonomy was associated with an expectation that everyone would be as self-reliant as possible, even though they could depend on others to give them food and help if necessary. Although Batek did not make a fetish of working hard or steadily, most seemed to feel guilty if they loafed for very long. Some people said, half jokingly, that if they did not do any work for several days in a row, the ghost of one of their dead ancestors would thump them on the back with a forefinger. Although most adults made regular efforts to support themselves and contribute to the food supply of the camp as a whole, there were some exceptions. For example, no one expected sick or elderly people to support themselves. The children and children-in-law of elderly people were especially obligated to help them, and elders also benefited from the general sharing of food in camp (see below). Nevertheless, many old people contributed significantly by helping to look after children, making things for themselves and others, and using their ritual knowledge for the benefit of the group.

A few people were, in our view, somewhat lazy, but Batek seemed willing to excuse this to some extent for various reasons. For example, a Semaq Beri woman who had married into a Batek group almost never gathered food like the other women. She depended on her husband to supply her with rice, which he obtained by trading forest products. People accepted this with equanimity, saying that because she was Semaq Beri, she was not "used to" digging and eating wild tubers. We also knew one man who seemed never to pull his weight. He was constantly in debt to traders and seemed to expect others to help him collect the forest produce needed to pay off his debts. We once asked some men why they tolerated such behavior. One answered with some surprise, "Because he's a Batek!"

The principle of personal autonomy provided both men and women the freedom to do almost anything they wanted to do. Husbands and wives often cooperated and worked together, but as equal, autonomous partners.

Respecting Others

Batek regarded each other as basically equal in their intrinsic value and therefore worthy of respect. Although some people, particularly shamans, were held in especially high regard, they neither expected nor received special treatment from others. All Batek felt that they deserved the same consideration as everyone else, and they were not shy in saying so. For example, when Kirk first started his fieldwork in 1971, a friend in the JHEOA advised him to take a few gifts for the headman at Post Lebir, to break the ice. So Kirk gave the headman a bush-knife and a few other store-bought items soon after arriving. Within the first week, nearly all the other men in the settlement came around asking when they would be getting their bush-knives. Although Batek accepted the idea that people who worked for others would be paid wages in proportion to the amount of work done, when payment took the form of gifts, everyone expected to be included. We never found an acceptable way to give thank-you gifts to the people who went out of their way to help us—a Western gesture that felt right to us—without hurting the feelings of others, who might have had little contact with us. We learned to restrict our gifts to such things as rice and tobacco, which could be given to the camp-group as a whole and then divided into equal portions for all families and individuals.

All Batek expected to be treated with respect by all other Batek, regardless of their personal relationships or feelings about one another. They considered it unacceptable to insult or ridicule someone, except in good-natured joking among friends. To hurt another person's feelings risked causing them to come down with a disease called *kaʔɔy* (K.M. Endicott 1979a:107, 109-110), which is akin to Western notions of depression. Batek believed *kaʔɔy* could cause a physical breakdown and even death. Its main symptom is extreme sadness, often expressed by uncontrollable sobbing. The disease was thought to reside in the heart and to make it hot. *Kaʔɔy* could be brought on by a variety of distressing experiences, including losing something or being frightened, but its most common cause was the sense of being mistreated or misunderstood by other people. When someone had an attack of *kaʔɔy*, all their close friends and relatives rushed to their aid in a dramatic expression of sympathy and social support.

In a typical case, Kirk once noticed a woman crying in her shelter with her eyes closed and her face turned toward the back of the shelter. When he alerted the others in camp, three women came rushing over. Two of them quickly began lightly stabbing their shins with a knife, as in the blood sacrifice, and then rubbed the blood on small pieces of palm leaf. They then took turns rubbing the blood on the afflicted woman's chest and stomach and throwing the leaves briskly away. The blood was supposed to cool the victim's heart, and at the same time the disease was thought to enter the leaf, which could then be cast away. Next, someone sent for her husband, who came immediately. He and the women began massaging his wife and comforting her. He also drew some blood from his leg and rubbed it on her. One woman drew an arrowhead-shaped design on the wife's chest and back with white lime paste, also to drive out the disease. When her sobbing subsided, they asked her what was bothering her. It turned out that she thought her father-in-law was angry with her. So her husband went to his father and got a little of his blood on a leaf, which he then rubbed on her stomach. Their ministrations went on for an hour or so, and by the end she was smiling.

In cases of *kaʔɔy* the onus was on the offender to make amends to the victim, for example, by giving some blood. If the offender did not, the rest of the group would be angry at him or her. People's concern about causing someone to contract *kaʔɔy* and getting blamed for it by the whole camp was a powerful sanction against mistreating others.

Batek also believed that Tohan would punish certain disrespectful acts, called *tolah* (Malay *tulah*), by causing a disease or an accident (K.M. Endicott 1979a). *Tolah* acts ranged from saying the true name of an in-law to killing someone. Batek expected people to show special respect to their elders and in-laws. It was considered *tolah* to say their true names, so kin terms, outsider names, nicknames, or teknonyms had to be used instead. People sometimes called elders *taʔ*, "grandfather," or *yaʔ*, "grandmother," out of respect, even though their actual kin relationship might be different. In addition, Batek prohibited using ordinary single-person pronouns when speaking to or about a parent-in-law or child-in-law.

Tohan's punishments varied in severity, depending on the seriousness of the offense. Minor offenses were usually punished by accidents. We were told, for example, that a man once urinated in a stream above where people were drawing water. A few days later, he fell out of a tree and hurt himself. For a serious offense, such as physically hurting someone, Tohan would send a fatal disease, *ʔaral tolah*, to strike down the offender.

Balancing the demonstration of respect for others and maintenance of personal autonomy was evident in the interaction with elders and in-laws. One way Batek showed respect for elders and in-laws was to listen to them, although they might not agree with what was said. For example, older people sometimes took it upon themselves to criticize and offer unsolicited advice to adolescents and young adults. The youths would listen but then make their own decisions. If an elder put too much pressure on a youth, it would infringe on the youth's personal autonomy and might even cause him or her to contract *kaʔɔy*. The effect was that elders did not have any actual authority over their juniors.

Helping Others

Batek felt a general obligation to help any other Batek who needed aid, although the feeling seemed to be stronger toward close kin and camp mates than toward occasional visitors from other areas. This obligation was expressed through numerous casual acts of assistance carried out in passing, with little notice or fanfare, as when someone helped another build a shelter or brought some firewood to another family. Although we made a point to pay for work done for us, people helped us regularly in minor ways with no thought of reward.

Adults felt a special obligation to help all youngsters, not just their own children. In addition to giving practical assistance to children with their everyday needs, adults willingly mentored and taught youngsters important skills and knowledge. For example, active hunters often took on teenaged boys as apprentices, teaching them and helping them hone their skills and getting help in return in butchering, cooking, and carrying back game. If a child were orphaned, other adults—usually aunts and uncles or older siblings, but sometimes more distant relatives—would raise him or her as their own. Step-parents treated their spouse's children the same as their own, even if they later divorced the child's parent.

Reciprocally, all able-bodied adults and adolescents took a hand in helping elderly and handicapped people as needed. Although such people tried to be as self-sufficient as possible, they willingly accepted help from others. For example, one man who was blind was amazingly capable at performing daily activities and would even walk from camp to camp alone at times, but he certainly would have had a much harder time without the general help that others freely gave him.

Some obligations to help others were somewhat formalized and were specified in terms of kin relationships. Adult children were expected to make special efforts to help their aging parents in any way needed. In the sharing of food, people gave portions to their parents and parents-in-law before giving them to other families in camp. Although this obligation did not require couples always to camp near the parents of one or the other spouse, it did obligate them to make certain that someone—perhaps one of the parents' other children—would stay with the parents if they did not do so themselves. Men were also expected to make a special effort to help and share food with their wife's parents. At the beginning of a marriage, especially if the wife were very young, a couple might make a point of camping with the wife's parents for a year or so to help them and give them things. If an elderly couple or widow or widower had only one child, the responsibility for caring for the parents would fall heavily on one couple. We knew of one case in which the husband continually complained about the burden of helping his widowed mother-in-law, and she in turn complained that he was neglecting her. Usually, however, the job was shared by several children, their spouses, and the camp-group as a whole, so it did not seem too onerous to any one person.

Sharing Food

The obligation to share food was a central principle of Batek social life (K.M. Endicott 1988; Lye 2004). Batek generally considered unharvested resources to be free to anyone for the taking, but once food was harvested or bought from a trader or shop, it had to be shared with other members of the camp. Sharing was done on the basis of generalized reciprocity: sharing without calculating exact returns for what a person gave and received from the sharing network (see Sahlins 1972). The usual procedure was for people to give shares first to their own children and spouse, then to any parents-in-law or parents present, and finally to all other families in camp. Small amounts of food could be consumed by the procurer's conjugal family alone, but if a family had more than it needed, it shared the surplus with other families, usually families living nearby. Usually food was shared only with other camp members, but sometimes temporary visitors from other areas would be included, especially if they were closely related to a camp member.

Normally the people who obtained the food decided how to share it, but occasionally other people asked them for food or just showed up at their fire at mealtime. Generally speaking, the amounts of food given were roughly the same for each family, although slight adjustments might be made according to the size of the family. A second stage of sharing might then take place if some families still lacked food. The result was that every family got some food unless, as happened rarely, no one had been successful in the food quest. Even when food was abundant, the sharing went on according to the same principles, thus taking on a ritualized character as each family gave portions of its excess food to other families and received portions—sometimes of the same kind of food—in turn. It was not unusual to see small children carrying plates of cooked tubers to neighboring shelters, while other children were bringing similar plates of food in return. (Schebesta saw Jahai Semang sharing food in this fashion in the 1920s [1928:84].) This apparently unnecessary distribution confirmed that sharing of food was an important ethical principle.

The obligation to share food applied to all foods obtained, but slight differences in the distribution procedure resulted from the different characteristics of the foods and the ways they were obtained. Vegetable foods, especially wild yams, were a reliable food source. Usually anyone who looked for them would get some, although the amount obtained was seldom more than three times the needs of a single family. Thus, there were usually several sources of vegetable food in a camp on any given day, and each source-family supplied between one and three other families. Batek obtained meat less regularly than vegetable foods and in sizes varying from less than an ounce to about sixteen pounds. Small animals, such as fish, frogs, birds, and bats, were usually consumed by the family that caught them. However, larger animals, such as monkeys and gibbons, were usually shared with the entire camp. Often the hunter gutted and partially roasted the kill in the forest, and he and his companions might eat the tail and internal organs. All food collectors ate some of the foods they obtained if they got hungry, and no one begrudged them that right. Hunters or other camp members cut the animals into a standard number of pieces—e.g., thirteen for monkeys—and gave the portions to that many families. If there were more families in camp, the pieces might be divided again. Within families, women often received slightly larger portions than men to compensate for their not eating meat during their menstrual periods.

Batek shared purchased foods and nonfood consumables, such as tobacco and kerosene, according to the same principles as wild vegetable foods unless they were obtained in unusually large amounts. If someone bought, for example, a whole gunny sack of rice (more than 100 pounds), he or she would usually dole it out to others gradually over a period of days or weeks. Occasionally the buyer would resell portions of the food to other Batek at cost, thus becoming, in effect, the purchasing agent for the group as a whole.

Sharing food was an obligation for Batek, not something the giver had much discretion over. The sharing obligation was enforced by strong social pressure. As one hunter said: "If I didn't take the meat back to camp, everyone would be angry at me." Recipients treated the food they were given as a right; no expression of thanks was expected or forthcoming, presumably because that would imply that the donor had the right to withhold it. The person who obtained the food could decide how to divide and distribute it, or he or she could delegate that job to someone else. There seemed to have been an element of randomness in who got food on a given occasion.

The ubiquity of sharing didn't mean that people always wanted to share, however. Once a young hunter returned to camp with two monkeys, which he divided up and shared with all the other families. Later he told Kirk that he and his children had cooked and eaten a third monkey in the forest. He said he was unhappy at having to share the meat with so many other people—it was an unusually large camp—as it made the portions so small. Supposedly anyone who consistently refused to share food would be excluded from the food-sharing network. Although we did not see this happen in Kelantan in 1975–76, Lye Tuck-Po reports that it often happened during her research in Pahang after 1993 (personal communication).

The food-sharing network was the Batek's safety net. Besides ensuring that everyone, regardless of productive capacity, had food regularly, the sharing network ensured that all men and women, whether married or not, had direct access to the foods usually procured by the opposite sex. And because food sharing was an obligation rather than a voluntary act, it did not give power to food getters over food recipients.

In theory nonconsumable goods a person made or obtained in trade, including cash, were considered personal possessions that did not have to be shared. In practice, however, the general obligation to help others led to a relatively even distribution of material wealth. Although sometimes people tried to hide their possessions, Batek frequently loaned and gave things to others. People also regularly borrowed other people's possessions, even without asking. When we gave gifts or payment to someone in the form of durable goods, such as clothes, we often saw them later being used or worn by someone else.

Nonviolence

Batek, like most other Orang Asli, considered all violence, aggression, and physical coercion unacceptable (see, e.g., Dentan 1968). To them being violent was something only outsiders would do. One man told us that the ancestors had forbidden Batek to engage in war. In former times, when Batek were attacked by slave-raiders, the Batek fled rather than fighting back.[1] Kirk once asked a Batek man why their ancestors had not shot the attackers with poisoned blowpipe darts. The man looked shocked at the question. "Because it would kill them!" he replied. Batek said that hurting someone was both *tolah*, punished by Tohan, and *lawac*, punished by Gobar and Ya?. We were told that if a person were violent during life, the superhuman beings would refuse to take the offender's shadow-soul to the afterworld after death. The offender was doomed to roam the forest as a malevolent ghost. Any human punishment for violence would be superfluous in light of these powerful sanctions from on high. Still, in answer to our hypothetical question about what people would do about a persistently violent person, we were told that the group would abandon that person, fleeing if necessary.

Except for occasional scuffles between small children and the odd swat from a frustrated parent, we never saw any Batek commit violent acts. Batek methods of socialization were very successful at curbing violent impulses in children at an early age. By the time they were old enough to play together without adult supervision, children rarely deliberately hurt each other. We never witnessed a violent altercation between adults, although we heard about a few instances. Once in the late 1970s, we were told, two men got into a physical fight over one man's wife, whom both wanted. While a few people tried to break up the fight, most of the group fled the scene in panic, fearing that Ya? would split open the earth beneath the camp and destroy it in a massive flood. One man said he grabbed the wrists of the two combatants and said, "Think of the sun; think of the earth; this will all dissolve." Such behavior was obviously regarded as a serious breach of the natural order of things. While we were in the field in 1976 we heard that a woman in another camp, whom we knew quite well, had hit her two-year-old boy over the head with a piece of bamboo and knocked him unconscious. The boy's grandmother was so angry that she hit the mother in turn. We were later told that the mother had actually killed two of her previous babies by hitting them. Some people said her behavior was a bit insane. As far as we know, she was never punished either by the superhuman beings or by society, although people were furious at her after the last incident.

The prohibition against violence removed the potential for stronger people to coerce weaker ones. Women and men alike were protected from abuse, spouse beating, and other acts of physical violence that are committed—and often accepted—in many societies.

Noncompetition

Competition, like interpersonal violence, was almost nonexistent in Batek social life. We never saw people deliberately trying to outdo each other or drawing attention to their accomplishments. Although people seemed pleased when they succeeded at something, Batek etiquette required people to be modest and self-effacing (see also Lye 2004:140). When we were weighing foods brought in, we sometimes found it difficult to determine who, in a hunting party, had actually killed an animal. People might say something like, "We got one leaf monkey," rather than stating who shot it.

Similarly, children's games were not competitive. In many hours of observing children's play, Karen never saw them playing in a way that created winners and losers. In the early 1970s when Kirk was staying at Post Lebir, the school teacher introduced the sport of soccer to the students. He divided them into teams depending on whether they were from the Aring or Lebir River. They spent many happy hours rushing back and forth across the playing field trying to kick the ball into the opposition team's goal. However, the main difference between this and soccer as we know it was that the teams took turns scoring! Once in 1990 we saw some adolescents playing cards in someone's shelter. They were having great fun drawing cards, discarding, and throwing their hands down triumphantly every few minutes. However, as far as we could tell, there were no agreed-upon rules to the game, and no one kept score.

In a sense the lack of competition was merely a side-effect of some of the other principles of social life, including the prohibitions against aggression and hurting the feelings of others. Competition creates winners and losers, and Batek avoided making anyone feel the pain of losing, since it might cause them to contract *kəʔɔy*. However, we have highlighted noncompetition as a separate ethical principle—even though it is the mere absence of something they had little experience with—because in some other egalitarian societies, such as those of New Guinea, competition is highly developed. We think the difference between competitive and noncompetitive egalitarian societies has a bearing on gender concepts and relations. The relative lack of competition in Batek society, we believe, helped prevent either sex from dominating or outdoing the other in areas in which one might have had inherent advantages.

Groups

Kinship Networks

Every Batek was part of a network of kin that potentially included all other Batek. When people met for the first time, they would try to discover whether they had any consanguineal or affinal relatives in common. If they could not find a precise connection, they would adopt kin terms appropriate to their sex and age. For example, someone from outside one's immediate family would be called uncle (*bah*) or aunt (b*ə*ʔ), older sibling or cousin (*to*ʔ), or younger sibling or cousin (*bɛr*). Adults often referred to all the children in a group as their children (ʔ*awã*ʔ), only mentioning a specific genealogical relationship when asked. Children grew up in a group of siblings and cousins, called a *səbɛrto*ʔ, differentiated by relative age but not by sex. In a sense Batek saw themselves as a single extended family.

For Batek the concept of descent amounted to little more than the recognition that a person came from a certain mother and father. Inheritance went, in principle, from both parents to all children equally, but, in fact, in this society of sparse possessions there was usually little for a child to inherit.

Conjugal Families

Conjugal families (*kəmam*), consisting of a married couple and their dependent children, were relatively stable groups in the general flux of Batek social life—despite the ease with which people could divorce—and therefore could be regarded as the component units of camp-groups, which split up and recombined throughout the year. A couple was considered a *kəmam* even after their children moved out of the family shelter, but a household without a conjugal pair (e.g., a widow with children) was not. Each conjugal family had its own shelter and cooking fire in forest camps.

Conjugal families were to a large extent self-sufficient economically. Given the Batek division of labor and people's free access to resources, a man and woman together could perform all the tasks necessary to support themselves, their children, and any elderly parents they might have. Husbands and wives generally organized their activities so that one person, usually the husband, could hunt or collect rattan or other forest products for trade, while the other spouse, usually the wife, could engage in food-getting activities with a high daily success rate, such as digging tubers (see chapter 4). But to overcome the vagaries of disease and aging as well as failures in daily food-getting efforts, conjugal families lived in camp-groups and participated in a food-sharing network. Camp living also provided conjugal families with more extensive social contacts and increased safety from tigers and other animals.

Both partners in a marriage had an equal voice in decisions affecting the household, including when and where to move, what economic activities to pursue, and how to use their money or trade credit. Couples made such decisions through a process of discussion and usually took action only after reaching a mutually agreeable plan. Sometimes one partner would be more insistent, and the other would give in. As often as not, it was the wife who would get her way. For example, we knew several couples in which the husband, who was from a different area, was living with the Lebir group because his wife, whose parents were Lebir people, refused to move to her husband's natal area.

Occasionally, when spouses could not agree, they would each do different things for a while. In 1990 we noticed an older man sitting forlornly on the

A family at home: Tanyogn (right) and Langsat (middle) in their shelter. Their adolescent son Pikas (left) sleeps in a separate shelter, but eats with them. They are surrounded by the products of their labor and the paraphernalia of life: a mound of tubers, a dart quiver, pandanus baskets and mats. A bundle of pith for dart making dries over the fire.

platform of his shelter which was no longer covered by the plastic tarp that had been its roof. He explained that his wife had wanted to catch a ride with a trader so she could go visit one of their grown sons near the Terengganu border. The husband had argued that the trip would not be worth the effort since they might not even find the son, but his wife packed her belongings and their plastic roofing and left with a group of other Batek in the trader's pickup truck.

Many prohibitions fostered the sense of autonomy and the habit of independent action by each conjugal family. Married couples had to maintain a certain physical and social distance from their parents and in-laws as well as from their siblings of opposite sex. Since shelters were not big enough to accommodate persons who had to sleep apart, the prohibitions on sleeping near certain close relatives caused adolescent boys and girls to live in separate lean-tos from their parents even though they might still eat together. Newly married couples might stay in the camp of one or both sets of parents, but they had to have a shelter and cooking fire of their own.

Camp-Groups

Batek always lived in groups of conjugal families and individuals who chose, for their own reasons, to camp together at a particular time. Camp-groups changed size and composition constantly, as some families moved into a camp and others left to join other camps or form new ones. When abandoning a campsite an entire group might move to a new location together or split into two or more new camp-groups; sometimes only a few families would break away to join other groups. Because of the danger from wild animals, mainly tigers and elephants, people did not like to camp in groups of fewer than three families. At the other extreme, camp-groups of over twenty-five families might form when it was easy to find food, as during the height of the fruit season, but such large groups usually could not stay together long, for they quickly depleted the resources in the neighborhood. The camps in which we lived in 1975–76 varied in size from four to twenty-five households, but usually numbered between five and ten. The average camp population was thirty-four persons, including eleven adult men, nine adult women, and fourteen children. Camps usually existed for a week to ten days, until the resources in the area had been thoroughly picked over.

People chose their camp-mates on the basis of common economic interests, kinship ties, and friendships. In theory a person or conjugal family could join any other Batek camp-group, but in practice people usually did not join a camp unless they had close relatives or friends in it. Often a camp contained a core of three or four families who were closely related through an elderly parent or grandparent, whom they were supposed to help economically. For example, the married children of an old widow might tend to camp together so that they could help to provide food for her. Similarly, the married children or siblings of a well-liked couple might tend to camp together much of the time. However, no families or individuals were required to camp together at all times. People could join another camp-group if they wanted a change of companions, if they got into a personal conflict with someone in their camp, or if they decided to join others in a particular economic pursuit. There were no formal criteria for camp-group membership or ritual process for joining or leaving a camp. One's presence and participation in the social and economic interaction of the camp was the essence of membership.

Few activities involved the camp-group as a whole, and those that did took place in a characteristically spontaneous, cooperative fashion. For example, building the large covered platform (*hayã? təbəw*) used for singing and trancing rituals required a lot of work by numerous people. Typically one person or a small group initiated the project, but if others did not agree with the timing or location, they simply did not join in. During the construction, people voluntarily undertook the tasks they knew best how to do, usually men cutting the poles for the platform and roof frame and bark sheets for the floor and women making the thatch and the paraphernalia for the singers and dancers to use and wear. Sometimes a project like this, which took several days to complete, was abandoned before it was finished, if other priorities distracted the workers to other tasks or even induced them to move.

Although camp-groups were transitory, they cooperated economically in a number of ways. Most importantly, the camp-group was the group in which the food-sharing network operated. People were obligated to share food with other camp members, but they had no obligation to send food even to close relatives who were not living in the same camp. In addition, camp-group members shared information on the resources of the area, thus making it easier for everyone to find food and trade-goods. Despite changes in its composition, the camp-group was the unit of long-term survival. By cooperating and sharing, camp-groups could protect themselves from dangers and could more effectively exploit the resources of an area than if they had done so as separate conjugal families.

River-Valley Groups

We use the term "river-valley groups" to refer to groups of people who normally reside in the watersheds of particular rivers. In 1975–76 there were two main river-valley groups of Batek in Kelantan State, the Lebir River people and the Aring River people. The Batek on both these rivers thought of themselves as distinct groups residentially, economically, and even socially, while simultaneously acknowledging their common identity as Batek. They referred to themselves as "Batek Lebir" and "Batek Aring." Although river-valley groups tended to stay in their own watersheds and use the local resources, they did not claim exclusive ownership of the land and its resources or actively prohibit others from camping and foraging there. However, there appeared to be a tacit understanding that each river-valley group would exploit the resources of its own watershed as much as possible—especially fruit trees, the only resource to which Batek made a vague group claim.

In 1975–76, people tended to camp in their own river valleys unless they were visiting relatives in the other watershed or looking for someone to marry. Because river-valley groups had relatively low populations, people often had to look beyond their own river valleys to find unmarried persons of a suitable age outside their circle of prohibited relatives. Some people grew up in one watershed and then moved to the other after marriage. Over time, they might come to identify with their spouse's river-valley group. Although there were several minor differences in religious customs and thought between Lebir and Aring people, there were no social barriers to interaction between them. In early 1976 the Department of Aboriginal Affairs brought most of the Aring and Lebir people together for a few months at Jentah, a spot on the Lebir just below the mouth of the Relai River, for an agricultural project. The two groups camped on opposite sides of the river but interacted on a daily basis.

Marriage and Divorce

People made their own decisions about whom to marry. Sometimes parents tried to influence their children's marriage choices, but it was up to the individuals to decide whether to heed their parents' wishes. Tanyogn said that when she was young, she had wanted to marry a man her mother disliked. So she didn't marry him, but she told us that she remained fond of him and extended help and friendship to him throughout their adult years. She married Langsat instead and had a companionable, loving relationship with him until she died. While Tanyogn had respected her mother's wishes, her parents could not have prevented her from marrying the man she wanted if she had been determined to go through with it. Indeed, some couples did marry despite parental objections, and many others married without even consulting their parents.

People were free to marry anyone except their half and whole siblings, parents, grandparents, uncles, aunts, children, nephews, and nieces. Sex or marriage with such people was considered incest (*cəmam*), an offense punished by Gobar, who would send a thunderstorm to topple a tree on the offender or cause a spark of lightning to enter the offender's foot and cause a crippling disease. Only two examples of incestuous marriages were mentioned to us; each case involved a niece and an uncle. In one case the girl died shortly after the marriage, and in the other all of the couple's children died within a few months after birth. People attributed these misfortunes to the improper marriages.

Batek were unusual among Semang in allowing marriage between first cousins. We knew of numerous examples of first-cousin marriage, including cases of siblings from one family marrying siblings from another family. This was not a prescribed or even preferred type of marriage alliance, however, but merely the outcome of the choices made by the persons themselves. Other Semang groups prohibit marriage to first cousins (Schebesta 1928; Benjamin 1985), possibly to ensure that marriage ties spread beyond the local group. Apparently, the random imbalances in the numbers of males and females coming to marriageable age at the same time among the Batek ensured that marriages into other river-valley groups and even other aboriginal ethnic groups were common. Sometimes a group of young men—or, less frequently, young women—would visit a distant group where one of them had relatives in hopes of finding a mate.

Foremost among the criteria for choosing spouses was mutual attraction. The Batek said that love or friendship (*sayɛŋ*) and physical desire or lust (*hawaʔ*) have a lot to do with the choice of marriage partners. One man stated that in addition to personal attraction, he and other men look for women who are industrious—who fetch water, firewood, and thatch, and who weave pandanus mats. He said they prefer to marry Batek women, rather than women from other aboriginal groups (such as the Semaq Beri), because the Batek women work harder. He also stated that they like women who have very curly (typically Batek) hair, because these women can wear flowers and bamboo combs in their hair. When we asked him what he thought Batek women considered when choosing a spouse, he replied that he thought they preferred industrious men who fetch firewood and thatch, dig tubers, and collect rattan.

Women, when asked what they look for in a man, gave responses that were very much based upon the qualities their own husbands possessed. Thus, one woman whose husband was an excellent hunter said that she liked a man to be a good hunter. Another said she married her husband because he had been to many towns (that is, he was worldly and sophisticated) and that she did not care that he was not a superior hunter. These women told us that we liked each other because we could both write!

People were also willing to consider partners of very different ages than themselves. We knew some couples in which one spouse was as much as thirty years older than the other. Usually the husband was older, but older wives were not uncommon. For example, after an epidemic on the upper Lebir in 1978, several of the surviving spouses married each other; in one remarriage the woman was about fifteen years older than her new husband. Young men occasionally married girls who had not yet reached puberty. The couple would live together, usually near the girl's parents, and the husband would raise the girl until she was old enough to assume the full responsibilities of marriage. But in most marriages involving wide age differences, at least one of the partners had already been widowed or divorced.

Marriages often grew out of sexual liaisons that began in adolescence or early adulthood. Adolescents who had become too old to stay in their family shelters sometimes lived in mixed-sex groups, although more commonly they occupied separate boys' and girls' shelters. Batek culture neither revered virginity nor encouraged young men or women to remain virgins until marriage. Rather, young people were expected to indulge their sexual desires. A couple might meet in one or the other's shelter at night when the rest of the camp was thought to be asleep, or they might arrange a tryst in the forest during the day. Sometimes it was difficult for an observer—and apparently for Batek, also—to distinguish the premarital relationships of young people from marriage, since there was no mandatory marriage ceremony. Young adults often went through three or four short-lived marriages, which might last only a few days or might continue for a year or more. Sometimes a couple had an on-again, off-again marriage for a few years before either settling into their marriage or divorcing once and for all.

For first marriages, it was customary for young people to ask permission of both sets of parents, although, as we mentioned above, this was not always done. It was also common for them to give gifts to each other and to their prospective spouse's parents. Usually the woman wove pandanus sleeping mats and baskets for her husband and herself to use in their new household. The man gave a few pieces of store-bought cloth (previously barkcloth was made and given) and some rice or other purchased food to his wife and her parents. The wife thus contributed to the marriage those products that were the specialty of women, and the husband presented purchased goods that men, as the major participants in the rattan trade, could more readily acquire than women. Although gift-giving was usual, it was not obligatory, and some marriages took place without it. There was no special Batek word for such gifts. The giving of gifts did not constitute bridewealth; it did not signify the purchase of the woman, her sexuality, or rights to her children. Rather, it was a gesture of good will and the son-in-law's first step in fulfilling his obligation to help his parents-in-law. If the marriage later dissolved, the gifts did not have to be returned, although some people expressed mild indignation about this when we asked them about it. Subsequent marriages might or might not occasion gift-giving.

Practical action rather than ritual defined marriage. There was no wedding ceremony, although sometimes a new couple gave a small feast. The true beginning of a marriage was when the couple set up house together and assumed the economic and social roles of husband and wife. They began to cooperate in food getting and to share their meals. The wife took on the responsibility of cooking for her husband, even though men as well as women knew how to cook all foods and did so during bachelorhood. They also began to help both sets of parents economically, to use the appropriate terms of reference and address for their affines, and to follow the proper avoidance behaviors toward them.

Ideally the couple would spend most of the first year of the marriage camping near the wife's parents, especially if the wife were very young, so that the husband could help his parents-in-law. The pair would then spend the next year with the husband's parents, helping them. After this, the couple could reside wherever they wanted to, although most couples tried to spend some time with both sets of parents. In practice the pattern of residence following marriage was highly variable.

Divorce was as casual and almost as frequent as marriage in the years of early adulthood. Most marriages of young people were in a sense experiments in having relationships and playing adult roles, and most of them foundered after a short time. Sometimes one partner, usually the girl, was too young to be willing to act as an adult married person. One girl who first married at around thirteen years of age had a series of separations from and reconciliations with her husband, who was a few years older than she. The reasons she gave for not wanting to be married to him were that she did not know how to cook for him and did not want to sleep with him. The first reason was unfounded if taken literally, for she clearly knew how to cook all the foods the Batek ate. The statement suggests, however, that she did not want to perform the role of wife.

Another common reason for divorce among young people was that the husband and wife wanted to camp with their own parents, who might be living in separate camps or even in separate river valleys. If both the husband and wife were unwilling to compromise by temporarily leaving their parents to live where the spouse wanted to live, the only solution might be divorce. Sometimes parents pressured their children to divorce if they did not like the child's spouse. Yet, few people actually divorced for such a reason if they were truly fond of their spouse.

After a series of marriages and divorces in early adulthood, most Batek entered into a more stable marriage, or, as Batek put it, they found someone who "stuck" to them. Such a marriage might last until one person died, although some ended in divorce after a period of years. A characteristic of these more stable marriages, which the marriages of early adulthood normally lacked, was the presence of children. It is unclear why early marriages usually produced no children, as couples did engage in sexual intercourse. Perhaps young wives experienced what has been called a "period of adolescent sterility" due to their reproductive cycles not being well-established. Pregnancies tended to solidify marriages, encouraging couples to adopt full adult responsibilities and duties toward each other and their child.

Divorce, like marriage, was easily carried out in Batek society. If a couple began to live in separate shelters, they were considered divorced. Since there was no bridewealth and no group or family interests vested in the marriage, there were no great impediments to divorce when the couple no longer wanted to remain together. Spouses were not so dependent upon each other that a divorce would cause economic problems serious enough to keep them in an otherwise undesirable marriage. Women and men could get their own vegetable and animal foods through their own efforts and the sharing network and could call upon other relatives for help when necessary. Both spouses could also build their own shelters, so they were not dependent upon each other for a roof over their heads. Thus, divorce did not present extreme hardship to Batek men or women, although economic cooperation between spouses did, of course, make life easier.

After a divorce of a couple with children, breast-feeding infants and very young children remained with the mother, while older children might live with either parent (the children themselves decided) or alternate between them. Divorced parents might live in the same camp or in nearby camps, thus facilitating visits with their children. When a divorced parent remarried, the new spouse took on a parental role toward the children that continued even if they in turn divorced. Thus the more divorces and remarriages their biological parents went through, the more "parents" the children acquired. This dispersion of parental responsibilities no doubt enhanced the security of children in a society in which either or both parents might die at any time by giving the children a number of potential foster parents. Similarly, affinal ties were maintained after divorce, with the result that one's affinal network increased with each divorce and remarriage. This gave older people a substantial number of "children-in-law" whom they could call upon for help. Thus, divorce in Batek society paradoxically helped create more, not fewer, ties between people.

Batek said there were both good divorces, in which spouses parted on friendly terms, and bad divorces, in which one or the other partner was emotionally hurt. Most former spouses seemed to accept the fact that people's feelings toward each other could change. When looking back on previous marriages and divorces, people seemed remarkably unbitter. Usually they said that the other person had broken off the marriage, but they seldom expressed anger or humiliation over having been rejected. Of course it is impossible to know just how much hurt, anger, jealousy, or disappointment people felt but suppressed even in "good" divorces. From early childhood Batek were not encouraged to display anger, although they were not—like Semai Orang Asli (Dentan 1968; Robarchek 1977)—trained to fear all strong emotions in themselves. They learned to control, disperse, vent, or bury their negative emotions or to "walk away" from anger by moving away from people with whom they were in conflict. However they managed to deal with their negative emotions, the result was that former spouses often lived in the same camps in apparent friendship and harmony.

Batek believed that people should wait some time after a divorce or a spouse's death before remarrying. The reason for the waiting period was to prevent the smell of the old spouse from mixing with the smell of the new spouse. The length of the waiting period varied, however, depending on personal circumstances and feelings.

It was prohibited (*lawac*) to sleep with or marry two siblings in rapid succession because the mixture of smells of the two siblings through the spouse would be offensive to Gobar. Breaking this prohibition, like breaking the incest prohibition, would result in Gobar's sending a crippling disease to the offender by means of a spark of lightning. Batek avoided the problem by waiting long enough for the smells to disappear before remarrying. The proper interval between marriages to siblings was a month, although if there were children by the first spouse, the interval was a year, because the children's smells would mix with the new spouse's smell too.

Extramarital affairs were fairly common. People joked that affairs were fine unless the couple had their tryst on a major path. Although spouses of the lovers might be hurt, angry, or jealous if the lovers were found out, and other relatives might become angry because of the social disruptions such affairs could cause, there was no means by which people could prevent men and women from engaging in extramarital relationships. Batek did not take special measures to prevent affairs or to punish those who indulged in them. They did not keep guard over their spouses or prohibit them from working in the forest away from the camp with people of the opposite sex. Their attitude was that no one could control the sexuality of anyone else in premarital, marital, or extramarital contexts.

Although Batek permitted polygamy, almost all Batek marriages were monogamous. The only stable polygamous marriage we encountered in a Semang group was among the horticultural Mendriq living to the west of the Batek, a case of a man with two wives. Among the Batek, polygynous marriages occasionally occurred when men, emulating the Muslim Malays, took second wives. These were always transitional situations, however, for one of the wives would eventually leave the marriage.

In a typical case, a man about twenty years old with a wife about the same age and a small baby took a second, younger wife, supposedly to help the first wife with the cooking and baby tending. Although the girls had been friends, they soon became rivals, and the younger one declared that she wanted the husband for herself. The original wife told the husband to choose one or the other or else she was leaving. In that case the husband divorced the second wife, but in some cases it went the other way. In general women did not like to share a husband, and they had no reason to tolerate such a marriage, since women were not dependent on husbands for food or shelter. Moreover, women could be reasonably sure of finding another husband, especially when women were in short supply, as on the upper Lebir in the mid-1970s. No woman we knew ever expressed a desire for more than one husband, though one woman said this was possible, but it might lead to the wife having twins.

Platonic Male–Female Interactions

Batek men and women, whether married or not, were free to interact socially and economically with members of the opposite sex. They were not limited to their own sex group for friendship, companionship, or work partners. Men and women who were married to other people sometimes worked together in the forest, out of sight of their spouses, and they visited one another freely in camp and between different camps. People sometimes gave gifts, such as bamboo combs, to members of the opposite sex out of friendship, without an obligation to reciprocate. Both men and women could maintain special friendships with people they might have married but did not, as in Tanyogn's case.

Batek believed that platonic relationships between persons of the opposite sex were possible. Indeed, Batek life was replete with close but nonerotic physical contact between males and females. A look around a Batek camp would reveal many instances of such contact. Family members in their small shelters, the floor space of which was only about five by seven feet, were constantly and unavoidably jostling one another. Babies were carried in slings that kept them pressed against the mother's or father's body. At night parents and their young children slept close together. Children playing in camp usually formed a tight cluster of bodies, often sitting on each other's lap, leaning against one another, or standing arm in arm. When around adults, young children often nestled into the adults' arms. Adolescents of both sexes lolled around in their shelters together in close bodily contact. Physical proximity and touching seemed to be the norm in Batek behavior.

One of the most common types of physical contact was delousing people's hair. The person being groomed either sat or lay in front of the groomer or lay with his or her head in the groomer's lap. Anyone could groom anyone else, regardless of sex, age, marital status, or closeness of relationship. It was not unusual to see a man or woman lying with his or her head in the lap of a member of the opposite sex who was married to someone else. In many societies, including our own, such close contact between two people would have been tantamount to admitting desire for each other or the existence of a sexual relationship between the two people. For Batek, however, the contact involved in

People of both sexes were often in close bodily contact with each other. In an oft-repeated scene, a mother searches her daughter's hair for lice.

delousing was no different from the other types of physical contact that they had from birth onwards. Batek, with their open shelters and open camps could readily observe that purposeful contacts, such as in delousing, as well as unavoidable jostling, did not necessarily indicate sexual intent. Indeed, the Batek did not even prohibit delousing between relatives who had to avoid each other sexually, even though the physical contact necessary for grooming was so close. This contrasts with the western Semang, who have strict prohibitions on touching between opposite-sex in-laws and close relatives (Schebesta 1954).

The acceptance of the existence of platonic relationships between members of opposite sexes had economic and social implications for Batek life. Since any man could work with any woman, a far greater number of work-group combinations occurred than would have been possible if the Batek were suspicious of mixed work parties. Also, the freedom of interaction enabled unmarried men to have access to female companionship and to goods, such as pandanus sleeping mats and baskets, which were made almost exclusively by women. Unmarried men were able to call upon female relatives and friends to build shelters for them in a new camp, so that they could go hunting right away, as the married men did. Similarly, unmarried women could gain access to male companionship and to rattan baskets made only by men.

A further effect of unrestricted interaction in Batek society is that there was not much social distance between the sexes. Batek male and female lives were far more integrated than in societies in which men and women could only turn to their own sex group for companionship.

Political System

Decision-Making and Group Coordination

The Batek had no formal political organization coordinating their activities. Decision making about all economic and social matters resided ultimately with individuals and conjugal families. Yet most decisions were not made in isolation. The very fact that families camped together implies some convergence of their interests and coordination of their decisions. Before a move, people discussed informally or in a meeting where to go and what to do. All interested parties, male and female, expressed their views, and those conjugal families that decided to do the same thing in the same area would move there together, while other families might go somewhere else. Usually husbands and wives jointly decided what activities they would pursue each day, but this too involved discussion with potential work-mates so that suitable work parties could be formed. Sometimes the interests of the camp-group as a whole were taken into account to ensure, for example, that when some people were collecting rattan, which did not produce an immediate return of food, others would be searching for food. Later the rattan collectors would share the food they obtained from the traders with those who had supported them before. These methods of decision making were cooperative without greatly impinging on the autonomy of the persons making up the families and camp-groups.

Leadership

Although Batek had no authority structure, they had two kinds of leaders: headmen and natural leaders (cf. Benjamin 1968). Headmen were introduced by Malays, while natural leaders developed within Batek society.

In Kelantan, headmen were called *penghulu*, the Malay term for "headmen of small districts."[2] Since the 1950s, they have been appointed by the JHEOA. But there is evidence in Batek genealogies that Malays had designated some Batek as "headmen," "commanders" (*panglima*), "ministers" (*menteri*), and even "kings" (*raja*) well before the JHEOA was created, probably in an attempt to create intermediaries through whom they could control the Batek. JHEOA officers tried to bestow the title *penghulu* upon people whom the Batek already looked to as their spokesmen and leaders (Ruslan bin Abdullah, personal communication; Howard F. Biles, personal communication), but, for one reason or another, the departmental officers did not always get it right. For example, two officially designated headmen were appointed because they had served in the military during the Emergency; they were not highly respected by Batek and therefore did not have much influence. When asked to recommend a new headman to replace one who died or retired, Batek assumed that they were supposed to look among the sons of the previous headman, following Malay custom, and genealogies show that headmanship did normally descend from father to son. People tried to choose the son with the best skills and personality for the job, someone who had the ability to communicate well with outsiders and a gentle manner with his fellow Batek. The JHEOA did not accept women as headmen, so people never recommended any. In 1975–76 there were two official headmen living on the upper Lebir, two on the Aring, and one at Kampung Macang, a half mile upstream from Post Lebir.

The headmen appointed by the JHEOA were supposed to represent vaguely defined groups of Batek in dealings with the JHEOA and other outsiders, in particular to convey the government's wishes to the Batek and to get them to do whatever the government wanted done. But as far as the Batek themselves were concerned, headmen had no authority over them. Batek saw the official headmen as like foreign ministers, who would carry their wishes and concerns to the powers that be. Because the interests of the Batek and the government often clashed, however, the headmen were usually unsuccessful. The job of headman, therefore, was highly stressful, since the headman could not satisfy the wishes of his "superiors" or his constituents. Many qualified Batek men rejected the job for that reason, despite the fact that it paid a small stipend.

What we call "natural leaders," on the other hand, were people whom the Batek themselves looked to for guidance. Natural leaders were usually older, intelligent, capable individuals—male or female—who had strong, charismatic personalities. They were said to have a "big name" (kənmɔh bəw), meaning they were known widely by reputation. They were leaders because people voluntarily turned to them for help and advice. But those who sought their advice could decide for themselves whether to follow it or not. Natural leaders did not seek power or influence; they merely served as a resource for people who wanted guidance. There was no Batek term for "natural leaders," but the Malay term for headman, *penghulu*, was sometimes applied to them even though they might not be official government-appointed headmen. Tanyogn, the female leader on the upper Lebir Batek in 1975–76, was often called Penghulu Tanyogn by other Batek and by Malay traders, although she was not recognized as such by the Department of Aboriginal Affairs.

Tanyogn exemplified the qualities of Batek natural leaders. She was highly intelligent and was an expert in many aspects of Batek life, including midwifery, herbal medicines, and religious matters. This made her an excellent source of information, and others often referred us to her for answers to difficult questions. She had a strong personality and impressive powers of persuasion. She participated vigorously in discussions and usually prevailed in arguments. She led by example. If something needed doing, she did it, encouraging other to pitch in as well. She routinely worked hard. When she and other women dug wild tubers, she usually came back to camp with more than anyone else. When she collected rattan for trade, she hauled as much as most of the younger men and women. Because Batek shared the food they obtained, Tanyogn's industriousness benefited the camp-group as a whole. She was concerned with the welfare of the group, not just her close relatives.

She and her husband, Langsat, took care of two orphaned boys. When she heard unattended children crying, she rushed over to comfort them. She helped sick parents by looking after their young children. When one of her nieces arrived in camp one day, Tanyogn built a shelter for her. When she saw us slip on a muddy path, she shoveled steps into the ground. Her sense of responsibility loomed large.

Tanyogn was fearless in dealing with Malays, and she knew how to manipulate them. For example, when some Malays took some corn from a Batek woman's garden, Tanyogn went to them and, threatening to report them to the JHEOA, demanded that they pay two gallons of husked rice, which they did. When some traders ordered the Batek to replace some bundles of rattan that had floated away in a heavy rainstorm, Tanyogn refused. They were foolish to leave the rattan by the stream, she bellowed. The Batek, she said, would have stored the rattan in the forest so it could not have washed away. She kept traders honest by having us weigh trade goods during transactions. Her actions made an impression on Malays and on fellow Batek. Long after her death she was remembered far and wide for her ability to *lawan gob*, "combat outsiders" (Lye 1997:426–427).

Tanyogn's ability to deal with Malays came partly from her personality and partly from her background. She had been interacting with Malays for most of her life. As a child, she had lived on the Relai and Lebir rivers at a time when many Malays lived along the riverbanks, and she and her family sometimes worked in their gardens in return for food, tobacco, and salt. They also traded forest produce to the Malays. For a while she worked for wages cutting rice at the villages of Limau Kasturi and Gua Musang along the railway line. When World War II broke out, she lived at Kuala Betis on the Nenggiri River—a meeting place between Malays and aboriginal Temiar. She had intermittent contact with Malay traders and government officials after moving back to the Lebir River.

Although Tanyogn was the only female natural leader we knew, there are hints in the literature suggesting that Semang cultures have long offered the possibility of a woman playing a leadership role. Speaking of the Batek he encountered in 1875, Miklucho-Maclay wrote:

> On several occasions, and in different places I heard accounts of Sakai [Batek] Rajahs, who are said to exist still and whom the people obey though these Rajahs do not live in any other style than the rest of the inhabitants of the forest. If such a Rajah dies his widow can claim to be considered as Queen. So I was often told and it is characteristic of the position of the Orang Sakai women as compared with that of the Malay women. (1878b:215)

Another group of Semang living in Patalung in southern Thailand apparently had a female leader in the 1920s, although the Austrian ethnographer Fr. Paul Schebesta (who visited her for less than two days) denied that she was actually the "chief," as the local Thais had claimed. He writes:

> Isan was a Semang woman whom the Siamese called the chief of the
> Negritos there, which she, of course, was not, as I knew when I met
> her. . . . Isan was, however, a very alert and voluble woman who had the
> ability to assert herself even with the men. Many other Semang women
> resembled Isan in this respect, but nowhere was leadership in the hands
> of a woman. (1954:227)

Although Schebesta's depiction of the strong position of Semang women in
general is consistent with our findings among the Batek, he seems to have
been unprepared to recognize a female leader when he saw one. However, I.
H. N. Evans, the director of the Federated Malay States Museum, also met
Isan, and he accepted her as the "ruler . . . to some extent" of her group
(1937:30–31). Certainly she exemplifies perfectly what we are calling a "natural leader."

Official headmen and natural leaders were not associated with specific
camps or clearly demarcated groups. The general flux of camp composition
resulted in some camps containing more than one leader and others containing none, although in that case one of the respected older people usually
became a temporary informal leader. When more than one leader lived in a
camp, they cooperated like everyone else. We seldom saw evidence of conflict
or competition between leaders. However, we did notice that one official
headman on the upper Lebir tended to camp separately from Tanyogn, possibly due to a clash of personalities.

Well-known shamans had some political significance. Although they did
not have power, they had influence in religious matters because of their
expertise. For example, one man said that he married an older woman at the
urging of a shaman he respected. Shamans took responsibility for making
sure that people behaved with proper regard for the superhuman beings and
the cosmos. To prevent cosmic catastrophes, shamans organized singing sessions to communicate with the superhuman beings, directing construction of
the dancing platform and large shelter, and leading the rituals. People sometimes gave food and fine mats to shamans after major ceremonies, but shamans could not demand gifts or extend their influence to other spheres of life.

Dispute Management

Batek did not vest natural leaders or headmen with the authority to pass
judgment on others or settle disputes. The disagreements that came up in the
course of everyday life were handled by the persons directly involved rather
than by an outside arbiter or judge. As discussed above, people almost never
used violence or threats of violence in trying to settle disputes; such behavior
was considered totally unacceptable. Instead, Batek used two peaceful ways
of dealing with disagreements. The first was to talk about them, either in a
direct discussion between the persons involved or in the form of loud complaints made to anyone who was willing to listen, sometimes done during the
evening hours in cross-camp arguments, discussions, or simultaneous mono-

logues. These discussions resembled the "talks" reported by Marshall as a key means by which the Ju/'hoansi of southern Africa resolved their disagreements (Marshall 1976). Among Batek, such discussions might lead to a consensus about who was in the wrong on a particular issue, and the group might try to bring the pressure of public disapproval on the offender to induce him or her to make retribution—emotional or material—to the victim. If tensions persisted, disputants employed their other method of dealing with disagreements: moving away from each other until tensions waned. Such separations were easily accomplished, as people could join up with other camp-groups at any time. People who tended to disagree frequently or otherwise not get along usually avoided one another altogether by not living in the same camp.

Conclusion

Batek ethical principles and social practices provided a basis for egalitarian relations between men and women. People were under a general obligation to help each other, especially through food sharing, but at the same time individuals, women as well as men, were free to make their own choices about economic activities, moving, companions, sexuality, marriage and divorce, and social roles. Only the Malay-imposed institution of headmanship favored men over women, but because headmen had little influence on Batek social life, even this did not offer men any clear social or political advantages.

Notes

[1] Miklucho-Maclay reported that in 1874–1875 some Batek were hostile to Malays and never lost an opportunity to take revenge on Malays for raiding them for slaves and other offenses. (He does not specify what form their revenge took.) Consequently, Malays were afraid to go into the parts of the forest where those Batek lived (1878b:213; see also Lye 2004:103, 105–106). We do not know how much credence to give this report. It is possible that some Batek did resist violently at times in the past, but we did not hear any Batek oral traditions to that effect (but cf. Lye 2004:106).

[2] By the 1990s, the JHEOA had taken to calling Batek headmen in Pahang by the Aboriginal Malay term *batin*, though the Malay term *penghulu* was still used in Kelantan. For details of headmanship in Pahang, see Lye 1997.

Chapter 4

Sharing the Work
The Gender Division of Labor

In this chapter we look at the kinds and amounts of work Batek men and women did. We begin by presenting our findings on how they obtained their food during the study period, and we compare the production of men and women in the major food-getting activities. We then describe who did non-food-getting jobs, such as making shelters and equipment. At the end of the chapter we discuss the question of why, given that men and women were free to pursue whatever activities they wished, the proportions of work done by men and women differed in many activities, even to the extent that some jobs were seen as the specialties of one sex or the other.

An Overview of the Batek Economy

In 1975–76 the upper Lebir River Batek were making their living through a mixture of foraging, trade, horticulture, and, very occasionally, working for outsiders (see also K.M. Endicott 1984; Endicott and Bellwood 1991). When we first arrived in September 1975, ten families were living at a clearing where they had planted about an acre of maize and other fast-growing crops. They were eating mainly maize from their garden and *gadoŋ* (*Dioscorea hispida*) tubers. Within a week of our arrival people grew tired of processing *gadoŋ*, abandoned the garden, and moved into the forest to join another group of Batek who were collecting rattan to trade to Malays. Rattan was in demand for making fish traps and furniture. Following established practice, the rattan collectors had contracted with Malay traders to supply them with a large quantity of rattan by a designated date. The Malays had given them an advance payment in the form of rice and flour, to free them to collect rattan rather than food. When these supplies ran out, people turned again to gathering and eating wild foods (a pattern we were to see numerous times), but continued collecting rattan for the traders until late November. Forming two or sometimes three separate camp-groups, people moved to new locations whenever they had exhausted the rattan and wild foods within about an hour's walk from camp. They lived on foraged food, traded food, and the few remaining crops at their abandoned garden that had escaped the predations of monkeys, pigs, and elephants.

From mid-December to mid-January, when the annual monsoon caused severe flooding, the Malay traders retreated to their homes near the village of Manek Urai, and we left for Singapore, in part to avoid the floods and in part to enable the Batek to concentrate on getting food without being encumbered by visitors during the most arduous time of the year. When we returned in February, people told us that they had spent the flood months divided into three camp-groups, all of which had moved away from the swollen main river to the upper reaches of small streams, where flooding was less of a problem and where wild tubers, game, and palm hearts and pith were more readily available.

After the flood season, the JHEOA started an agricultural project on the middle Lebir River just below the mouth of the Relai River. With the promise of rice and other free rations, JHEOA personnel induced all ninety Batek from the upper Lebir and seventy-six Batek from the Aring River to take part. These people formed several camps on opposite sides of the Lebir, cleared some forest, and planted maize, cassava, and a few other crops. While living at the clearing, they subsisted on the rations given by the JHEOA, food foraged from the surrounding forest—which quickly became depleted—and small amounts of agricultural produce they earned by doing farm chores for a few Malay families who were planting crops nearby. When the government rations ran out at the end of April, the Batek abandoned the clearing and went back to nomadic foraging and collecting rattan for the traders. In addition to hunting game and gathering a wide variety of wild tubers, they collected large quantities of honey, some of which they ate and some they traded for rice, flour, tobacco, cloth, candy, and costume jewelry. Occasionally they returned to their clearing to retrieve a few ears of corn. By mid-June, when we had to leave, they had begun to gather significant quantities of seasonal fruit. They told us that when the fruit season reached its peak, in July and August, they would move into the choicest fruit groves and live on nothing but fruit and game.

As this brief chronicle shows, Batek combined a wide variety of economic activities in a single year and shifted from one to another as opportunities changed. Their selection of opportunities was not random, however. It was based on a calculation that took account of their food preferences and the ease or difficulty of procuring the foods (K.M. Endicott 1984). Normally they would drop any other work to gather seasonal fruit or honey. When those were not available, they would collect forest produce to trade for such foods as rice, flour, and sugar. Lacking opportunities for trade, they would turn to gathering wild tubers and other vegetables. They would attempt to grow their own crops only when the JHEOA ordered them to and gave them seeds, shoots, and, most importantly, rations to tide them over until the crops were ripe. In practice they would work at farming only until the rations ran out. Regardless of their other activities, they hunted and fished regularly, as game and fish were their main sources of protein.

Their pattern of movement followed from their choice of economic activities. When they were not participating in the agricultural scheme, people moved camp every week to ten days, depending on when they exhausted nearby sources of food or rattan. If they had rice or flour on hand, however, they might remain at a campsite even after they had finished off the area's wild foods. When deciding where to move next, people chose destinations they thought would have food or trade goods in the vicinity. If their expectations proved incorrect, they moved on after a night or two. They did not follow a preplanned itinerary, but instead made their decisions on the basis of past experience and new information brought in by people searching for resources.

Getting Food

The old stereotype of man the hunter and woman the gatherer obscured the fact that in many hunting and gathering societies men also obtained vegetable foods and women obtained animal foods (Estioko-Griffin and Griffin 1981). The stereotype also exaggerated the importance of men's contributions to the food supply. By weighing all of the food a group of !Kung San (Ju/'hoansi) of Botswana obtained during a month in 1964, Richard Lee made the startling discovery that women were bringing in two to three times as much food by weight as men (1968). The drama and excitement surrounding men's big game hunting and people's love of meat tended to overshadow the contribution women made by quietly and steadily gathering vegetable foods, such as mongongo nuts, and killing small animals.

To avoid false impressions about the nature and amount of Batek men's and women's contributions to the food supply, we weighed all the food brought into camp during the study period, and we recorded the length of time people spent getting the food in as many instances as possible. We classified all meat-getting activities (except for fishing) as hunting and all plant-getting activities as gathering, regardless of whether men or women did them.

The data presented below are based on work diaries collected on ninety-three days, at intervals, over a period of nine months. We compiled the work diaries when the people were living nomadically, foraging for food and collecting rattan for trade, not while they were participating in the JHEOA agricultural scheme, although we include small amounts of cultivated food obtained from their abandoned gardens in our data. All seasons are represented in the data except the fruit season of July and August—the easiest period for getting food—and the flood months of December and January—the most difficult period. We weighed and recorded only the foraged and traded foods that people brought into camp, so our records do not reflect the food they consumed in the forest. Our records also exclude the small amount of food obtained by children.

During the period of data collection, the population of the camps was constantly changing. We therefore present the data in the following tables in terms of "instances of work" by men and women without identifying workers by name or specifying the daily population of each camp. By instance of work we mean continuous participation in a given food-getting activity on a single day. In cases in which several people worked together in a food-getting activity, we credited them all with instances of that type of work and divided the yields equally among all the workers. If a person did the same type of food-getting work twice in a day with a long break or another activity in between, we recorded it as two instances of the activity and recorded the yields of each instance separately. Because we were not able to time every instance of work that was done, the following tables include a category called "timed instances" and another category called "total instances." The total hours of work recorded in the tables are based upon the timed instances only, not the total instances of that activity. The recorded weights of animals are the whole, unbutchered weights, and the weights of vegetable foods are the raw, unprocessed weights.

Blowpipe Hunting

Batek used several methods to obtain game, including blowpipe hunting, smoking animals out of holes, digging them out of burrows, clubbing or spearing them, and chopping down trees in order to reach nesting game. Of these methods, blowpipe hunting was the most frequent and productive, undertaken in 61 percent of all hunting trips during our period of study and providing 70 percent by weight of all game obtained (see tables 4.1, 4.2, and 4.3).

Blowpipe hunters used blowpipes to shoot poisoned darts at tree-dwelling animals such as monkeys, gibbons, squirrels, birds, civets, and bearcats. Batek made their blowpipes from thin tubes of bamboo, one-half to one inch in diameter, fitted together to form a straight, double-walled tube from five to six feet long (K.M. Endicott 1972). A mouthpiece made from a bulb of resin enabled the hunter to form an airtight seal between his lips and the blowpipe. Hunters carved their darts from splints of palm wood, capped them with cones of pith, and coated the point with poison made by concentrating the sap of the cɛh tree (*Antiaris toxicaria*; Malay *ipuh*). They charred their dart shafts near the point so that if a wounded monkey tried to pull a dart out, the embedded tip would break off, leaving the poison in the flesh. Hunters carried their darts in bamboo quivers, about four inches in diameter and a foot long, strapped to their waists with cords. The blowpipe was a lightweight, easily portable weapon with an impressive range: hunters could shoot accurately into the lower stories of the forest canopy, more than 100 feet above the ground. For reasons that will be explored later, most blowpipe hunting was done by men.

Men hunted individually or in groups of two or three, rarely more, because larger groups were more likely to make noise and scare off the game. Often an experienced hunter was assisted by a young man who was learning to hunt. Because leaf monkeys, the usual quarry, normally feed in the lower tree branches in the morning and afternoon, spending the middle part of the day resting in the treetops beyond the reach of the blowpipe, hunters left camp around 8:30 to 9 AM and returned in the late afternoon, although they would start later if they had to make a new supply of darts first. Occasionally hunters went out just for a few hours in the afternoon. Hunters took their blowpipes, quivers of darts, bush-knives, and a few leaf-wrapped embers or a store-bought cigarette lighter to light their cigarettes or to start fires if they needed to smoke an animal out of a hole or cook an animal before returning to camp.

To find a troop of monkeys, hunters often had to travel into the forest a considerable distance from camp, since monkeys avoided areas near camps and areas where foraging parties were regularly working. Hunters walked quickly to the area they had in mind, then began their search, moving slowly

The most productive form of hunting was with blow-pipes and poisoned darts. Here a hunter aims his blowpipe at a monkey high in a tree.

and quietly, scanning the treetops for movement, listening for the crashing sound of monkeys leaping from tree to tree, and smelling the surrounding vegetation for the odor of monkey urine. They also scanned the ground and the bases of trees for signs of burrowing animals, such as pangolins and porcupines. Although monkeys were their primary quarry, hunters pursued any type of animal they came across. Often they worked their way along ridgetops to get a good view of the trees in the valleys on both sides.

When they spotted a troop of monkeys, one of the hunters would creep silently to the base of the tree that the nearest or most accessible animal was in. If he saw a *bateyoh* (*Hylobates syndactylus*; Malay *siamang*), a large, black gibbon, or a pig-tailed macaque (*Macaca nemestrina*; Malay *beruk*), the hunter might imitate its cry to induce it to come closer. He quietly aimed his blowpipe upward and shot a series of darts until confident that the animal had been hit at least once, preferably several times. Since the blowpipe makes only an abrupt popping sound when shot and darts are almost silent in flight, animals often were not frightened off even when one of their number had been hit. Sometimes wounded animals tried to flee, but they went only far enough to get out of sight of the hunters. The hunters then sat down, relaxed, smoked cigarettes, and talked in whispers as they waited for the monkey to die. A mature monkey might take as long as an hour to feel the full effects of the poison and fall to the ground. As soon as the crash gave away the monkey's location, the hunters rushed in. If the animal had any strength left, it might make a futile attempt to flee before the poison finally stopped its heart.

On a good day, a party of hunters killed several monkeys. Sometimes, however, hunters might not see any game or might only wound an animal. The poison didn't always work. Successful or not, hunters returned to camp by late afternoon or early evening, after an average of six hours of hunting.

If hunters made a kill early in the day, they might butcher and cook the animal and eat a bit of the meat before returning to camp with the remaining meat tied up in leaf bundles. Otherwise, they brought the unbutchered animal back to camp. Either way, they shared all the meat brought into camp with the other camp members. Considering the large amount of meat that was brought into camp during the ninety-three days of data collection (see table 4.1), hunters took seriously their obligation to share the food they obtained.

Between hunting trips hunters kept busy with ancillary activities. They spent many hours maintaining their blowpipes: heating them gently over low fires in order to straighten the shafts and dry the bamboo, which otherwise would rot from the high humidity in the forest. Hunters also spent part of each day making new darts to replace those previously used and lost. At almost any time of the day, someone would be working on a blowpipe or making darts. Sometimes hunters continued to prepare darts far into the night, working by the light of a resin torch, in anticipation of an early start the following day.

In the course of hunting or other work in the forest, people collected the materials for darts—pith for the cone and palm wood for the shaft—whenever they found them, keeping them for eventual use. Collecting the sap for dart poison, on the other hand, could require a full day's work if the most accessible poison trees were far from camp. Hunters cut V-shaped grooves in the bark of the poison tree and let the sap drip into a bamboo tube. They made the poison by repeatedly coating a bamboo spatula with sap and drying it over a fire until it formed a thick, sticky coating. The spatula was then stored in a covered bamboo container for future use. To poison a set of new darts, the hunter heated the spatula and rolled the dart tips in the softened poison. New batches of poison were constantly being made to replace what had been used or had to be discarded if the poison proved too weak to kill.

Table 4.1 summarizes the blowpipe hunting activities of the upper Lebir Batek during the study period and shows that men were the major participants in blowpipe hunting, accounting for 98 percent of the instances of the activity and all of the meat obtained. (Once a girl killed three birds with a blowpipe, but we did not include the food obtained by children in our data.) Men managed to procure some meat 87 of the 179 times they went blowpipe hunting, a success rate of 49 percent. Women accounted for the remaining 2

Making new blowpipe darts was a daily activity for Batek men. A young man rolls the tips of his darts in the sticky poison and lays the darts on a split piece of bamboo to dry.

percent of instances of hunting and came back empty-handed. Batek women and men alike said that women who went blowpipe hunting did it mainly for fun; the data indicate that women were not highly involved in the activity.

Table 4.1   Blowpipe Hunting

	Total Weight (Lbs.)	Total No. Instances	Average Lbs. per Instance	No. Timed Instances	Total Time Recorded (Hrs.)	Average Time Worked (Hrs. per Instance)	Average Yield (Lbs. per Hr.) of Timed Instances
Men	883.32	179	4.93	102	610.75	5.99	1.09
Women	0	3	0	1	2	2	0

Curiously, most Lebir Batek women showed little or no interest in blowpipe hunting even though, in contrast to some foraging societies, they were not prohibited from doing it. The Ju/'hoansi, for example, strictly prohibit women from hunting or even touching hunting equipment (Marshall 1976; Lee 1979; see Shostak 1981 for a case of a Ju/'hoansi woman hunting—and other Ju/'hoansi considering her actions to be deviant). We observed a few young Batek girls using borrowed blowpipes to hunt birds and squirrels with their male contemporaries or by themselves. We came across only three women who kept up an interest in blowpipe hunting into their adult years. The most enthusiastic woman blowpipe hunter we met was Chinloy, a married woman about sixteen years old. She owned her own blowpipe, which had been made by Langsat, an expert blowpipe maker who had supplied blowpipes to several of the men.

The hunting these women did differed from that of the men in some significant ways: the women's hunting was more recreational than serious; they mainly went after birds and squirrels as young boys and girls do, rather than attempting to hunt larger game; and they hunted in short spurts close to the camp rather than in more distant areas of the forest where the larger game would most likely be found. Although during our period of study these women failed to kill any animals with their blowpipes, they nonetheless seemed to enjoy the activity. Any food they might have procured would have been welcome, of course, but the group clearly was not depending upon the blowpiping efforts of women to provide meat. Batek women did not undergo the intensive training in hunting that men did, but it remains debatable whether this was a cause or an effect of the low numbers of women doing blowpipe hunting and the low success rate of those who did.

Because Batek depended upon male rather than female hunters to provide meat for the group, blowpipe hunting was a serious responsibility for the men. Many men seemed to enjoy hunting, and they spent a large portion of their time doing it. Others were enthusiastic about it during the first days at a

Chinloy, one of the few women who took an active interest in hunting, had her own blowpipe, but she carried her darts in her hair instead of in a bamboo quiver.

new camp, when game was relatively close and easy to find, but subsequently preferred to concentrate on other activities, such as rattan collecting. Even in the course of other activities, however, men kept their blowpipes close at hand in case they came across game or they decided to do some hunting along with their other work.

Although hunting was a vital part of food getting, Batek did not imbue it with the value and cultural emphasis that some other foraging societies did. Instead, Batek viewed hunting as one of a range of vital economic activities. People respected good hunters but did not ridicule poor ones. They knew that hunting ability was variable and that many factors influenced success, including differences in eyesight, lung strength for blowing darts, age, physical abilities, as well as circumstances surrounding specific hunting attempts. Accordingly, some people who rarely succeeded at hunting turned their attentions to other food-getting activities and left hunting to those more likely to succeed.

Girls as well as boys were free to practice blowpipe hunting, as these young girls are doing. By early adolescence, however, most girls had given it up, while boys were entering a period of serious training and practice that would enable them to become effective hunters.

Other Hunting

Hunters almost always took blowpipes when they went hunting, but often they would return to camp later that day with game obtained by other means. They employed specialized methods to procure several common animals: hornbills, bats, porcupines and pangolins (scaly anteaters), tortoises, and bamboo rats. Although people usually did not specifically set out to find these animals, sometimes they would see signs of them in the course of other activities, and later a hunting party would set out to try to get them. An advantage of hunting these animals was that they could be "stored" in their nests, holes, or burrows (see Ingold 1983). Hunters could be reasonably sure that the animals would still be in the same location at a later time, should they be unwilling or unable to go after them right away. This was not true of monkeys and other animals that roamed more freely; hunters had to take immediate advantage of opportunities to kill such game.

Hornbills were one animal that people could delay hunting until they had the time and inclination. The female hornbill and her brood nest for up to three months a year in a hole in a tree, safely walled in by the male, who seals the entrance with mud, leaving only a beak-sized hole through which he passes food. People found the nests by watching where the male hornbill went to deliver its supplies of food. The birds then became easy prey for hunters, who would climb the tree and chop through the mud wall to reach the trapped birds. If the tree was too large to be climbed easily, the hunters would cut it down before breaking through the nest walls. The male hornbill, like other birds, could be brought down with a blowpipe dart. Since hornbills were obtained by climbing or chopping down trees or by blowpiping, usually men rather than women got them.

Some species of bats lived in holes in trees, which could be spotted when the bats left at dusk to look for food. People would chop down the trees during the day when the bats were asleep inside. As the tree hit the ground, the startled bats would fly out of the hole, and the hunting party would club as many as possible. Hunters did not bother climbing bat trees because too many bats would escape through the open hole. Usually men both felled the trees and clubbed the bats, although sometimes women, especially young women who did not have children to look after, helped with the clubbing.

The bases of hollow trees and holes in the ground were the hideouts of porcupines and pangolins, which could weigh up to twenty-five pounds. People who found their burrows would make a pile of dry leaves and twigs outside the entrance, set fire to it, and fan the smoke into the hole. The smoke either drove the animal out of the hole, so the hunters could kill it with a club or bush-knife, or asphyxiated it in its burrow, in which case they could dig it out. Any combination of men, women, and children might participate in hunting porcupines and pangolins.

Similarly, men, women, and children caught tortoises on the banks of streams and rivers and in shallow water. People prodded mud or masses of rotting vegetation with a stick, hoping to hear and feel the telltale thump as the stick hit a tortoise shell. It was harder to capture the larger tortoises, which weighed upwards of sixty pounds and lived in deep pools in the streams. Usually men dove into the pools, speared the tortoises, and dragged them to the surface. If large tortoises were caught far from camp, the hunters would cook them, discard the shell, and carry only the meat back to camp.

Women were far more involved in hunting bamboo rats (*Rhizomys sumatrensis*), bamboo-eating rodents that weigh up to six pounds. People could hear them chewing on the roots of bamboo, as the sound resonated through the stems, or spot their droppings and then search for the entrances to their burrows. Working alone or in groups of two or three, the hunters used metal-tipped digging sticks to dig down one of the entrances to the bamboo rat's burrow. If there was no sign of the animal, they would dig down another entrance, and so on until they trapped their prey. With someone stationed at each entrance to club the bamboo rat if it tried to escape, the diggers thrust their digging sticks into the burrow until the animal was killed or wounded enough to give up fighting. If brought up from the burrow still alive, they clubbed it to death with digging sticks or the blunt edges of their bush-knives.

Tables 4.2 and 4.3 document the participation of men and women in methods of hunting other than blowpipe hunting.

Table 4.2   Nonblowpipe Hunting (excluding hunting of bamboo rats)

	Total Weight (Lbs.)	Total No. Instances	Average Lbs. per Instance	No. Timed Instances	Total Time Recorded (Hrs.)	Average Time Worked (Hrs. per Instance)	Average Yield (Lbs. per Hr.) of Timed Instances
Men	263.45	63	4.18	40	225.75	5.64	0.96
Women	6.52	12	0.54	8	13	1.63	0.3

Table 4.3   Hunting Bamboo Rats

	Total Weight (Lbs.)	Total No. Instances	Average Lbs. per Instance	No. Timed Instances	Total Time Recorded (Hrs.)	Average Time Worked (Hrs. per Instance)	Average Yield (Lbs. per Hr.) of Timed Instances
Men	84.65	28	3.02	15	60.25	4.02	0.72
Women	24.4	11	2.22	8	25.5	3.19	0.72

As in blowpipe hunting, men were more active than women in these hunting methods, both in frequency of attempts and yields. Still, women procured 2 percent by weight of the animals hunted by nonblowpipe methods and 22 percent of all bamboo rats. Probably women were relatively active in hunting bamboo rats because it was an activity they could do during the course of other foraging; it could be done by individuals or by larger groups, even with young children present; and it could be accomplished relatively quickly, usually in under an hour. Also, since bamboo rat hunting required the same equipment used for digging tubers, women could go after bamboo rats as the opportunity arose without having to plan in advance and carry special equipment.

Fishing

Batek used several methods of fishing: rod and line, hand, net, and poison. (In recent years they also used spearguns.) During the study period, rod and line fishing was the most frequent method used, especially by women, who often took their children fishing as a way of filling in an hour or two after completing other work. People made rods on the spot out of palm fronds by stripping the leaves off the stems and attaching store-bought or traded lines and hooks. Most fishing was done either early or late in the day, when streams were shaded. When people found a school of fish, they called their companions over, then followed the school upstream or downstream until they either caught some fish or gave up. The fish in the forest streams generally were very small, rarely more than a few ounces, and hourly yields of fish were low, as table 4.4 documents. Even a few small fish, however, made a welcome sauce when boiled. Usually people managed to catch only enough fish to feed their own families, although when the amounts were great enough, they shared with other families as well.

Fishing with nets, bought or traded from Malays, was done by men rather than women, perhaps in imitation of Malay practice. The most common method of net fishing was to stake out gill nets, measuring about three feet wide and twelve feet long, in the main river or in one of the larger side-streams. Fishermen put them out in the evening and hauled them in in the morning, usually yielding several good-sized fish. A few people also used circular casting nets in shallow waters, a method that also could produce a good catch under favorable conditions. Not many Batek owned fishing nets, how-

Hook-and-line fishing was recreational as well as economically productive. Using palm frond stems for rods, traded lines and hooks, and worms for bait, two women with babies on their backs spend a few hours fishing in hopes of getting the ingredients for a tasty sauce.

ever, and those who did own them did not always use them even when camping near the rivers and larger streams that were most suitable for net fishing. In contrast to the rural Malays who relied extensively on net fishing to provide much of their protein, Batek net fished only sporadically.

Batek also occasionally poisoned fish with poisons made from bark or roots. Fish poisoning was most effective in a section of a small stream that people could easily dam up or that had been dammed naturally by a fallen log or leaf-clogged rocks. A large group of men, women, and children would work together to pound the poison out of the bark or roots and release it into the stream. Stunned by the poison, the fish would drift to the surface and could be picked right out of the water. Although in his previous fieldwork Kirk had seen people get substantial amounts of fish by poisoning, people used this method only once during our period of study.

Table 4.4 documents Batek fishing, almost all of which was by hook and line.

Table 4.4   Fishing

	Total Weight (Lbs.)	Total No. Instances	Average Lbs. per Instance	No. Timed Instances	Total Time Recorded (Hrs.)	Average Time Worked (Hrs. per Instance)	Average Yield (Lbs. per Hr.) of Timed Instances
Men	40.34	43	0.94	22	73.5	3.34	0.35
Women	36.19	82	0.44	59	166	2.81	0.19

The table shows that women fished almost twice as often as men and obtained 47 percent by weight of all fish caught. In fact, women procured more fish than any other type of animal food. Fishing, however, accounted for only 6 percent by weight of the animal foods Batek obtained.

Gathering Tubers

Wild tubers were the vegetable staple of the Batek diet throughout the year, except during the fruit season. Batek ate at least twenty species of wild tubers, the most frequently obtained and best liked of which was *takop* (*Dioscorea orbiculata*). Wild yams (*Dioscorea* spp.) and other types of tubers grew throughout the lowland forest; people could find one or more species reasonably close to any camp (see also K.M. Endicott 1984; Endicott and Bellwood 1991; Lye 2004).

The tool kit needed to procure tubers was simple and easily portable: wooden digging sticks tipped with chisel-like metal blades fashioned from old bush-knives or small metal shovel blades obtained by trade. Sometimes people sharpened one end of a straight stick with a bush-knife to form a simple

A common activity of women in forest camps was gathering wild tubers, a staple of the diet. Here a typical digging party sets out. The women carry their babies in slings on their backs. They, and one girl, carry metal-tipped digging sticks; a boy shoulders a blowpipe.

digging stick on the spot. Gatherers also used pandanus baskets or cloth slings to carry the tubers or other vegetable foods back to camp. If they gathered more food than these containers could hold, they wrapped the excess in large leaves, tying the bundles securely with vines.

Digging tubers required considerable knowledge. First, people had to know where to dig. Sometimes they knew in advance where yams were growing: the gatherers themselves may have previously spotted the vines put up by the plants, or other people may have reported such discoveries to them. Sometimes people kept these locations in mind for a year or two and went to them only when they thought the tubers would be ready to harvest. Batek said, for example, that the frequently exploited *takop* tuber was best after its vine has withered and died. People would scan the trees for the dry dead leaves, then search the ground for the fragments of the vine that would reveal the location of the tuber. If no one had prior knowledge of sites where tubers were growing, people would comb the area until they found what they were looking for. Knowing the habits of the different species, they focused their searches on the most likely places. For example, *gadoŋ* preferred the sandy banks of rivers and streams, and *takop* usually grew on slopes away from streams. Of course, people also had to know how to dig, so they could bring up the tuber without expending more energy than it was worth. Diggers worked the soft laterite soil efficiently, continually assessing the twisted course of the tuber as they tried to avoid digging any more than necessary. Even so, sometimes a woman would have to dig down so deeply that she would disappear into the hole.

Women set out on their gathering trips shortly after most hunters had left camp. Each woman carried her digging stick and a basket or cloth sling, as did accompanying children who were old enough (age ten and above) to do some digging of their own. The group generally walked for twenty minutes to an hour until they located some vines. Wild yam plants tend to grow in clusters, as they reproduce both from the root and from "winged" seeds, which may sail a little way from the mother vine before sprouting. After inspecting various vines to try to determine which were at the stage of development most likely to yield good-tasting tubers—something never known for sure until the tuber is dug up—each woman selected a vine that looked promising. Making sure that everyone was within sight or earshot of each other, the women unloaded their equipment and set out cloths or large leaves for their young children to sit on. The women then knelt down and began digging where the vines entered the ground, each thrust of the digging stick loosening the reddish soil, so the digger could scoop it out by the armload.

With her baby asleep on her back, a woman inspects a piece of the tuber she is digging up to see if it is at an edible stage of maturity.

When the first piece of a tuber was unearthed, the digger broke it open to assess whether the tuber was firm and starchy enough to make good eating: if it was not yet mature it would be sticky inside; if it was too old it would be shriveled; either way, it would be bland. If the digger decided to reject the tuber, she moved on to another vine, after covering the plant's root, so it would continue to live and produce more tubers. A tuber that looked good would be dug to its end, each section of the tuber being inspected as it came to the surface, the good pieces being piled high and any poor-quality sections tossed aside. The favored *takop* tuber is long and thin and can twist and turn to a depth of five feet or more. Often people had to dig more than one hole to recover the whole tuber; sometimes two people coordinated efforts, each digging down to a different section of the same tuber.

When they finally got all the tubers from a particular vine, the gatherers chose between digging somewhere else or returning to camp. If they thought they already had enough food, say twelve to fourteen pounds, they stopped work even if the day was still young. Rather than trying to store tubers, people dug only what their families and other camp members could eat in a day or two. Sometimes, however, if it was getting late in the afternoon or a thunderstorm was threatening, diggers stopped work before filling their baskets

Occasionally people gathered more tubers than they could eat immediately. Here Tebu threads pieces of *takop* (a species of wild yam) on a strip of rattan so he can dry them over the fire to retard spoilage.

and returned to camp, probably hoping that others had fared better. Women returned to camp between about 2 to 4 PM, after a work day of just under five hours (see table 4.5).

Children—even infants—did not seem to interfere greatly with the tuber-digging routine, although occasionally a fretful or sick child preempted a digging trip. Mothers did not even stop work to suckle the infants they carried in slings on their backs; they just swung the babies around to their breasts and continued to dig. Sometimes a mother would place an older infant (age two to three) on the ground near older siblings (age three to ten) and leave it to the infant to clamber over and hang onto her to nurse while she was digging. Young children (age three to seven) spent their time watching their mothers, playing with small digging sticks, or playing in the trees with other children. Older children might do some digging. Some mothers carried a few playthings for their children. On one expedition, for example, Dusun stopped for a cigarette break, took out her pandanus pouch, and proceeded to empty out a plastic baby bottle, a flashlight, a bamboo comb, a bottle of hair oil, two empty bottles, two knives, a metal file, her cigarette and fire-making equipment, and a live pet bat, which kept the children busy while the mother got on with her work. Mothers might cook a few newly dug tubers if their children were particularly hungry, but usually they waited until they returned to camp.

Occasionally mothers, grumbling that young children would not be able to walk far or fast enough, tried to discourage their children from accompanying them on gathering trips. We once heard a couple of women trying to convince their children to stay at home by telling them that there were many leeches in the forest; the children were not deterred. Sometimes, however, children themselves opted to stay in camp with older siblings or an adult. No doubt the women enjoyed their occasional child-free gathering trips, but they did not always get more food when they were unaccompanied by a full entourage of children.

Of the twenty or so species of tubers the Batek exploited, the *takop* (*Dioscorea orbiculata*), which was tasty and succulent either roasted or boiled, formed by far the largest single source of tubers (56 percent of the total weight obtained during the study period), even though the individual tubers were not huge. Three other species—*rɛm* (*Dioscorea prainiana*), *kasuʔ* (*Dioscorea pentaphylla*), and *gadoŋ*—could be dug up in large quantity in a matter of minutes. *Rɛm* and *kasuʔ*, which grow close to the surface, could weigh thirty or forty pounds each; if people came across these tubers, even in the course of other work, they would usually stop to dig them up. Batek said, however, that *rɛm* could be bitter or so tasteless that only children would eat them. The *gadoŋ* tuber had a different drawback: in its natural state it contains the bitter and toxic alkaloid dioscorine (Burkhill 1966), which must be leached out before it is edible. Although a few women and/or men could dig up over a hundred pounds of *gadoŋ* within twenty minutes, the processing required at least one full day and usually two. Batek regarded *gadoŋ* as tasty when properly prepared, but they did not bother with it unless they were staying in a place long enough to process it in large amounts. Nonetheless, *gadoŋ* was a useful food resource; even rural Malays relied on it as a famine food (Burkhill 1966).

Although women took primary responsibility for gathering tubers during the study period, there were several circumstances under which Batek men also turned to this work. If the hunt proved unsuccessful or if a hunter happened to come across a tuber-bearing plant, especially a *rɛm* or *kasu?*, he might make a digging stick and go to work. Older men who were no longer effective hunters dug tubers frequently. Bachelors, too, dug tubers at times for themselves and to share with others. Sometimes husbands and wives went digging together, especially in the years before or after raising children. When wives were sick or wanted to rest, their husbands might dig tubers for their families. Perhaps most importantly, however, men turned to gathering rather than hunting or other tasks when people were short of food, since tuber digging was the food-getting method that was most likely to succeed.

The success rate for gathering tubers was 93 percent for men and 95 percent for women, whereas the success rate for hunting by all methods was 59 percent for men and 69 percent for women. (This surprisingly high success rate for women's hunting would have been considerably lower had women attempted more blowpipe hunting.) In a now-classic article on the Ju/'hoansi foragers of southern Africa, Lee demonstrated that "hunting is *a high-risk, low-return* subsistence activity, while gathering is a *low-risk, high-return* subsistence activity" (1968:40; his emphasis). Batek hunting and gathering followed the same pattern, suggesting that Batek men as well as women turned to gathering tubers when they could not afford to fail at food getting. Table 4.5 shows the involvement of Batek men and women in gathering tubers.

Table 4.5   Gathering Tubers

	Total Weight (Lbs.)	Total No. Instances	Average Lbs. per Instance	No. Timed Instances	Total Time Recorded (Hrs.)	Average Time Worked (Hrs. per Instance)	Average Yield (Lbs. per Hr.) of Timed Instances
Men	1558.25	145	10.75	89	415.75	4.67	2.56
Women	3010.5	341	8.83	257	1148.51	4.47	2.23

Tubers comprised the Batek's greatest single source of food by weight during the study period. Women, gathering 2.3 times as often as men, produced 66 percent by weight of all the tubers. That men produced 34 percent by weight, however, shows that men contributed significantly, even though they dug tubers less often. When men did gather tubers, they averaged higher hourly yields and longer periods of work than women, as well as greater yields per instance of gathering. Men's higher yields were probably due in part to their being unencumbered by children.

Other Gathering

In addition to tubers, Batek gathered several nontuberous vegetable foods, including banana flowers, ferns, wild ginger, mushrooms, nuts, palm cabbage, and palm pith. These vegetable foods were collected opportunistically by anyone—man, woman, or child—who came across them. The first three were available throughout the year; mushrooms were seasonal. The most important nut, *pənacɛʔ*, was available from September to November. Another nut, large, oily, and edible after boiling, was *tawɔɲ* (*Hodgsonia capniocarpa*; Malay *kepayang akar*), available from July to August. Palm cabbage from several species of low-growing palms was the "fast food" of the forest, easily obtained by slashing away the tough leaf sheaths surrounding the stem of the palm to expose the soft, edible inner shoot. Palm cabbage could be eaten raw or cooked and was available year-round. A few species of palm trees contain thick cylinders of edible pith which was extracted by chopping down the tree and splitting open the trunk.

The seasonal food to which the Batek looked forward most was fruit— the many species of fruit that grew wild in the forest and domesticated fruits from abandoned Malay orchards (see also K.M. Endicott 1979a; Lye 2004). Their great love of fruit was expressed in their belief that the superhuman beings eat nothing but fruit. Batek reported that during the yearly fruit season, July to August, they lived off fruit to the near exclusion of all other foods.[1] Fruits that fell to the ground when ripe were collected by men, women, and children alike. However, many species of fruit had to be cut down from the tree trunk or branches. Although Batek women readily climbed trees to collect fruits growing on the lower limbs, they usually left it to men to climb the taller trees. Still, not all men were comfortable climbing to the extreme heights at which some fruits grew; the men who enjoyed climbing—or at least did not mind it—took on the task of going after the loftiest fruits.

To climb thin tree trunks, the climber put his arms around the tree, placed his feet against the trunk, and "walked" up it. If the trunk was too thick at the base for a climber to fully embrace, he would pull himself up a vine until he could transfer to the lower branches of the tree. Alternatively, he would climb a small tree adjacent to the one he wanted to climb, then get the smaller one swaying so he could reach over and pull himself into the branches of the larger tree. Or he might construct a vine ladder of rattan between the two trees and climb across it (see below). Climbers used bush-knives to sever the fruit-bearing stems or branches, letting them drop to their companions waiting below. Occasionally people chopped down fruit trees if they could not climb them and if they were in an area they seldom visited. Although we found it surprising that people would cut down a fruit tree, even if only rarely, Batek seemed unconcerned. They seemed to regard fruit as an inexhaustible resource.

Indeed, Batek reported that during the fruit season food was so abundant that groups far larger than usual routinely camped together. In addition to being a time of increased socializing, the fruit season was a key time for sing-ing and trancing sessions, which included rituals for thanking the superhu-man beings who, according to Batek beliefs, created fruits for the Batek to enjoy (see K.M. Endicott 1979a).

Another source of food, this one more sporadic than seasonal, was agri-cultural produce. Some Batek planted a few crops at the behest of the JHEOA, which had been trying since the mid-1960s to get the Batek to aban-don nomadic hunting and gathering in favor of swidden ("slash and burn") farming. Although other Semang groups, such as the Mendriq, had adopted agriculture to the near exclusion of hunting and gathering, Batek treated agri-cultural efforts as little more than an additional foraging technique. They were willing to plant crops as long as the JHEOA supplied them with rice and other foods—intended to tide them over until the first harvest—but as soon as the rations ran out or they wanted more or different foods, they aban-doned the fields and moved into the forest to hunt and gather.

Before they deserted the JHEOA-sponsored agricultural project in 1976, we asked the group if anyone was planning to stay and guard the fields; one man replied, "You can stay if you want, but you will be the only ones here. We're leaving." People returned periodically to the gardens to collect what-ever they could find, but the pickings were slim. Only a few vegetables—mostly ears of corn—escaped the ravages of wild pigs, elephants, and other animals. The Batek approach to agriculture at that time seemed little different from their approach to hunting and gathering: people did what they wanted to do, not what the agricultural cycle required.

Not surprisingly, then, when Batek did undertake agriculture, individual men and women involved themselves to whatever extent they wished. Both sexes helped to clear the undergrowth, and men felled the larger trees and did most of the burning. Men or women interested in establishing their own plots did so. Other people helped them or continued to procure wild foods in the vicinity. Both men and women planted the rice and vegetable seeds and the stalks of cassava (*Manihot utilissima*; Malay *ubi kayu*) supplied by the JHEOA or occasionally obtained from Malay farmers, and anyone who was so inclined weeded the gardens. Batek shared the small amount of cultivated food they produced with as many people in camp as possible, as they did with wild foods.

Table 4.6 documents the nontuberous vegetable foods Batek gathered; the few vegetables, mainly corn, that they grew during two short-lived agri-cultural stints within the period of study; and the few fruits they collected before the onset of the fruit season. The pattern of procuring nontuberous vegetables and fruit resembled the pattern of gathering tubers: women, work-ing twice as often as men, produced 61 percent of the foods by weight, while men produced 39 percent. But the work contrasted with tuber gathering in that women averaged slightly higher yields per instance of work than men.

Table 4.6   Procuring Other Vegetable Foods

	Total Weight (Lbs.)	Total No. Instances	Average Lbs. per Instance	No. Timed Instances	Total Time Recorded (Hrs.)	Average Time Worked (Hrs. per Instance)	Average Yield (Lbs. per Hr.) of Timed Instances
Men	198.75	23	8.64	11	27.5	2.5	3.73
Women	307.2	51	6.02	37	66.75	1.8	4.1

Collecting Honey

During the honey season of 1976, from April through June, Batek obtained so much honey that they went for days at a time eating little else but honey and bee larvae, and still had enough to sell or trade to Malays in return for rice and goods. It may well have been a bumper year. Although Batek could always count on getting some honey, the amount of honey depended on the number of trees that flowered and whether storms blew the flowers off the trees, which varied somewhat from year to year.

Honey collection was a dramatic and tricky job, best undertaken at night when the bees were least active. Because bees' nests were often in the tallest trees in the forest, hanging like hammocks from the underside of limbs, only the most adept and bravest climbers—usually younger men—attempted to get honey. One or two people were needed to scale the trees, and a few others helped on the ground. Sometimes young women who did not yet have children to look after participated in the ground crew, but we knew of no cases of women collecting honey by themselves.

Since most of the hive-bearing trees were too thick to climb directly, people constructed elaborate systems of "vine ladders" out of a very strong species of rattan (ʔawey ləŋ). From a smaller, climbable tree, they tossed a weighted fishing line over a low limb of the honey tree, attached the rattan vine to the fishing line and pulled the rattan over the limb, and then secured the two ends of the rattan to a smaller tree. They climbed these ladders, which were arranged at about a forty-five degree angle from the vertical, by grasping one vine in each hand and walking up the vines, gripping them between their toes. The honey-collectors also made one or more rectangular baskets out of broad sheets of bark and attached them to smaller rattan lines, which would be used to haul the baskets aloft.

After dark the climber would begin his ascent, carrying an unlit torch of dry leaves, a bush-knife, and a source of fire—a cigarette, store-bought lighter, or firestick—and dragging the line to the bark basket behind him. When he reached the hive, he lit the torch and waved it under the hive. Injured or stunned by the smoke and heat, the bees tumbled to the ground in a cascade of embers. The climber then pulled up the bark basket, held it beneath the hive, cut the hive loose, and lowered the basket on its rattan line to the ground crew. Honey collectors suffered however many bee stings they got resolutely if not gladly; they seemed to regard honey as being worth a little discomfort. In the days following honey collecting everyone in camp feasted on honey and honey-soaked larvae, raw or boiled, and a few people made the beeswax into candles. Table 4.7 gives details of honey collecting.

Table 4.7   Collecting Honey

	Total Weight (Lbs.)	Total No. Instances	Average Lbs. per Instance	No. Timed Instances	Total Time Recorded (Hrs.)	Average Time Worked (Hrs. per Instance)	Average Yield (Lbs. per Hr.) of Timed Instances
Men	500.51	77	6.5	42	172	4.1	1.17
Women	73.3	8	9.16	4	12.75	3.19	1.11

Men collected 87 percent by weight of all the honey and were involved in over nine times as many instances of honey collection as women. In this sample women averaged higher yields per instance than the men because the few times women participated in honey collecting, the ventures happened to be unusually productive. In keeping with our methodology of evenly dividing the yields among all participants in joint food-getting efforts, the data in Table 4.7 represent men's and women's shares of these joint efforts.

Collecting for Trade

Batek took advantage of various trade opportunities presented by the Malay and Chinese demand for forest products. For Batek, collecting tradeable products was basically an extension of collecting forest products for their own use: they simply expanded the number and types of goods they normally collected for themselves.

Both men and women collected and traded some kinds of forest products. These included rolls of thatch made from the *cəmcom* palm (*Calamus castaneus*); plants used by Chinese or Malays as medicines or aphrodisiacs; resins; special woods, such as the fragrant *gaharuʔ* (or *baŋkol*) wood (*Aquilaria* spp.; Malay *gaharu*); rattan vines (*Calamus* spp.); and certain foods, such as the seed pods of the leguminous *həntaw* tree (*Parkia speciosa*; Malay *petai*). Other forest products were generally collected only by men or only by women because only one sex normally worked with them. For example, women usually collected pandanus (*Pandanus* spp.) for trade because they were the specialists in weaving pandanus articles. Similarly, Batek men, as the main hunters, had access to certain products the Malays and Chinese wanted, such as the highly prized beaks of the *Rhinoplax vigil* hornbill, the solid casque of which Chinese craftsmen carved like ivory.

Batek were very active in collecting and selling rattan. Batek themselves used long, thin rattans for lashing and as rope. For the trade market, they collected both the thicker rattan, ʔawey manaw (*Calamus manan, Calamus ornatus*; Malay *rotan manau*), used primarily for furniture frames; and several species of thinner rattan, ʔawey baraŋ, used for fish traps and, when split, as bindings for furniture frames. Malays were happy to let Batek collect the rattan for them, in part because many Malays feared the forest as the home of evil spirits (*hantu*). Traders came into the forest only to negotiate deals with Batek. They came up the river in outboard boats bringing cash, rice, flour, salt, sugar, tea, tobacco, cooking pots, metal knives, fish hooks, cloth, and trinkets to trade. Individuals or groups of Batek would contract to collect a certain amount of rattan, usually hundreds or even thousands of pieces, by a certain date. The traders would advance the Batek some rice, money, or goods, reserving the balance of payment until the rattan was delivered. Then the Malays either left and returned at the agreed-upon date or camped on a nearby sandbar, outside the forest, until the rattan had been collected. After cutting down the rattan, the Batek carried or rafted it to a designated collection point, and the Malays took it downriver on rafts made of bamboo provided by the Batek.

Sometimes Batek collected rattan without being under contract and rafted it to town themselves, so they could sell it directly to the Malay and Chinese buyers. They could get a higher price that way, and it gave them a

Rattan collectors transported their rattan to an agreed-upon collection point where they turned it over to the traders. Here two men arrange piles of thin rattan. Some bundles of thick rattan lean against a boulder in the background.

chance to buy a wider selection of goods than they could get from the traders. But then they had to find a way to get back home. Sometimes they got a motorboat ride back with traders or with officials from the JHEOA; otherwise they had to walk, which would take several days.

Men were more active than women in collecting rattan. The only women who regularly did rattan work were young women who had not yet had children and a few older women, like Tanyogn, whose children were old enough to look after themselves. Rattan work was not very compatible with the care of very young children: workers had to go far from camp to harvest all the rattan in an area, and they routinely carried loads exceeding 100 pounds.

The first step in the collection of *ʔawey manaw* was to climb the tree that supported the rattan vine. The crown of the rattan plant, which looks similar to the crown of a palm tree, hooks itself onto the upper branches of forest trees, and the vine trails down to the ground. Since the crowns of rattan vines might be fifty to a hundred feet in the air, it was men, rather than women, who climbed up and cut the vines free. A few people on the ground—women and men—pulled the vines down, a hard job if the vine was tangled in tree branches. They then dragged the rattan to a level place and cut it into nine-foot lengths. Several pieces—whatever people thought they could carry—were bundled together and tied at each end with the rope-like thin rattans. Each person carried his or her own bundle of rattan to the collection point or to a place where the rattan could be placed on rafts and floated downstream.

ʔawey baraŋ were far easier to collect. A man or a woman could pull them down without having to climb the supporting tree. One variety of thin rattan could be coiled into large hoops, which were easily carried over one's shoulder. Most of the thin rattans, however, were cut into nineteen-foot lengths, tied in bundles of twenty-five strands, folded in the middle, and dragged out of the forest by men and women. If the rattan was to be floated downstream, men constructed rafts from bamboo, as women professed not to know how. But women as well as men took part in loading the rattan and poling the rafts to the collection point.

For a variety of reasons, men were more active than women in carrying out trade transactions. Usually the persons who collected the goods—mostly men—also did the trading. And male Chinese and Malay traders sought out Batek men rather than women when arranging contracts and negotiating exchanges. Participating directly in trade transactions brought no personal advantage, as the resultant money, food, and goods were shared with all the people who had contributed to the trade effort, including people who had kept up the food supplies so others could concentrate on collecting rattan.

If trade required Batek to travel to a village or town, a few people went on behalf of a larger group. More men than women made trips to the villages downstream, but there were no rules or prohibitions concerning who could go. Any man or woman who wanted to make the trip did so. The few women who went along tended to be young, unmarried women or married women who did not yet have children. Other women let their husbands know what they wanted from town. During the study period, only men went to Kuala Krai, the major town of the upper Kelantan area, because free accommodations were available to men at a hostel that the government ran for Orang Asli school boys. It was easier for women to go along on trips to the village of Manek Urai, where they and the men could sleep on their rafts.

Table 4.8 shows that men did rattan work 3.3 times more often than women. In fact, men's 284 instances of rattan collecting exceeded their frequency of involvement in any other activity. Even hunting—by blowpipe and all other methods—totaled only 270 instances.

Table 4.8   Rattan Work

	Total No. Instances	No. Timed Instances	Total Time Recorded (Hrs.)	Average Time Worked (Hrs. per Instance)
Men	284	153	850.25	5.56
Women	86	62	290.05	4.69

The significance of the high frequency of rattan work emerges when we see what the Batek got out of trade. Table 4.9 shows the foods they obtained from trade, mainly of rattan, but also from the more sporadic sale of pandanus, fragrant wood, honey, and other forest products for which we have no quantitative data. Some of the money men and women earned from us—in payment for helping us with chores or translating texts and songs—was also spent on the traded foods that are documented in table 4.9.

Men's trade efforts yielded three times the total amount of food by weight as women's efforts did. Women obtained more cultivated vegetables than any other food category. They earned some of this food by harvesting fields of Malay farmers to whom they traded forest products. A significant feature of Batek trade was that the foods they received in return or bought

Table 4.9   Foods Obtained Through Trade

Food	Men's Yield in Lbs.	Women's Yield in Lbs.	Total
Rice	1,076.63	106.54	1,183.17
Flour	207.98	14.92	222.90
Sugar	53.21	9.98	63.19
Tinned Meat/Fish	2	7	9
Cultivated Vegetables	106.85	348.1	454.95
Cooking Oil	7.98	1.33	9.31
Total Weight	1,454.65	487.86	1,942.51

with their cash proceeds were almost entirely plant foods, mainly rice, flour, sugar, and cultivated vegetables, not canned meat or dried fish. This suggests that they felt they were getting enough meat from their own efforts. They also preferred the taste of fresh meat.

Work Groups

Batek carried out their food-getting and other activities both in single-sex and mixed-sex groups. The composition of the work groups depended upon the nature of the work being done and the friendships and common interests of the persons involved. People with similar work interests who enjoyed working together did so. Hunting parties, for example, consisted of men who liked to hunt together. Gathering parties consisted of women who wanted to dig in a particular area together. Rattan collecting parties often consisted of both men and women, whoever wanted to work rattan that day. There were no rules about who could or could not work together. Every imaginable configuration of workers occurred at one time or another: husbands and wives, adolescents of one or both sexes, old people with young, mothers or fathers with opposite sex children, married persons with other married or unmarried persons of the opposite sex. Work groups changed in composition from day to day, depending on individuals' changing interests and on the changing interests of their potential companions.

The only work group that had some degree of stability was the married couple. It was not unusual for a couple to go foraging together, accompanied by their children. Some couples seemed to especially enjoy working together. But whether a couple worked together or separately, people viewed the work of men and women, husbands and wives as complementary.

The productive capacities and the actual productivity of the husband–wife unit underwent many changes over the span of a couple's life together, influenced by such factors as health, age, personality, and the numbers and ages of dependant children. Young, newly married couples basically continued the work patterns of their bachelorhoods. The men spent many hours hunting and collecting rattan. The main activities of women in the pre-motherhood years were getting food, collecting rattan, making pandanus mats and baskets, and constructing the family shelter at each new camp. When a couple had children, they obviously had to produce more food to feed them. Parents did not expect their children to work at food getting, although whatever small contributions children made of their own accord were welcome. Not until the children were about fourteen years old would they begin to provide much of their own food. During the teen years the children became increasingly independent, but this independence did not cut them off from the family food supply. Still, as the children began to procure increasing amounts of food, parents could adjust their own food-getting efforts; the dependency relationship of children to parents gradually changed into a relationship of mutual sharing and help. As the parents grew older and began to lose strength and health, their children increasingly compensated for their parents' declining productivity.

The aging wife and husband also continued to make adjustments within their own relationship; whoever was the stronger of the two tended to be the more productive. Often, but not always, this was the younger partner. Thus, in many older couples the wife was the main provider of food. Because of failing eyesight, slower reflexes, and the like, older men were usually not very successful at hunting and turned instead to digging tubers on their own or with their wives. Older women generally kept up their gathering activities. Husbands and wives usually adjusted to each other's changes in productive capacities with understanding and compassion. For example, Tanyogn, who was about forty-seven years old, was more productive than her husband, Langsat, who was about fifty-five. Whenever Langsat's foraging efforts failed, Tanyogn explained that he was old and therefore could not work hard, and she attributed his lack of success to unfortunate circumstances rather than to any fault on his part.

Men's and Women's Contributions to the Food Supply

It is reasonable to suppose that in a predominantly hunting and gathering society the contributions of the two sexes to the food supply would affect their degree of equality as we have defined it.[2] Presumably, if one sex as a group were dependent upon the other for food—and thus for survival—the sex supplying the most food could exercise some control over the other sex. Therefore, it is worthwhile to examine the contributions of Batek men and women to their total food supply.

One way to compare men's and women's food contributions is by the gross amounts of food obtained by each sex. Since there were more men than women in the population studied—and therefore more males than females contributing to the group's food supply—table 4.10 shows the amounts of food by weight obtained *per person* during the study period. As this table shows, women procured slightly more food by weight per person than men, even though men as a group supplied more total food.

Table 4.10   Weights of Food Procured per Person

	Total Weight of Food Procured (Lbs.)	Average Daily Population	Pounds Procured per Person (93 Days)	Percent of Food Produced per Person
Men	4,983.92	11.25	443.0	49
Women	3,945.973	8.62	457.8	51

Another way to compare the food contributions of the sexes is by the amounts of calories each contributed to the diet. As we were unable to obtain the actual caloric values of Batek foods, the figures presented in table 4.11 are an approximation, based upon the Western foods listed in caloric charts most closely resembling them; the figures for hunted meats were based on the caloric value of lean beef, fish on nonfatty fish, tubers on yams, other vegetables on silver beet, and so on (Coursey 1967; Osmond and Wilson 1968; Davis 1954). Again, we take into consideration the fact that men outnumbered women in the study population.

Table 4.11 shows that at the level of individuals, men averaged 1.76 times the number of calories contributed by women. The reason for this is that men's food-getting efforts concentrated on foods that were relatively high in calories, while most of women's work was directed toward collecting tubers, which were lower in calories. This difference is largely due to men providing most of the meat and traded foods, which had higher caloric values than the wild vegetable foods obtained by women. (Indeed, this may explain in part why the Batek were so interested in trade: trade provided well-liked and relatively high-calorie foods—especially rice, sugar, and flour—that had the extra advantage of being more storable than many wild foods.) Traded foods accounted for 42 percent of the total calories in the Batek diet during the study period, wild foods supplying the other 58 percent.

Table 4.11   Calories Supplied per Person

	Total Calories Supplied	Average Daily Population	Calories Supplied per Person (93 Days)	Percent of Food Produced per Person
Men	4,385,430	11.25	389,816	64
Women	1,907,403	8.62	221,276	36

Still another way to assess men's and women's contributions to subsistence is to compare the amount of time each sex spent in food-getting activities, as shown in table 4.12, which includes time spent collecting rattan because rattan was traded for food. Batek men spent an average of 28.7 hours

Table 4.12   Average Food-Getting Hours Worked per Person

	Total Hours Worked	Total Person Days	Hours Worked per Day	Hours Worked per Week	Percent of Hours Worked per Person
Men	4,287.1	1,046	4.1	28.7	58
Women	2,332.4	802	2.91	20.37	42

per week in food-getting activities (including collecting rattan), and women spent an average of 20.37 hours per week in the same activities. On average, then, men worked 1.4 times longer than women in food-getting tasks. In addition to the time spent obtaining food, Batek men and women spent several hours per week processing and cooking the food and a few more hours maintaining and replacing their food-getting equipment. The total number of hours men and women worked each week, then, was less than the forty hours typically worked in industrial societies.

Most Batek approached their economic activities enthusiastically. They did not sharply distinguish work from leisure activities. Although people considered some jobs more difficult than others—they rated rattan collection and tuber digging as the hardest—they seldom complained that they had to work too hard or too much. Indeed, they considered their means of food getting far more attractive and far less arduous than the alternative of growing their own crops in the tropical sun.

The economic data, as presented in all the preceding tables, demonstrate that there is no single, all-encompassing way of assessing men's and women's contributions to Batek subsistence: for example, women provided slightly more food per person by weight, but men contributed over twice as many calories per person. What is clear from the data is that both men and women made substantial contributions to the food supply and that neither sex was dependent upon the other. But, as we discuss in chapter 7, there is more to gender egalitarianism than contributions to the food supply.

Chores and Crafts

Processing Food

Batek cooking was basically very simple, and everyone—even young children—could do it. Foods were roasted directly over the fire, boiled in a cooking pot, or cooked in a length of bamboo placed on the fire. There were a few tendencies shaping the organization of cooking, however, which prevailed much of the time. Generally each family cooked its own food in its own shelter. The wife took charge of cooking the bulk of the rice or tubers for her family, but the husband and children pitched in. When a family was roasting tubers, for example, the wife might begin the cooking, but the husband and children would put more tubers on the fire and take them off and scrape the ashes off when they were done.

Meat cooking often involved men to a greater extent. Hunters sometimes butchered and partially or fully cooked game in the forest, so when they reached camp it only needed to be distributed. A woman who had procured meat, as in the case of bamboo rats, might prepare and cook the meat herself or delegate the job to her husband or children. When an animal, such as a monkey, was brought back uncooked, the hunter, another man, or some older children, usually boys, went to work on it. Someone placed the animal directly on the fire to singe the fur, then scraped it off with a stick. The carcass was cut open to expose the entrails which were taken out, the edible parts roasted or boiled, and the inedible parts discarded. The task of cleaning the intestines frequently fell to the children. They did this and other jobs the adults were happy to avoid, such as plucking the feathers from flea-ridden hornbills, with great enthusiasm.

After the initial preparation, the cook skewered the carcass on a stick and thrust the stick into the ground at an angle, so the carcass would roast over the fire. Alternatively, the cook might cut up and boil the carcass. When the meat was fully cooked, it was cut into pieces and distributed to as many people as it would feed. If there were large quantities of meat, more than enough to go around the camp, some of the meat was dried over the fire on racks made of green wood. Dried meat kept for four or five days, but it usually got eaten sooner.

Processing poisonous foods was the only time-consuming food preparation. Both men and women processed such foods, the most common of which were the large *gadoŋ* tuber and the *pənaceʔ* nut. They processed *gadoŋ* in large quantities to make the effort worthwhile. Usually a camp as a whole decided to devote the necessary one or two days to processing it. The camp members would consider whether there was already enough food in camp to last until the *gadoŋ* was ready. If not, some people might try to get some non-poisonous tubers to tide them over. Even though *gadoŋ* was processed in large enough quantities—often over 100 pounds—to feed a whole camp for at least a couple of days, not everyone in the camp helped in the processing work.

A few men and women dug up the tubers and brought them into the camp; then one or two people—generally women—would begin the processing. Workers would come and go during the processing, which might last most of the day, depending on the amount of *gadoŋ*. It was not uncommon for one person to work steadily throughout the day, while other capable men and women lounged around the camp. The workers did not seem to mind this. Whoever wanted to work did so; whoever did not stayed out of it. Many people said that they did not mind doing such work, although they would not like to do it every day. Some people had little patience for it, however. On one occasion a woman got so fed up with processing *gadoŋ* that she went off digging for nonpoisonous tubers and her husband took over the processing and looked after one of their children at home while his wife was out in the forest.

Gadoŋ tubers look like large, irregularly shaped potatoes about six inches across, and processing *gadoŋ* involved several steps. *Gadoŋ* had to be peeled, cut into chunks, and then either sliced wafer-thin and boiled for about half an hour or boiled first and then sliced. After all the *gadoŋ* had been boiled and sliced, it was placed in open-work rattan baskets that had been lined with large leaves. The basket would be taken to a nearby river or large stream and secured in the water so the current could leach the poison out of the slices of *gadoŋ*. The basket was left in place for twelve to twenty-four hours, depending on how fast the water was flowing. When people thought that the poison was gone, they retrieved the basket, boiled some of the *gadoŋ* slices in fresh water, then tasted it. If anyone felt dizzy or sick after eating it, they placed the *gadoŋ* in the river again for more leaching. When it was at last cleansed of its poison, people boiled it or steamed it over the fire in containers of green bamboo, then ate it freely. *Gadoŋ* could be stored in bamboo containers and used as rations while people moved to a new location, but because of the lengthy preparation *gadoŋ* required, Batek did not like to spend too much time in an area where it was the only kind of tuber they could find.

The seasonal nut *pənaceʔ*, available from September through November, had to be leached of its poisonous hydrocyanic acid (Burkhill 1966) before it was edible. Men and women alike helped with the processing work. Usually men climbed the *pənaceʔ* trees to cut down the nuts, which grow within a husk about four to six inches in diameter. Back in camp, the processors, who might be men or women, pounded open the soft husk to expose the approximately twenty-four nuts embedded in pulp. They cut the nuts away from the pulp, scraped them clean, and then boiled them with a few green palm leaves. Once the *pənaceʔ* nuts had been boiled, their shells were cracked open with a rock. The processors cut the kernels into slivers before placing them in leaf-lined rattan baskets or cloth sacks, but sometimes they left the kernels whole and strung them on a rattan fiber. The nuts were placed in the river for leaching for one night if they had been sliced or for two nights if they had been left whole. Then people boiled them again and tasted them. If no one felt ill after the initial tasting, the *pənaceʔ* was ready for eating, although people said they could eat only small amounts at a time or else they would get stomach aches. This might have been due to the relative richness of the nuts, incomplete leaching, or the rapid spoilage to which *pənaceʔ* seems prone. Burkhill (1966) reports that oil processed from the nuts turns rancid quickly and can cause diarrhea. Batek kept the *pənaceʔ* slivers in bamboo containers for as long as the supply lasted.

Collecting Water and Firewood

Both men and women collected the everyday necessities of water and firewood. Water containers were made by piercing the mid-segments of five- or six-foot-long pieces of large-diameter bamboo. Some people also used plastic buckets obtained through trade. Fetching water was not an onerous job, since Batek always camped on the banks of a river or stream, and anyone in a family who noticed that a water container was empty would fill it. Similarly, everyone collected firewood as needed. Both men and women frequently returned to camp from their food-getting or other activities with a load of firewood slung over their shoulders. When a family's firewood supply was low, any member of the family would fetch more from the surrounding forest. Probably women brought in more firewood than men in total, however, as men spent more time away from camp. Everyone, including children, made and tended cooking fires at the family hearth. Children of both sexes also helped collect firewood and water when they were so inclined or when their parents asked them to.

Building Shelters

Every time people moved camp, they had to build new lean-to shelters. After a couple selected a house site, the husband would cut three saplings for the house supports, stick them into the ground, and then rush off to hunt before animals fled the area. The wife handled the rest of shelter building. She searched for long fronds of the low-growing *cəmcom* palm to make into thatch. She cut the fronds, piled them up, and carried them on her back, looking like an oversized beetle as she made her way back to camp. With a quick stroke of a bush-knife she de-thorned the stem, then folded all the leaflets to one side. Bundling three fronds together to form a shingle about seven feet wide, she lashed the palms to the house supports. Construction usually took about an hour to an hour and a half. Sometimes women also made platform floors for the lean-tos, but usually left it to the men to split bamboo into a flat mat or to lay a series of smooth, strong sticks across some small logs to create a floor about six inches above the ground. During the course of living at a camp, either the wife or husband might make repairs to the shelter, adding more leaves to a leaking roof or sometimes moving the house to a different location.

Upon reaching a new campsite, women constructed lean-to shelters for their families. Lesoh (left) folds palm fronds into thatch "shingles," while her mother, Tanyogn, lashes shingles to poles to form the shelter's roof.

Men, especially bachelors and adolescent boys, sometimes constructed their own lean-tos, although female relatives often did it for them or helped them.

Occasionally men built four-walled Malay-style houses which were raised on posts. The frames were made of wooden poles lashed together with rattan, and the walls and floor were made of split bamboo or sheets of bark. People constructed such houses only when they expected to live in one place for many weeks, as when planting gardens. They readily abandoned the houses, however, whenever they decided to move on, even if they had only just completed them. Sometimes Batek built Malay-style houses for show. During one agricultural stint in 1971, Aring River Batek constructed Malay-style houses at Post Aring at the urging of the JHEOA. The houses were too hot, however, so people lived in lean-tos in the forest and pretended to occupy the houses when JHEOA officials visited.

Making Tools, Clothing, and Equipment

Women and men alike made most of the tools and goods they needed for everyday life, with only a few items being the specialties of one sex or the other. Hunting equipment was made by men since they were the primary hunters; sometimes men who were especially skilled at making blowpipes made them for other people. However, some women knew how to make darts and carry out basic blowpipe maintenance. Both sexes made digging sticks by cutting a sapling to length, carving one end to a point, or lashing on a metal blade with rattan. The blades were fashioned out of old bush-knives or even lids from cooking pots that had been obtained through trade. Women as well as men worked metal by heating it in an ordinary fire, cutting it with a bush-knife, and, using the butt end of an axe for an anvil, hammering it to shape. (After about 1980 most digging sticks were tipped with small metal shovel blades obtained by trade.) Women and men alike also carried out such tasks as sharpening knives and digging stick blades with sharpening stones or files, and carving and attaching new wooden handles to their knives.

Everyone manufactured many items of everyday equipment on the spur of the moment, including tongs made from bamboo, raspers made from thorny stems, and torches made from leaf-wrapped chunks of resin held in place by a forked stick. Rather than permanently keeping and transporting a variety of tools, people made much of their equipment from materials on hand or easily found in the forest.

They satisfied their clothing needs easily. Both men and women made their own loincloths by simply tearing pieces of cloth acquired through trade or at village shops into the required lengths. All Batek adults and even some children could do simple sewing repairs on traded cloth goods, using store-bought needles and thread. Both sexes also made flower headdresses, the same designs being worn by men and women. Rattan armbands were made and worn mostly by men, but some women could make them as well. Both sexes made decorative bamboo combs.

Barkcloth, which the Batek traditionally used for loincloths and carrying slings for infants or possessions, was no longer being made in 1975–76. People considered manufactured cloth to be more comfortable and durable, although a good piece of barkcloth would last several months. Some people still knew how to make barkcloth, however, and when we asked them about it, they gave us a demonstration. Most of the work was done by a mixed group of teenagers, following the instructions of the older men and women. They first cut down a *cɛh* tree (also the source of dart poison), which was favored over other suitable trees because the barkcloth from it is especially white. After carefully peeling off the bark in five-foot long sheets, workers laid each piece on a log or over a tree stump, then pounded it with heavy sticks for an hour or so until the fibers spread and softened like felt.

When Batek still made barkcloth for regular use, they would cut cross-hatch designs into the pounding sticks in order to achieve a smooth, decoratively patterned spreading of the bark fibers. One older man made such a pounding stick for the demonstration, and the barkcloth he made did indeed have the best texture. Some of the teenagers working on the barkcloth periodically held up their lengths of cloth to a parent or other adult and asked if the bark needed more pounding. When the barkcloth had become smooth and soft, the workers took it to the stream and rinsed it over and over again, wringing and twisting it to remove the poison and wood splinters. Then they hung it over branches to dry.

Basketry was among the few craft activities in which one sex or the other specialized. Batek made baskets out of three different forest materials: bark, rattan, and pandanus. Bark baskets were made by men and women alike by peeling sections of bark from certain species of trees, then folding over the corners of the pieces of bark and stitching them in place with lengths of split rattan. These baskets were used primarily for collecting honey, but might be put to other uses as well.

Rattan baskets were the specialty of men, although people said that a few women knew how to make them too. These baskets were woven in a hexagonal pattern (like the cane-work of Breuer chairs) and were especially useful as receptacles for holding foods that were to be leached in the rivers; the open-work design allowed the water to flow freely over the food. Rattan baskets could be made fairly quickly, the actual construction taking only an hour or so once the rattan had been found and split into useable strips, a procedure which also took little time. Men also made cruder rattan baskets on the spot for carrying game back to camp if a hunter did not have a cloth sling or pandanus basket.

Pandanus baskets, as well as pandanus mats and pouches, were the specialty of the women. Pandanus weaving was time-consuming; it might take several days, for example, to complete a large sleeping mat. Batek women preferred the variety of pandanus they called *rəmadul*, because they liked its strength. People said that the deity Tohan gave them the *rəmadul* plant specifically for making pandanus objects. The *rəmadul* leaves are about five feet

The definitive work of women was making mats and baskets from pandanus leaves. Chinloy splits the leaves into uniform strips by drawing them through a cutting device made of tough root fibers. Women often decorated their hair, ears, and waistbands with flowers and fragrant leaves.

long and taper to a point from a maximum width of about four inches. Women noted the location of *rəmadul* plants whenever they ran across them in the forest. When they needed new baskets or mats, they returned to one of these plants, cut off the mature leaves, and, before carrying them back to camp, sliced off the sharp tips and the thorns that ran up and down the edges and central spine of each leaf.

To prepare the leaves for weaving, women split them into strips, using a cutting instrument made of fibers from the stem of the *patiʔ* tuber. Women preferred this tool to a knife because it would split the leaf along the grain, producing even strips, while knives could too easily cut across the grain. Women adjusted the width and length of the pandanus strips according to whether they were to be used for baskets, sleeping mats, or small pouches. They dried the strips over the fire and softened them by pulling each strip over the edge of a smooth piece of wood or bamboo a few times.

Batek used the same weaving technique for all the pandanus objects they made. The weaving was usually done on the diagonal, a method that produced a tight weave without requiring a frame. Only the square bottom of the large back-baskets called *hapəʔ* were woven on the square, a process that required more effort than diagonal weaving to hold the pandanus strips in place. The weavers finished the outer edges of each type of pandanus item in a different way. The *hapəʔ* basket edge was the most involved, requiring five steps. Rattan straps were attached to the largest of the baskets so they could be carried as backpacks.

Pandanus items were functional in design and usually not highly decorated. Sometimes women varied the weaving patterns or colored some of the pandanus strips with natural vegetable or store-bought dyes. Some people made and reserved dyed mats to sit on during ritual singing and dancing sessions.

Pandanus weaving was a skill that required instruction and practice. Girls began to learn the techniques when they were about eight to ten years old. Their mothers and other women showed them how to prepare and weave pandanus and supervised their efforts. People expected all adult women to know how to weave pandanus, and, indeed, women made all the sleeping mats, baskets, and pouches the Batek used every day. Bachelors would be given whatever woven items they needed by close female relatives, or, they might buy them or trade for them from a young unmarried woman. People kept their baskets and mats for months, until they became too tattered to use.

Batek said that men did not know how to do pandanus weaving, that it was something the women did. Occasionally, however, a man or boy joined in. We saw some boys around four and five years of age being shown how to weave by an older woman after they had come over to her and started fooling around with some scraps of pandanus. They were laughing at each other's attempts and gave up after a few minutes, saying they could not do it right. The woman said she was just teaching them in play and that the children would just play around at it. We also saw Pay, a married man in his late twenties, spend a few hours one day helping his mother, Tanyogn, weave a large sleeping mat. She told us with obvious pride that, unlike most men, Pay knew how to weave. No one else seemed particularly surprised at or interested in what Pay was doing; no doubt they were used to the fact that he was accomplished at whatever he did, whether it was blowpipe hunting or, as he was demonstrating that day, pandanus weaving.

Another craft that was the specialty of women was plaiting the long rattan waistbands (*nɛm*) women normally wore. They made their waistbands from a type of rattan called *təŋwɛŋ*. They scraped the thorns off the rattan, peeled back the bark to get at the usable fibers, then pulled the fibers away from the inner core of the rattan. Pulling the fibers through the split end of a stick that had been stuck into the ground, they separated the useless short or weak pieces of fiber from the stronger strands. Women tied the ends of several of the rattan fibers to a stick or post stuck in the ground, then plaited them, splicing in more strands as the ends of the previous strands were reached in order to create one long cord. When a woman considered her waistband long enough, she knotted the end of it. Women dyed waistbands orange by boiling them for about an hour in a pot containing the fruits of certain species of rattan, then hung them over the fire to dry. They made new waistbands whenever they wanted and whenever they could find the right rattan. Waistbands lasted several months, and even after a woman replaced hers, pieces of her old one might be worn by her young daughters or used by her husband or sons as single-stranded belts.

Usually women wove pandanus baskets and mats, but a few men also knew how. Here Pay helps his mother, Tanyogn, weave a pandanus sleeping mat.

The characteristic woman's garment was the multiple-stranded waistband. Here a woman plaits a new one while wearing her old one. She also wears a necklace and bracelet made of black fungus rhizomes that were thought to ward off certain diseases. Strips of pandanus for making pouches dry on a stick at the left.

Explaining the Division of Labor

Batek Explanations

Batek were well aware of the general patterns of male and female work, but they seldom tried to characterize the gender division of labor as a whole. Significantly, no one ever told us that men hunt and women gather. The closest to a general statement we heard was when one man told us that men hunt and women weave pandanus, a statement probably based on the facts that these two activities were almost exclusively done by members of one sex, they both required specialized skills, and they took up substantial portions of men's and women's work time.

When we asked why women or men were more active in particular activities, Batek often explained it in terms of presumed physiological differences between the sexes. For example, as mentioned in chapter 2, one reason they gave for the predominance of men in blowpipe hunting was that men had stronger breath than women. Tanyogn, one of the fittest women we knew, told us that she could not blow a dart hard enough to pierce the skin of an animal. People also explained some men's specialties in terms of their supposed greater strength, especially in the upper body and arms. This was given as the reason why men did most of the more challenging tree climbing, why they chopped down most large trees, and why they carried bigger loads of rattan than women. Men's greater strength was also cited as the reason why men more often than women did the jobs, such as blowpipe hunting and searching for *gaharu?* wood, that might bring them into contact with tigers and elephants. Supposedly men could fight off or get away from dangerous animals better than women.

On the other hand, Batek believed that women were physiologically better equipped than men to care for small children, presumably because only women could nurse them. People explained women's lack of participation in some jobs in terms of incompatibility with child care. For example, when we asked Tanyogn and Langsat if children affected hunting trips, they told us about a particular younger couple that had small children. They explained that when the wife and her children went along with her husband on a hunt, she and the children would stay some distance behind the husband, because the children always laughed and made a lot of noise. People also said the children would tire quickly on the long walk and would want to be carried by their father, thus interfering with his hunting efforts. In fact, men did not take their children on hunting trips, even when the children begged to go, except on those rare occasions when their wives went along.

Batek further explained the specialization of men and women in particular jobs in terms of the knowledge and skill needed to do them. People often said that they didn't do a job usually done by members of the other sex because they didn't know how. For example, Tanyogn said that she did not know how to sneak up on game like her husband, Langsat, did. She explained that when she went along with Langsat on a hunt, she would wait in one spot while he sneaked up on the animals. Then she admitted that she *could* sneak up, but only slowly.

According to some myths, the deity Tohan and the original people (Batek ?asal) taught the Batek how to do certain jobs, transmitting the knowledge through dreams, but they taught some of the jobs to only one sex. For example, Tohan taught men how to obtain and use dart poison and how to hunt; he didn't teach women these things because they didn't have strong enough breath. Supposedly Tohan taught only women how to weave pandanus and how to make thatch for their lean-tos and for the large ritual shelters. Tohan taught other skills, such as making barkcloth, to both sexes.

Still other skills, according to informants, were not taught by Tohan at all, but were figured out by Batek themselves or were learned from Malays. The most significant task they learned by themselves was digging wild tubers. People said that the original human couple became hungry as they walked around the forest, so they dug up some tubers and cooked them over the red flower that was used as fire until true fire was obtained from a superhuman being in the form of a sambhur deer. Similarly, people figured out for themselves how to get honey. People told us that the Batek of long ago learned how to process the poisonous *gadoŋ* tuber from Ya' Kedat, a Malay *hantu* (evil spirit), whose husband had made the *gadoŋ* poisonous in order to kill her. Informants said that Batek learned to fish from Malays.

Batek acknowledged that individuals varied in their knowledge and skills—even in the areas of specialized knowledge Tohan presented to a single sex group. For example, some men were good at hunting and others were not, and people expected and accepted these variations. Furthermore, Batek acknowledged that individual ability and interest might cut across sex lines. But in general they expected men and women to gravitate toward doing the kinds of work that they were inherently best suited to do.

Conclusion

We see no reason to doubt the Batek's own explanations of the influence of physiological differences on the gender division of labor. According to their reasoning, it is most practical and efficient for men to concentrate on work that requires blowing power and upper body strength—including blowpipe hunting, tree climbing, chopping down trees, and carrying heavy loads—and for women to focus on jobs that are compatible with caring for young children—such as digging tubers, digging up bamboo rats, hook-and-line fishing, and craft work. Our data bore out the pattern of work effort that would be expected. The division of labor resulting from each sex building on its strengths ensured that all necessary tasks got done.

The Batek value system did not give high prestige to some jobs while devaluing others. Therefore people had no motivation except personal interest to try to do the jobs normally done by the other sex. People seemed content to do the jobs associated with their sex, and they got satisfaction from doing them well.

Notes

[1] As we were unable to be with the Batek during July and August of 1976, we have no quantitative data for that period. Our data do include the few fruits that ripened earlier in the year, and we were able to observe the methods people used to gather that fruit. Informants explained to us their fruit-gathering strategies and the general pattern of activities they would follow during the July–August fruit season.

[2] Cross-cultural studies of hunting and gathering peoples have not shown a simple correlation between women's making a large contribution to the food supply and their having high status or autonomy (see, e.g., Sanday 1974, 1981; Hayden et al. 1986; R.L. Kelly 1995).

Chapter 5

Growing Up Batek

Among the many lessons children learn while growing up is how to be men and women. Socialization practices differ widely from society to society, both in their methods and their goals. The roles mothers and fathers play in raising children are part of the broad spectrum of the gender roles that children learn. Moreover, the ways adults treat boys and girls and the expectations they place on them shed light on a people's gender concepts. Child rearing methods both express and perpetuate gender concepts, values, and behaviors.

Conception, Pregnancy, and Childbirth

Batek said that couples must copulate many times over a period of months in order to cause the blood in the womb, which would otherwise be expelled through menstruation, to begin to coagulate into a ball, which becomes the fetus. Women claimed to know nothing about semen (*lǝnas*) and its role in pregnancy, and they seemed embarrassed by the subject. Men, too, were discrete about the topic. One man told Kirk, in confidence, that *lǝnas* causes conception, but that men keep this information secret from women. After conception, the fetus grows steadily, whether or not the couple continues to have sex. When the fetus has developed hands and feet, Tohan sends some life-soul (*ŋawaʔ*), which enters its head and heart, causing it to begin to breathe. About the same time, the fetus develops an individual shadow-soul (*bayaŋ*), which is associated with consciousness and volition. After that, the mother may feel the fetus begin to move. Batek expected male children to resemble their fathers and females to look like their mothers because Tohan makes them that way.

During pregnancy there were no prohibitions on a woman's eating habits or on her activities, including sexual relations. She continued her normal activities for as long into her pregnancy as she felt able. According to Batek, if a woman were still breast-feeding a child when she became pregnant with another child, she would notice a steady decline in her milk supply from about the third month of pregnancy onward, resulting in a forced, though gradual, weaning of the nursing child. Nevertheless, Batek mothers did not force a child to give up milk entirely; if a young child wanted milk, parents bought powdered milk when possible. When lactation started up again toward the end of pregnancy, mothers might let a child resume nursing and continue after the new baby's birth.

When a Batek woman went into labor, the husband and a few helpers quickly constructed a special birth house in the forest, a short distance outside the camp. People said that superhuman beings instructed them to do this, although occasionally labor proceeded too quickly to make this possible. Tanyogn gave two further reasons for building separate birth houses: that giving birth in the family shelter would make it dirty and that after the birth, the birthplace was a prohibited space to everyone except the mother, who was permitted to return to keep a fire going beside the placenta (see below). Batek avoided building a birth house next to a stream to ensure that floods did not wash the house away after the birth. If the house washed away, Tanyogn explained, the baby would miss its birthplace and would suffer uncontrollable crying spells called *sabɛn*. Distancing the birth house from streams also helped prevent blood *lawac*, which occurs when menstrual or postpartum blood washes into a stream and creates a smell that is offensive to the thunder-god and the underground deity.

The birth house was similar to an ordinary lean-to shelter, but it always contained a platform of bark, sticks, or bamboo, which was sometimes covered by an old mat or cloth. A backrest was constructed of sticks driven into the ground at an angle so the woman could lean against it while giving birth. A fire built close to the platform kept the mother warm.

At all stages of the process, other Batek aided a woman giving birth. Before the husband took the woman to the birth house, people gave her medicines and recited spells to prevent her from suffering postnatal fevers accompanied by chills called *mɔryɛn*. Some of these medicines were drunk as infusions; others were burnt near the mother's abdomen; and still others were burnt to ashes, then made into a black paste and applied to the mother's body in horizontal lines across the abdomen and back and in vertical lines below the breasts. Both men and women could recite spells and apply medicines; whoever had the expertise did it, even if the man was not the husband of the woman in labor. This, however, was usually the only male role in the childbirth procedure. (We were told that men *could* be midwives, but we did not know of any such cases.) In the birth house the woman was normally attended by a midwife and two or three assistants. Some people said it was inappropriate for men to be present for the birth, but others said that the husband and other men could attend if they wanted to.

The midwife was generally a woman who had had children of her own and had attended enough other births to be well acquainted with the procedure. This typically was an older woman, but young women, including teenagers, could also serve as midwives. One woman said that she began acting as a midwife at about age fifteen. She said she simply knew what to do—no doubt from observing numerous previous births.

Tanyogn, an experienced midwife, explained that in the birth house the mother reclines against the backrest and spreads her legs underneath a draped cloth. The midwife reaches around the mother's abdomen and massages it in the direction of the pelvis in order to bring together the knees and elbows of the baby. The midwife then presses downward on the woman's abdomen to push the baby down. (Whether or not this technique actually affects the position of the baby, the massaging probably helps to distract the mother from the pain.) When the baby begins to emerge, the midwife reaches one hand over the mother's near leg and the other hand under it and receives the baby in her hands. She does not pull the baby or otherwise assist in the birth; Tanyogn appeared quite shocked when we asked whether more invasive procedures, equivalent to using forceps, were ever used. She said that the baby emerges of its own accord, along with the umbilical cord and then the placenta. She added that the baby cries as soon as it is born, without slaps or any other outside intervention.

The midwife immediately places the baby between the mother's feet, then bathes the mother and baby with cool water to prevent the infant from developing a fever. The midwife ties the umbilical cord with a piece of thin rattan, and then cuts the cord with a sharp sliver of bamboo. According to Tanyogn, they do not cut it with a metal knife because that would cause a burning sensation inside the baby. The baby is then wrapped in a cloth to keep it warm. A cloth is tied around the mother's waist and a heated stone placed on the cloth to warm her. The midwife or her assistants may massage the mother to make her more comfortable. The midwife puts the baby to the mother's breast, and when the mother feels ready to walk back to camp, she rejoins her family in their shelter. The parents give gifts such as cloth to the midwife for her help, though she may be given less if the baby dies.

Batek used various safeguards against postnatal health hazards to both mother and baby. To prevent the mother or baby from suffering *məryɛn*, a fire was kept burning near the placenta, which was left in the birth house and covered with a pandanus mat. The mother returned regularly to the birth house to keep the fire going for three or four days or until the placenta had shriveled and dried. Another anti-*məryɛn* measure was for the mother to drink hot medicinal teas, which were also supposed to stimulate the flow of milk. A further health measure was to keep an infant's umbilical cord stump after it had fallen off; if the umbilical stump were discarded after birth, the baby would miss it and would suffer *sabɛn*. The stump was wrapped in a small piece of cloth, and the baby wore this bundle as a bracelet until it could walk or until the bracelet got lost.

For one or two months after childbirth—probably until the cessation of the lochia flow of blood—the mother maintained the same food prohibitions that women followed during menstruation. If a new mother were to eat prohibited foods, she and/or her baby would suffer dizziness. Similarly, the midwife avoided eating meat on the day she assisted with the birth and washed the baby, lest the smell of the meat cause the baby to suffer dizziness. The father and family of the new baby were not subject to any such prohibitions, however. The mother resumed all her normal activities whenever she felt well enough, though some Batek said that women should not bathe in streams or rivers for a month or two after giving birth, as during menstruation.

After birth the baby was given an "original name" (*kənmɔh ʔasal*) or "flesh name" (*kənmɔh sec*) (see chapter 3). Some people said the baby is named immediately after birth, while others said that naming is delayed for a few days or even weeks. The name was chosen by the midwife, father, or both parents (see also Lye 1997). Often the name referred to the stream nearest the birthplace or to something the mother saw the day of birth—such as a particular flower, rock, or leaf. Names were announced to the camp with little or no ceremony, although occasionally new parents provided a small feast for camp members.

Batek did not practice infanticide for social or demographic reasons, though some occasionally may have killed severely deformed babies (Lye Tuck-Po, personal communication). We knew a few children with minor abnormalities, such as a second thumb, but these children were treated the same as other children. People said they desired boys and girls equally, and because disease kept the Batek population low enough relative to resources, they apparently had no need for systematic infanticide.

Batek regarded twins as a normal occurrence. Women were known to have died from bearing twins, but there also were cases of Batek women successfully giving birth to healthy twins. According to one female informant, people tried to avoid having twins by taking care not to "twin" firesticks, that is, not to carry two firesticks at once. This same informant said that twins could also be caused by a woman having two lovers at the same time, though she later commented that a woman's having two lovers would more likely cause divorce than twins.

The difficulties of birth and disease did take their toll on the Batek. About 25 percent of Batek children were stillborn or died within the first two years after birth. Malaria was one of the prime killers of infants. If a child lived to age five, however, it would most likely survive into adulthood. People said that if they buried a stillborn baby in the ground, as some other Orang Asli groups do, it would become a *kəwãʔ*, a ghost that tries to suck passers-by, as though the unfulfilled need to suckle survives after death. Lebir River Batek avoided creating *kəwãʔ* by giving all deceased infants the same kind of tree burial they gave to adults (see K.M. Endicott 1979a), a procedure that was thought to help the shadow-soul escape to the afterworld.

Batek considered the ideal spacing of children to be three to four years, after the previous child no longer needed milk and was somewhat independent of its mother. The ideal spacing, however, was not always the reality. Many Batek siblings were only a year or two apart in age. People considered close spacing of babies to be a hardship, but those to whom it happened accepted it. As far as we know, Batek did not resort to abortion. Some people said that they avoid sexual intercourse for several months following child-birth, while others said that people resume sex right away; it seems to have been an individual matter. Batek reported that the roots of various wild plants could be used by women and men as oral contraceptives (*ʔobɛt nɛŋ ʔawaʔ*, "medicine no children"). We do not know whether the contraceptives were actually effective. Two long-married but childless couples were said to have used contraceptives successfully, but these same couples were also said to be sterile. We got the impression that few couples regularly used contraceptives; indeed, people normally said that they like having children. Some couples may have taken contraceptives to prevent too close a spacing between preg-nancies, but it is more likely that extended birth spacing was caused by the suppression of ovulation resulting from extended breast-feeding.

Childhood

Batek treated babies of both sexes the same and with tremendous affec-tion. Babies were constantly held and indulged by parents and older siblings until they could walk. Because they were breast-fed, infants spent most of their time with their mother, in a cloth sling on her back or at her breast dur-ing the day and sleeping next to her at night. Breast-feeding might continue for three or four years if the mother did not become pregnant again. But fathers, too, played a major part in the social life of infants, taking obvious pleasure in holding, carrying, cuddling, and playing with their sons and daughters. Furthermore, such indulgence was not confined to immediate family members. All adults and older children took an active interest in the babies in camp, and they showered them with affection. Tanyogn, for exam-ple, lit up when she saw her baby grandson after an absence of some weeks, and she immediately gave him a large piece of monkey meat, even though he was still too young to chew it.

From the very start, mothers fed babies on demand, letting the infant determine the frequency and duration of nursing. Other caretakers also treated babies with the same kind of physical comforting and stimulation. Going everywhere their mothers or fathers went exposed even the youngest infants to the work and leisure activities of women and men. As infants grew, parents gave boys and girls equal freedom to explore their surroundings, including letting them crawl across camp. Parents allowed children of both sexes to play with all the family possessions, except quivers of poisoned darts, which were stuck safely out of children's reach high in the thatch roofs of their shelters. The favorite toys of children about eighteen months of age were knives, including large bush-knives. It was common to see baby boys and girls hacking away at everything within reach, including the support poles of the family shelter. They wailed in anger if anyone tried to take their knives away.

Two- and three-year-old boys and girls spent most of their time playing together near their mothers. They accompanied their mothers on fishing and gathering trips, walking when their mothers would not carry them and playing alongside the women while watching them work. Their play reflected what they saw. Both boys and girls especially enjoyed play-digging for tubers near their shelters or at the edge of camp. Gripping their digging sticks like adults, they dug down for roots, pulled them out of the ground, and brushed off the dirt. "This is a piece of *takop*," a little girl pretended as she tossed an inedible root into a basket.

By about three and a half to four years of age most children played with five- and six-year-olds in mixed-sex groups. Their imaginative activities could spring up at any time. One afternoon children who had just come back to camp after accompanying their mothers on a gathering trip were ready for some fun. Two young boys climbed into the trees and cried "*Mbok, mbok!*" Monkeys! The game was on. A couple of three-year-old boys grabbed their miniature blowpipes and showered the "monkeys" with clay pellets. Two more young boys and a five-year-old girl ran to the trees and quickly climbed up to join the monkey troop. They flung themselves from vine to vine, clambered up to the higher branches, slid down, and flung themselves some more. "Come down!" a worried father called up to them. The monkeys just laughed and climbed even higher. They came down only when they grew tired of their strenuous frolic.

Children learned to dig by observing their parents doing it and by practicing. This boy and girl are play-digging in camp. They brought a rattan basket to carry back whatever they dig up.

Despite occasional parental worries, as long as children remained within earshot they were allowed to do almost anything they pleased. They chopped down trees. They built fires and cooked food. They pretended to smoke porcupines out of holes. They carried sticks on their shoulders like bundles of rattan or firewood. Many children enjoyed pretending they were moving camp. They packed up a few items in baskets or cloth slings, carried them to another part of camp, and constructed play shelters out of leaves and sticks. Placing cloths or mats on the ground, they lay down and pretended to sleep. Chiro', a particularly imaginative five-year-old boy, liked to construct elaborate shelters out of upright poles and all the cloth he could find. Less frenetic activities included delousing each other's hair and—while we were there— listening to our tape recordings of Batek songs, an activity that easily kept children occupied for hours at a time.

Each camp was like a new playground. In a campsite filled with vines, vine-swinging became the popular activity. If there were a spacious sandbar, children might set up a log drum, then sing and dance around it. A fallen tree extending over a stream invited hours of imaginative water games. At one such site a group of boys and girls ranging from three to six years of age began swimming together. (Children learned to swim mainly by observing older children and practicing it themselves.) Then they jumped off the log into the water, yelling "Farewell!" or "I'm dead!" or even an English "Bye-

Children's play often mimicked the serious endeavors of adults. Here some children practice the rituals used to communicate with the superhuman beings. Those on the left, dressed in sweet-smelling leaf decorations, dance in a circle, while those on the right beat a log drum suspended from rattan vines.

bye!" When one child held his hands up like claws, growled, and ran after the others, everyone began playing tiger, with much spontaneous role switching between tigers and people—and who was chasing whom. Then whirring like motors, the children pretended to be boats. After an hour and a half the kids drifted off to their shelters to eat some food or take a rest.

Play was free flowing, inclusive, and cooperative. Games did not have set rules; rather, children shaped their activities as they went along. They joined in and dropped out at will. No one was deliberately excluded from any activity. Youngsters who could not keep up because of their age and more limited abilities found other things to do. When older children were in camp, the younger children sometimes tried to play with them; at other times they watched the older children and then imitated them after the older children had left to do something else. Sometimes the older kids were happy to have the younger kids join in, as when they held singing sessions that could last for hours. Cooperative rather than competitive, Batek play did not produce winners and losers or gendered rivalries. Instead, play consisted of like-minded children having a good time doing things together, much like the noncompetitive adult activities on which most play was modeled.

From about six to ten years, children still got together in mixed-sex groups, but they increasingly practiced adult skills. During those years children learned more about their environment and technology through observation, questioning of older children and adults, and some instruction. Everyone practiced fishing, digging tubers, catching frogs, and other food-getting activities. Although parents did not expect children to produce food, youngsters seemed to enjoy their attempts and sporadic successes. Imitating animal sounds, learned from hunters, was a favorite activity. Boys and girls observed hunters making blowpipes and darts, and they watched older children hunt birds and squirrels with blowpipes and slingshots in the forest near camp. It was not unusual to see a group of young boys working on their blowpipes in one shelter, a group of teenagers working on theirs in another shelter, and a group of three- and four-year-olds sitting in a third shelter making play blowpipes by drying small pieces of bamboo over a fire. Girls joined in the hunting activities to varying degrees. Many of them carved darts, and some hunted with the boys or on their own. Once a six-year-old girl shot three birds with her father's blowpipe while hunting with some boys. Another time she and another girl saw a squirrel in a tree at the edge of camp and grabbed their uncle's blowpipes from his deserted shelter. "He won't mind," they assured us. The squirrel got away but the hunters came back grinning.

Adolescence

By about age ten, children spent more and more time practicing adult activities, and the activities of boys and girls gradually diverged. Boys hunted birds and squirrels further from camp and spent more of their in-camp hours making darts and quivers. As they entered their teen years, boys got their next lessons in hunting by going out with experienced hunters. Fourteen-year-old Mah, for example, regularly accompanied Pay, an accomplished hunter in his twenties, assisting him while developing his own hunting skills. Boys did not always wait to be invited to accompany hunters. "Fathers worry about taking young kids hunting," two teens reported. "They even worry about us. But we go out anyway and follow them." Although a few of the girls continued to hunt with boys their own age, as far as we know, girls neither sought nor received further training from adult hunters.

Instead, girls turned to the company of women. Adolescent girls especially looked to single teenaged girls and young married women for fun and companionship. They relaxed together in camp, playing flutes, singing, and decorating their faces with white lime paste. The women let the girls try on their clothes, and they dressed up together in headbands of fragrant leaves. Although girls were already developing their own house-building skills, they sometimes shared shelters with the young women, occasionally even when a husband was present. Girls and young women dug tubers together, often working with some of their mothers. In camp girls learned how to weave pandanus baskets and mats by watching and helping the women and practicing on their own.

Although no one depended on the work of youngsters, by age twelve or thirteen boys were hunting, girls were gathering, and both were collecting rattan so often that they were essentially already following adult behavior patterns. By age fourteen to sixteen young women and men were skilled workers, contributing more significantly to food getting, living in separate households from their parents, and entering into their first marriages. And through it all, young adults continued to have fun. Once some young men opened a play shop, imitating Indian and Chinese shopkeepers and traders, where they "sold" pieces of cloth to customers wielding scraps of paper as money. One young married man enjoyed spending his leisure time shooting at squirrels with a slingshot, as teenaged boys often did. For Batek, being an adult did not mean giving up the playfulness of childhood.

The gradual change from the mixed-sex play groups and identical activities of early childhood to the frequently single-sex work groups and complementary activities of adulthood took place without overt pressure or coercion from adults. There were no rituals that formally inducted children into prescribed adult roles. Nor did Batek assign children to age-grades or other categories with set time frames marking children's progress from childhood to adulthood. Rather, adults expected children to learn skills and to mature socially at their own rates. Multi-age playgroups exposed children to activities appropriate to all ages and levels of maturity. Physical maturity was regarded as a separate matter from an individual's readiness for marriage or the full economic responsibilities of men and women. Children seemed to slip into appropriate gender role behaviors by aligning themselves with the positive role models of same-sex adults. Children saw that both men and women approached their work and their leisure with confidence and enthusiasm. They saw adults having good times when they worked and being playful when relaxing. Even in the absence of prohibitions against engaging in activities usually done by members of the opposite sex, children seemed to gravitate easily to the behavior patterns of their own sex. In short, both men and women seemed satisfied with their lives, and children readily identified with same-sex adults.[1]

Parenting

Although prolonged breast-feeding kept infants closely tied to their mothers, and the organization of labor resulted in young children accompanying their mothers on numerous gathering trips, Batek did not define child rearing as women's rather than men's work (see also Lye 1997). Fathers were involved in all phases of child rearing (K.L. Endicott 1992). Men shifted into the fathering role even before their babies were born, when they built special lean-tos outside camp for their wives to give birth. Fathers often participated in naming their babies. First births led to the renaming of both parents as well; the man became known as Father of So-and-So, the woman as Mother of So-and-So. These teknonyms publicly linked both parents to their first-born child, regardless of its sex.

Both parents devoted considerable time to their children, from infancy onward, although mothers spent more time overall on child care, especially when their children were young. But hunting almost never required men to be away from camp during all their children's waking hours, so even the most active hunters were still available to their children for many hours a day. Fathers often carried their small children while visiting other camp members and even when talking with traders. Children could be found at their father's side while he made darts, cleaned and dried his blowpipe, and butchered game. Fathers as well as mothers bathed their children, cleaned up their excrement, and took them outside camp to relieve themselves. Both parents played with their children, cooked for them, fed them, and slept near them. Fathers often made toys—including blowpipes, swings, and climbing ladders—for their children's amusement.

When a new baby preoccupied a mother, older children became even more dependent on their father for comfort and attention. Children were as openly affectionate toward their father as they were toward their mother, and attachments to fathers and mothers appeared to be equal in intensity. Often when a father left camp to hunt, a young son or daughter would run to the edge of camp and cry out for him. Such wails went up for mothers, too, if they tried to go off to work without taking their children along. "Children miss their parents," Tanyogn explained. "They are afraid they won't come back."

When parents wanted to work unencumbered, they might put their older sons and daughters in charge of the younger children. This was not a perfect solution, for sometimes the caretakers drifted off to other activities, leaving their siblings to their own devices. This was probably why parents did not rely on sibling caretakers too often. But usually older siblings took their duties seriously, comforting children who cried for their parents, soothing those who hurt themselves, and looking out for them even when everyone else was playing. Since child care duties fell equally to boys and girls, all Batek were well versed in child care by the time they reached adulthood.

Even so, there were variations in the skills and dedication parents brought to child rearing. Tanyogn and Langsat, for example, looked out for their children continually, even tracking down their grown children in other camps if they were worried about them or missed them. Tanyogn paid keen attention to the needs of other people's children as well. She and Langsat took care of two orphaned youngsters. If Tanyogn heard crying, she investigated and tended to any child who was not receiving care from others. She carried other women's babies if the mothers needed a break or were sick. And she kept an eye on the activities of the older children, her own and others, calling to them to come down from trees or refrain from doing any other activity she thought was getting too dangerous.

Pengasih and Pales were another couple who brought great care and patience to raising their family, which included seven children under the age of twelve. Pengasih usually carried both her nursing infant and her two-year-old daughter when she went gathering or did other chores. Pales frequently had a child in his lap when he was in camp. When the couple's three-year-old son Rangoy went through a period of tantrums, they handled him with extreme patience. One day, for example, Rangoy cried hysterically after tripping and spilling his bowl of grated tubers and honey. Pengasih carried him across camp to their shelter and handed him to Pales, who held him on his lap and hugged him while she grated more tubers for him. Still sitting in his father's lap, Rangoy ate the new food and gradually calmed down. Pengasih told us that having many children was a lot of work, but she and Pales were rarely out of good humor when tending their children.

Not all parents were well suited to child rearing. One divorced mother who tended toward laziness in everything she did, seemed scarcely to care about her eighteen-month-old son. She was the only mother who routinely left a nursing child behind when she went out for more than a short while. In camp the child followed her around as best he could. She usually ignored him when he cried. One rainy day when both of them were sick, she gave him a plate of food to take to Tanyogn's shelter. He got his foot tangled in the underbrush, but his mother did not come to his aid. Instead, Tanyogn's son dashed over to him and took the plate. The child untangled himself and returned home. On the rare occasions that his mother played with him, poking, tickling, and playing hitting games with him, he laughed heartily. By the time he was two years old, however, he was living with his father in another camp, and his mother seemed happy to be on her own.

Unusual though it was for such a young child to live with the father rather than the mother, the fact that in cases of divorce children could live

with either parent or alternate between them demonstrated that Batek
regarded child rearing as the responsibility of men as well as women. There
was no economic detriment to children's welfare in being with one parent
rather than the other. Since both men and women could provide food for
their families through their own efforts and through each camp's food-sharing network, children could be supported by either parent. Whether or not
fathers or mothers gave emotional support to their children had more to do
with an individual's personality than gender. Some fathers doted on their
children; some mothers remained aloof.

In many societies fathers are distanced from close interactions with their
children because fathers play an authoritarian role. Batek placed neither parent in this position. Although parents had the responsibility to teach their
children proper social and religious behavior, they did not have the kind of
authority over children that many, if not most, societies assign to adults.
Mothers and fathers shared equally in the little authority that Batek parents
had over their children.

The very idea of parental authority was problematic for the Batek
because they believed that coercing a person could cause the person to suffer
the depressive condition *kaʔɔy* (see chapter 3). The challenge for parents,
then, was to teach their children without coercion. Adults quietly taught by
example, performing their work and leisure activities in full view of their children. As children tried out the skills they observed, parents offered any explanations and assistance the children needed. Parents did not pressure children
to do things before they were ready, able, and willing. Parents verbally cor-
rected children who misbehaved, but they did not hold them responsible for
breaking rules they did not yet understand. That is why when young children
broke *lawac* rules, a parent, usually the mother, performed the blood sacrifice
on their behalf rather than expecting her children to do it. When parents were
annoyed with their children, they told them so with a sharp, "Stop! You're
making me angry!" But parents did not really expect obedience. As one
father said with a shrug, "Children don't listen. They don't know any better."

The main way parents tried to control the behavior of their children without inducing *kaʔɔy* was by invoking the authority of a third party: the thunder-god, Gobar, tigers, or outsiders. Gobar was the punitive authority figure
for both adults and children, as he unleashed violent thunderstorms to punish
transgressions of various *lawac* prohibitions. For example, one day when children were down at the stream slapping the water with pieces of bamboo, a
mother shouted out, "*Lawac!* Gobar doesn't like the noise." When children
were laughing while watching a swarm of butterflies on a sandbar, another
mother called out, "*Lawac!*" The children looked a bit sheepish, but kept
right on laughing. An hour later a thunderstorm blew in, letting them know
that Gobar always has the last laugh.

Parents also used the threat of tigers to scare children out of certain activities. Building on the very real physical threat tigers posed, parents used the
tiger as a bogey figure. If a child wandered too far away from camp, for exam-

ple, a parent would call out "Tiger, tiger!" so the children would run back to camp. This warning taught children to be aware of dangerous situations, and it was also an effective technique for controlling children. When young children tried to follow older children into the forest, the older ones might tell them, "We're going far. There will be tigers!" and the younger kids would stop in their tracks. Despite a sharp decrease in the tiger population in Peninsular Malaysia, the fear of tigers remained strong in Batek culture, ensuring the continuing potency of the tiger as an authority figure (see also Lye 2004).

The other third-party threat parents used to influence children's behavior was the outsider, *gob*, usually meaning Malays. Parents might tell a misbehaving child that the *gob* would come or that a *gob* was watching. (Sometimes we were the *gob* in this scenario.) Sometimes such threats seemed blatantly manipulative, especially when people played on the shyness toward strangers that very young children often exhibit. But as with the tiger, Batek had good reasons to teach children to be wary of strangers. Until around 1920 Malays raided the Batek for slaves (K.M. Endicott 1983). Slave-raiders would kill the adult men and capture the women and children. Memories of those times remained painfully alive. One family recalled losing a child while working for a surveying crew sometime after World War II. Some incident caused the couple to suspect that the surveyors were actually slave-raiders. The family fled, but one child became separated from the group. The family looked repeatedly for the boy, but never found him. When parents tried to scare children into good behavior by reminding them of the *gob*, they were simultaneously reflecting, fanning, and utilizing fears of being abducted by slave-raiders.

Resorting to third-party authority was a roundabout way to control children, but that was very much the point: it was a way for parents to teach appropriate behavior without being authoritarian. Parents took advantage of the generally true assumption that children would fear and avoid things that might actually harm them. This disciplinary technique allowed both parents to be equally close to their children, for no parent had to endure the social distance that could result from playing a punitive or authoritarian role.

However, very occasionally a parent would hit a child. The Batek word for "to hit," *sakɛl*, also means "to kill," and most Batek considered both acts to be abhorrent (cf. Dentan 1968). Some people, however, said that it was all right to hit children "a little bit, to teach them." Although most parents considered hitting a last resort, frustration sometimes got the better of them. For example, early one morning a mother who had very little patience with her young son, slapped him when he wouldn't stop crying. The slap only made him cry harder, waking up the whole camp. Another mother lost her patience as she tried to clean her squirming baby's backside, slapped the child's back with an open palm, and let him go. The only case of serious child abuse we came across involved a woman who apparently beat two of her children to death and knocked another one unconscious (see chapter 3). Batek regarded her violent outbursts as insanity.

That Batek children constantly saw mothers and fathers fully sharing parental responsibilities undoubtedly influenced their concepts of gender. From the start, children received nurturance, comfort, affection, instruction, and aid from both parents. In many societies children experience a far more divided kind of parenting, such as nurturance from mothers only and discipline from fathers only. Such parental "divisions of labor" both reflect and reproduce a society's beliefs about "innate" abilities of males and females. Batek daughters and sons saw that mothers and fathers were capable of performing the same range of activities and interactions. This gave children their first impression of what their own capabilities were.[2]

Instilling Batek Values

The need for teaching without coercion was a result of the contradiction between the basic Batek values of personal autonomy and social responsibility. On the one hand, parents were not supposed to interfere too much with the will of the individual child. On the other hand, parents had to teach children how to behave properly. Children had to learn to be self-reliant, to share, to obey *lawac* prohibitions, and to be nonviolent. Children had to learn to balance individual freedom and adherence to moral principles, and parents had to gently but persistently teach them how.

Parents fostered self-reliance in their children in a number of ways. They let even the youngest of children explore their surroundings and try different skills and activities. They let children take risks—including using knives, making fires, and climbing trees—and they intervened only when they thought their children's activities far exceeded their abilities. When children cried, parents did not immediately rush to their aid. Rather, they sized up the situation and let children deal with most problems on their own.

Parents instilled the sharing ethic early. They accepted babies' possessiveness, in part out of fear of causing *kaʔɔy* and in part out of a pragmatic recognition of the limitations of children's social capabilities. Once children could walk well, adults explicitly taught them to share food by handing them plates of food to deliver to other families. But parents tolerated lapses in sharing as an inevitable part of childhood. For example, when Kaloy once dropped his piece of meat, his younger brother Rangoy gave him some of his. But Kaloy wanted a bigger piece, so he bit Rangoy. "Kaloy is like a fish—he bites," his mother said, laughing. "He is ignorant. He doesn't know any better." Possessiveness also extended to objects. One young boy, for example, closely guarded the toy raft he was playing with, holding it tightly against his body if anyone came near. One child who seemed to want to play with him offered him a leaf, but he just hugged his raft even more tightly. Each child went his own way. Adults usually ignored such incidents. The general expectation seemed to be that if someone wanted something so badly, others should not interfere. Sometimes this meant returning objects one had taken. One day, for example, Tekem snatched a sarong that Yem was playing with. When Yem got upset, Tekem handed back the sarong. Even parents would give in. After eighteen-month-old Pon cried for the knife her mother took from her, her mother gave it back. There were times, however, when parents refused to give in to their children's wishes. When one young boy rummaged in someone else's shelter for a pair of sunglasses, his parents insisted that he take off the glasses and return them to their owner. He did so without an argument.

Lessons in the many *lawac* prohibitions that guide Batek life took place over a period of many years. Parents did not hesitate to verbally correct children who inadvertently committed *lawac* acts. Adults took every violation as an opportunity to teach children correct behavior, but they did not hold young children responsible for transgressions that they did not yet understand. As children grew up, they gradually took more responsibility for their actions, obeying *lawac* rules and performing blood sacrifices if they violated them.

One important tenet of Batek ethics that children had to learn was that aggression and violence were unacceptable.[3] Batek began curbing aggression early. When one- and two-year-olds hit each other, whether deliberately or accidentally, adults immediately separated them and tried to distract each one with a new activity. Toddlers and older children were explicitly told not to bother each other, but it took a long time before they learned this lesson. Siblings were especially apt to annoy each other. They made faces at one another, threw things at one another, and hit each other. Living in tight quarters, they were constantly bumping into each other. Sometimes what one sibling intended as play, another saw as an annoyance. One day, for example, a smiling two-year-old flopped down in her older sister's lap, but she didn't get the warm reception she obviously expected. Instead, her older sister cried out, "Stop it!" and hit her. No one intervened in this case. But sometimes adults headed off aggressive acts in the making. When a young boy threatened to throw a stick at another child, some adults shouted at him not to do it. Parents seemed to expect a certain amount of hitting but expected children to outgrow it. As Tanyogn said, "They stop when they realize how it feels."

People seemed to think that the best way of dealing with aggressive behavior was to let it play itself out. They had a number of techniques to make that happen. Often people laughed at children's aggressive behavior, making what seemed important to the child appear trivial and amusing, thus easing the tension of the situation. Sometimes people tried to distract the aggressive child. If they saw a child about to hit someone, people might cry out, "Stop it!" Parents did not normally punish children for aggressive acts and only rarely struck children to teach them not to hit others. Instead, adults minimized their reaction to aggression and let children learn at their own pace that acting aggressively was not something Batek do. As children became more aware of adult behavior, they saw that adults did not hit each other, act possessive about food or objects, or display explosive anger. The absence of an adult model of aggression for children to follow was probably the greatest factor in socializing children to be nonaggressive.

That children of both sexes were socialized out of aggressive behavior—in the same way and to the same degree—had implications for the development of gender role concepts. Batek did not expect men and women to act very differently in interpersonal interactions. For example, men were not supposed to be aggressive and dominating, nor were women expected to be deferring and meek. Batek boys and girls did not have to grow up in radically different ways. Their socialization guided each individual toward a confident independence coupled with a sensitivity toward others, rather than creating vastly different masculine and feminine personality types. Batek highly valued the right of each individual to make and act upon his or her own decisions and their freedom from the authority of others. Their dislike of aggression and discouragement of aggressive behaviors seemed to be correlated with these values. Had aggression been allowed and fostered in one sex, coercion and domination of others would have been the logical and possibly unavoidable consequences, with physically stronger males intimidating and aggressively controlling women. Batek society's ethic of nonaggression placed men and woman on a level playing field.

Notes

[1] Draper's (1975b:611) assessment of Ju/'hoansi gender-role acquisition is relevant to the Batek as well: "Beatrice Whiting (personal communication) has pointed out that since both men and women of the hunting and gathering groups of !Kung have equal power, girls should have little conflict in identifying with the same sex parent. Possibly in this egalitarian setting (and others) learning of sex roles can proceed largely by identification for both sexes and without the need for overt instruction as it occurs in many other societies in secular and ritual guises."

[2] When Chodorow hypothesized the kind of parent–child relationships that would contribute to "social equality between men and women and their relative freedom from certain sorts of psychological conflict" (1974:66), she came close to describing the realities of Batek socialization: "Most important, boys need to grow up around men who take a major role in child care, and girls around women who, in addition to their child-care responsibilities, have a valued role and recognized spheres of legitimate control. These arrangements could help to ensure that children of both sexes develop a sufficiently individuated and strong sense of self, as well as a positively valued and secure gender identity, that does not bog down either in ego-boundary confusion, low self-esteem, and overwhelming relatedness to others, or in compulsive denial of any connection to others or dependence upon them."

[3] Writers on nonaggressive and nonviolent societies generally accept that all people experience aggressive feelings at some point during their lives (see, e.g., Montagu 1978; Draper 1978; Dentan 1978; Marshall 1976). In nonaggressive societies, however, there is no cultural encouragement of, sanction for, or acceptance of aggression. Nonaggressive societies socialize children out of such behaviors. The socialization of Batek children to be nonaggressive contrasts sharply with the encouragement of aggressive behavior lavished on boys by the Yanomamo, the classic example of a society in which aggression is a valued attribute of manhood. Yanomamo boys: "are encouraged to be 'fierce' and are rarely punished by their parents for inflicting blows on them or on the hapless girls in the village" (Chagnon 1968:84).

Chapter 6

Continuity and Change in Batek Gender

So far we have presented the egalitarian gender concepts, gender roles, and gender relations of the Batek as the outcome of a particular constellation of ethical principles, social practices, and material circumstances. Their ethical principles together with the ability of every adult to survive without depending on particular other people seems to have produced a society in which every man and woman had wide freedom of action without sacrificing the security of group support. But it is easy to mistake a description of a given state of affairs for an explanation, to imply that certain features are the causes of others. One test of an explanation is whether it can account for changes, or absence of changes, in a system under study when external circumstances change. In this chapter we look at the effects of a change in the Batek economy—from a nomadic foraging-trading economy to a semi-sedentary horticultural-foraging-trading economy—on gender concepts, roles, and relations among one group of Batek in 1990. This change was caused ultimately by government-sponsored development schemes, in the form of logging and plantation agriculture, and government programs aimed at changing Batek culture (see also Dentan et al. 1997).

1990: New Conditions, New Responses

In early 1990 we returned to Post Lebir by road. The road was part of a vast network of roads built to serve the rubber and oil palm plantations that had replaced the rainforest throughout the Lebir River valley, from its mouth near Manek Urai to the border of the National Park (Taman Negara) in the south (see map). In Malaysia, land that is not privately owned is considered

127

state land, and the use of that land and its resources is a major source of revenue for each state. In the early 1970s the state of Kelantan began the process of "developing" the Lebir valley by dividing it up into timber concessions that were sold to logging companies or to business concerns that hired logging contractors. Logging was not only a source of revenue in itself, but was the necessary first step in converting the land to plantation agriculture. During the 1970s and 1980s logging roads spread throughout the Lebir River valley, and the logging companies extracted the valuable timber at a furious rate (K.M. Endicott 1982). Some companies even poached logs from the National Park, a rainforest preserve, leaving behind areas of massive erosion where logging roads cut into the hills and riverbanks.

After removing the valuable trees from concession lands, logging companies were required to cut down all the remaining vegetation and burn it off, leaving nothing but bare earth and ashes. At this point either the federal government land development agency (FELDA) or the Kelantan state government equivalent (KESEDAR) took over the job of converting the land into plantations by bulldozing more roads, terracing the hillsides, and then planting oil palm and rubber tree seedlings. The rainforest, with its thousands of species of plants, was thus replaced by a new "forest" of only two species, nourished by chemical fertilizers and protected from weeds by herbicides. These plantations were of two types. In one type the land was parceled out in ten-acre plots and allotted to landless Malays who were promised title to the

Logging not only destroyed the rainforest in the Lebir River valley, it also exposed the soft laterite soil to tropical downpours, thus causing massive soil erosion. In this typical temporary logging camp, the general devastation is evident.

land in return for living there, making certain improvements, and, eventually, paying back the cost of developing the land. In the other type, the development agency retained control of the plantation and ran it as a commercial venture, using mostly Thai and Indonesian laborers. By 1990 some of the more remote plantations were still being logged off, while others already had trees at varying stages of growth, and some were already producing rubber and oil palm nuts.

The development of the Lebir River valley was done without any consideration for the Batek. According to federal and state laws, Batek had no rights over the land they had lived on for centuries; legally they were squatters on state land. In fact, even if they had had the money to buy land, they would not have been permitted to do so, because most of the Lebir River valley was classified as a Malay Reservation, an area in which only Malays could purchase land. The only compensation the Batek were given for the loss of the resources and the land they depended upon for their livelihood was about $1,000 (Malaysian 3,000 *ringgit*) for some durian trees that were cut down when a plantation was built on the upper Aring River. Batek were not offered any allotments or jobs in the land settlement schemes, nor did they want them. The JHEOA discouraged Batek from working for logging companies, and Batek quickly gave up any thought of working for the contractors who were building the plantations after one contractor, who asked a group of Batek to burn some brush for him, cheated them out of their wages.

Even the Batek's right to live at Post Lebir was tenuous. Although the JHEOA, a federal government agency, had applied to the state government for 1,000 acres of land surrounding Post Lebir in the 1950s, the state had been unwilling to grant even a Temporary Occupation License, which must be renewed every year and can be revoked at any time. In 1990, the JHEOA had stopped making improvements at Post Lebir because the government was contemplating building a dam on the Lebir just above Kampung Lalok to generate electricity and control downriver flooding, that would flood Post Lebir and the bottomlands along the Lebir, Aring, and Relai rivers, including areas already under plantation use. (Apparently that plan was later shelved, since in 2004 Post Lebir still existed, a large new school had been built there, and government agencies were building concrete block houses for Batek families at Kampung Macang, just up the road from the post.)

In 1990, the only place the Batek had a relatively secure right to live was in the National Park, which straddles Kelantan's southern border with Pahang. The park is almost entirely within the area occupied by Batek since at least as early as the nineteenth century. According to federal laws concerning Orang Asli and the regulations of the Department of Wildlife and National Parks, which manages the park, Batek had the right to live in the park and to gather wild foods and hunt game—even protected species—for their own subsistence. However, they were not allowed to collect rattan or *gaharu?* wood for trade, although they could collect them for their own use. This led to some resentment, since Batek did not see why they could no longer trade rattan from one of the few remaining patches of rainforest in the area. On the whole, however, Kelantan Batek in 1990 had favorable feelings toward the game wardens who protected the park. The game wardens treated Batek with respect, did not try to make them change their way of life, and gave them wage-earning jobs from time to time. A group of Batek living in the Pahang side of the park in the 1970s often camped near the park headquarters at Kuala Tahan, where they worked as firewood collectors and as guides for tourists. In 1990 one man said he had worked for a time shooting elephants with tranquilizer darts, clipping their ears, and putting radio transmitters around their necks. He also worked for tourists who wanted to photograph tigers from blinds at night. He gave up this kind of work as too dangerous, however, after he was chased up a tree by an enraged bull elephant.

Because of the widespread destruction of the Batek's resource base and the unrelenting pressure from the JHEOA to settle them at Post Lebir (the department even closed the medical post on the Aring River in the mid-1970s to force the Batek to go to Post Lebir for medical attention), we expected most if not all of the Batek from Kelantan to have settled in the vicinity of Post Lebir by 1990. When Kirk had last visited them in May and June of 1981, more than twenty Batek families had established houses at Kampung Macang. The total number of people who had houses in the vicinity of the post, including Batek Teh and Batek Te', was 184, in forty families. Although many of the Batek families represented were in the forest collecting rattan and *gaharuʔ* wood at the time, they had cleared land and planted crops near the village. Rubber tree seeds furnished by the JHEOA had also been planted, and a herd of thirty-three cows, also provided by the department, grazed nearby. Nine young men had joined the Malaysian army and were in training at an army base near Kota Bharu, the state capital. People said there were no more Batek living in the Aring River valley, which had already been logged off and was full of outsiders who were converting the area into plantations. The Batek still seeking rattan and *gaharuʔ* wood were staying on the upper Lebir and its eastern tributaries, where substantial tracts of forest still survived. But logging was going on at a rapid rate, and we reasoned that by 1990 there would be little option for the Batek but to settle at Kampung Macang and adopt an economy based on subsistence farming and rubber tapping for cash, as the JHEOA had intended.

Part of the reason we were eager to study a group of Batek who had been forced to change their economy was to see whether the economic changes and sedentarization had undermined the conditions that produced egalitarian gender relations in 1975–76. In a comparative study of nomadic and recently settled !Kung (now called Ju/'hoansi) in Botswana, Draper had found that the status of women declined in the group that had settled down and adopted an economy based on "agriculture, animal husbandry, and a small amount of gathering." She concluded that the

> features of sedentary life that appear to be related to a decrease in women's autonomy and influence are: increasing rigidity in sex-typing of adult work; more permanent attachment of the individual to a particular

place and group of people; dissimilar childhood socialization for boys and girls; decrease in the mobility of women as contrasted with men; changing nature of women's subsistence contribution; richer material inventory with implications for women's work; tendency for men to have greater access to and control over such important resources as domestic animals, knowledge of Bantu language and culture; wage work; male entrance into extra-village politics; settlement pattern; and increasing household privacy. (Draper 1975a:78)

On the other hand, perhaps the social underpinnings of male–female egalitarianism among the Batek would prevent the development of power and prestige differences between men and women even if women became economically dependent upon men.

What we found when we reached Post Lebir was a shock. Far from being a large and thriving community, the settlement was smaller than in 1981. Adjacent to the prefabricated schoolhouse, medical hut, and dwellings that formed the post was a small village of seventeen houses, fifteen of which were small bamboo and thatch dwellings raised on wooden posts. The other two were new wooden plank houses built for the headman and one other man by the JHEOA. The inhabitants were mostly Batek Teh and Batek Te' who had been settled at the post since the late 1960s. Thickets of cassava and banana plants grew between the houses, and across the road was a grove of rubber trees, the source of the residents' meager income.

Kampung Macang, the Batek village just up the road, now contained only fourteen houses, in various stages of disrepair, and most of them were empty. Only three families were in residence along with a few adolescents and several school-aged children. The only sources of food in evidence at Kampung Macang were some seasonal fruit trees, not yet bearing fruit, and a few banana plants. The rubber trees across the road were overgrown with weeds, and people told us that they had ceased tapping them for rubber over a year before.

The post itself looked more dilapidated than it had in earlier years. With the forest around it removed, it lay hot and dusty in the sun, and the grass in the area between the buildings, which had once formed a tidy playing field, had been allowed to grow to knee height. The only new building was a Muslim prayer hall that had been built by the Kelantan State Department of Religion. Electrical wires stretched from poles by the road to several buildings, but were not connected; a gas-driven water pump in a shed by the prayer hall was out of service. When we saw that the Batek village at Kampung Macang had become a virtual ghost town, we realized we'd have to modify our research plan.

By questioning some Batek and JHEOA employees at the settlement we were able to piece together a picture of where the missing Batek were and what they were doing. Different groups had adopted different strategies for dealing with their radically changed circumstances. The upper Lebir people with whom we had lived in 1975–76 had moved into the National Park on the upper Lebir and its tributaries and were spending some time across the Pahang border on the streams flowing into the Tembeling River. They had deliberately removed themselves beyond the reach of the roads. They were living by foraging and trading rattan and *gaharu?* wood, as before. The most disheartening news about the group was that our friend Tanyogn had died a few years earlier, from a disease that affected both her stomach and throat, although some people claimed that a Malay trader killed her by means of magical spells after she had refused to sell him a mat at a price far below its value.

The people who still had houses at Kampung Macang—who were originally from the Aring River—were in the forest on the Terengganu border collecting thick rattan for a trader from Kampung Lalok. They were using Kampung Macang as a base camp to which they returned briefly between rattan-collecting trips. They were living entirely off the proceeds of trade. The bulk of the Aring people had returned to the upper Aring River valley, where they were living in the National Park and in the area bordering it. They were foraging and collecting forest produce for trade, and some, it was said, had planted crops the year before and intended to do so again. There was considerable movement of personnel back and forth between Kampung Macang and the upper Aring community.

We found out later why the Batek had refused to settle down at Kampung Macang. The foremost reason was that they wanted to avoid pressure to "become Malays." The overall goal of the JHEOA was "the eventual integration and assimilation of the Orang Asli population with the national society" (Jimin et al. 1983: 55, 110), by which they meant absorbing the Orang Asli into the Malay population (Dentan et al. 1997). According to the Malaysian constitution, a Malay is a person "who professes the religion of Islam, habitually speaks the Malay language [and] conforms to Malay custom" (Malaysian Government 1982, Article 160[2]). Since most Batek could already speak Malay, assimilating them into the Malay population required that they be converted to Islam and induced to adopt a Malay style of life. Despite the Federal Constitution's guarantees of freedom of religion for all citizens, the JHEOA stated that "the propagation of Islam among the Orang Asli population is part of the term[s] of reference given to the Department" (Jimin et al. 1983:90) and that "religion would be the binding bond in the integration process" (Jimin et al. 1983:91). Consequently, from the late 1970s onward, JHEOA officials and government-supported Muslim missionaries had pressured the Batek to adopt Islam. They promised such rewards as motorbikes and wooden houses to those who would convert and threatened to withhold government assistance and programs from those who refused. The Kelantan State Department of Religion built the prayer hall at Post Lebir, paid a religious teacher to visit the school each day classes were in session to teach the schoolchildren how to pray, and sponsored religious training sessions in the state capital, Kota Bharu, for any Batek men who were interested.

Most of the Batek Teh and Batek Te' who lived permanently at Post Lebir had declared themselves to be Muslims, although the degree to which

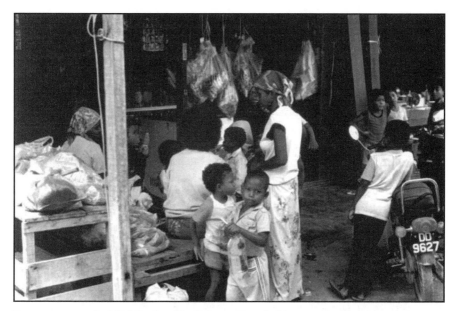

It was common in 1990 for families living at Post Lebir to catch rides with traders so they could shop at Kampung Lalok, about ten miles away by road. Dressed in Malay style, they bought food, toys, cloth, and trinkets.

they actually followed the prescribed practices varied. All of them had adopted Malay-style names and had been issued identity cards indicating their religion as Islam. Four men were known to have been circumcised, a few prayed from time to time, but almost no one followed the dietary laws unless Malays were present. Several of the Batek men who had houses at Kampung Macang had studied the religion and identified themselves as Muslims while in the presence of Malays, although they generally reverted to their Batek patterns of behavior when camped in the forest. A small number of other Batek men had adopted Islam at one time, but later had given it up. Because schoolteachers routinely bestowed Malay names on all schoolchildren and JHEOA census-takers recorded everyone's religion as Islam unless they strenuously objected—which many were too shy or too intimidated to do—the bulk of the people who maintained a presence at Kampung Macang were regarded by the government as Muslims, although their actual commitment to the religion varied from moderate to nonexistent.

The vast majority of Batek—those who fled from Kampung Macang or refused to move there in the first place—refused to become Muslims and complained bitterly about the pressure to adopt Islam that was applied to them when they lived there. Many people said it was *tolah*, a serious violation of the social and natural order, for a Batek to become a Muslim, comparing it to an animal changing its species. One man told us about a Batek man who converted to Islam and then contracted a disease in which "his heart died and his body rotted, but his eyes were still alive." Some Batek speculated that the deities might destroy the world if the Batek adopted Islam *en masse*.

Those who rejected Islam did so for numerous reasons. One was that they already had a religion, as they realized once they began to compare their worldview and rituals to those of the Malay missionaries. For example, some Batek explicitly compared the Malay practice of praying to their own singing to the deities, the Malay prayer hall to their own covered dancing platform, and the Malay prohibition against eating pork to their own prohibition against eating the sambhur deer, which, according to Batek myth, gave fire to humankind. Some said that Allah was merely the deity of the Malays, equivalent to the Batek creator deity Tohan. The missionaries were asking the Batek to substitute an alien view of reality for one that had evolved over many generations, one that gave meaning to their experiences, from thunderstorms to illness and death. As one man said, "We can't just forget our superhuman beings."

People also frequently mentioned the practical disadvantages of becoming Muslims. Their foremost concern was that most of the animals they ate, including monkeys, were forbidden by Islamic dietary laws. To give up those sources of meat would have been a serious dietary deprivation, and it would also have contradicted their belief that the superhuman beings created those animals for them to eat. People also objected to the inconvenience of having to pray five times a day, and Batek men were less than enthusiastic about the requirement that they be circumcised. The fasting month (*Ramadan*; called *Bulan Puasa* in Malay) was another major disadvantage of Islam in Batek eyes. Those Batek living at Post Lebir who converted to Islam or who merely allowed themselves to be listed as Muslims on their identity cards discovered that they could be arrested if they were seen eating, drinking, or smoking in the daytime during the fasting month. To most Batek the benefits of converting to Islam were not as obvious as the disadvantages.

Poverty was the other reason people commonly gave for leaving the settlement. The Batek who moved to Kampung Macang in the late 1970s planted rice for a few years, but soon ran out of new land to clear. They planted most of their fallow rice fields with rubber trees and reduced their gardening efforts to growing corn, cassava, peppers, and squash in small plots along the riverbank and between their houses. In the 1980s the rubber trees were mature enough to tap. But people who tried to make a living from the proceeds of rubber tapping found that they could not make enough money to support their families. The price received for rubber was so low that their expenses outstripped their meager income. The Batek Teh and Batek Te' living at Post Lebir who continued tapping rubber complained that they had nothing but cassava and bananas to eat. In addition to the economic hardship, people considered rubber tapping monotonous and unpleasant work compared to foraging and collecting forest products to sell. One man complained that they had to tap the rubber trees early in the morning when the undergrowth was damp and full of leeches, and he added that it was hard work cutting new grooves in the bark of each rubber tree. Most of the Batek who still maintained houses at Kampung Macang used it mainly as a base camp. They spent most of their time in distant patches of forest collecting forest products to trade, which they preferred to rubber tapping or growing crops at Kampung Macang.

Some Batek refused to live at the settlement simply because they felt too exposed there, both to the heat of the sun, which they considered dangerous to their health, and to outsiders, who upset their peace of mind. As one man put it, "I can't live surrounded by outsiders. But I don't mind having outsiders on one side if I have the forest at my back." Strangers passing Kampung Macang on the road often came in and snooped around without a thought of asking permission. Some Malays made it a point to ask the Batek what they were eating, as if they had the right to stop them from eating foods that were forbidden by Islam. Women were often subjected to unwanted attention from male intruders, especially when their husbands were not around. Although we did not hear of any cases of sexual assault, sexual harassment was common, and many women expressed fears that outsiders would rape or beat them. In the forest Batek felt safe and free to be themselves, but at the settlement they had no defense against outsiders and the pressures they brought.

Because so few people were living at Kampung Macang, we decided to try to find the Batek who had moved back to the upper Aring River and were said to be planning to clear some fields and plant crops. A few days later, guided by two Batek men from Kampung Macang, we drove through miles of oil palm plantations to the headquarters of the Aring Lima Plantation, which bordered Taman Negara on the upper Aring River. After a day of searching for Batek, we finally found them. We drove up a disused logging road on the edge of the plantation that climbed into secondary forest. A bundle of rattan lying beside the road told us we were finally on the right track. After a further half-hour's drive over the rutted and eroded logging road and across a narrow, crumbling log bridge, we reached a small clearing where we were greeted by several Batek women and children. They led us along a path through the clearing, between tree stumps and fallen trees, then across a small brook to what looked like a typical forest camp—with the exception that the shelters, instead of being covered with thatch, had roofs of plastic sheeting.

It was an emotional meeting for us and our surprised but welcoming hosts. Most residents were people Kirk had lived with in the early 1970s, but a few were friends from the upper Lebir in 1975–76. Now they were living by foraging and trading forest products, but they were planning to extend their clearing and plant a full range of crops. Shoots of corn were already growing along the streambank. We decided it would be worthwhile to study social change in this group, as they seemed to be committed to a relatively sedentary life based in part on farming. We anticipated, however, that they would still be moving fairly often, and because we had our two young sons with us, we decided that Karen and the boys would return home while Kirk carried out five months of research, and Karen would rejoin him for the last few weeks without the children.

Within a couple of weeks, most of the Batek living in the area, 132 people, had formed a large camp in the forest a half mile up the stream. They had come together to perform the singing and dancing ceremonies that remind the superhuman beings to send down seasonal fruit blossoms. In the center of the camp was a large bark-covered dancing platform, which was without the usual lean-to roof, since the weather had been quite dry. Over the next few weeks the camp—which was too large to stay together very long—gradually broke up, as groups of people who wanted to look for rattan and *gaharu?* wood split off and moved into areas that had not yet been picked over. Finally, the remaining families moved to a new location deeper in the forest and thus nearer to the rattan supplies, but still within walking distance of the new clearing. For the next few months that group divided its time between foraging, collecting forest produce, and preparing its fields. It eventually moved closer to the clearing, and when we left in July, people were building substantial houses in their fields, and some had already moved into them. Families that did not want to plant crops moved here and there, sometimes forming one or more camps in the forest nearby, sometimes venturing into the upper reaches of the Aring or Relai rivers in search of *gaharu?* wood, and occasionally camping with the farming group.

Kirk made his base with the farming group, which, when the road was not too muddy, could be reached by a four-wheel-drive car. He also camped with one of the more nomadic groups for a short time and spent ten days at Kampung Macang, where he studied how the families using that settlement as a base camp carried on their lives. Thus, he was able to compare the male–female relations in several groups that varied in their degrees of sedentarization and exposure to the outside world.

Gender Concepts, Roles, and Relations in 1990

Gender Concepts

The conceptions and evaluations of males and females among the upper Aring Batek in 1990 were essentially the same as those of the Lebir Batek in 1975–76. The tendency to think of most superhuman beings as male–female pairs was still strong, even when applied to new entities. For example, the people who were planting crops had adopted the Malay belief in the earth spirit (Malay *hantu tanah*) and the rituals addressed to it. When asked what sex the earth spirit was, our informant replied, "We always think of spirits as married couples."

Division of Labor

Trade had become an even more important part of the Batek economy in 1990 than it had been in 1975–76. Both farming and nonfarming groups were obtaining most of their food and supplies by trading forest produce, mostly rattan and *gaharu* wood, to Malay traders who came in by four-wheel-drive pickup trucks every few days. Batek received rice, flour, sugar, and a variety of delicacies, including bread, crackers, cookies, oranges, noodles, chocolate milk, and Popsicles. Presumably, when the farming group's crops were ready for harvest, the reliance on traded food would diminish. People were still getting most of their protein through hunting and fishing, but wild vegetable foods had become mere supplements to the diet. Trade had also brought people unprecedented amounts of material goods, such as plastic sheets for roofing, cotton blankets, mosquito nets, fishing nets, mats, flashlights, radios, cassette recorders, and plastic toys. Whereas people had once had only a few articles of clothing, now most families had one or more suitcases full of bedding and clothing: shirts and trousers and thong sandals or plastic shoes for men; sarongs and blouses for women; shirts and shorts for children. Some men even had cans of insect repellent, which they sprayed on their shoes to prevent leech bites.

The work routines of the women in the farming group varied little from day to day. One woman in her mid-twenties, married with two young daughters, described her typical day. In the morning she made tea with condensed milk and sugar, which formed the family's morning meal. Later she washed clothes and bedding and hung them on rattan lines to dry. Around midday she cooked rice, and, if her husband came back to eat, they had a family meal together. During the heat of the day, she bathed herself and her children and then rested while the children napped or played. In the afternoon she worked at various tasks, such as planting crops, digging tubers, or fishing. About 4 PM she gathered some firewood and then cooked the evening meal. If there were no rain, she might do a little more work in the fields or the forest after eating. After putting the children down to sleep, she visited with her husband and friends.

Women's work routine in 1990 differed in several respects from that of 1975–76. One difference was that most women's activities took place in or near the camp. Women made few of the expeditions that had been so common before, in which large groups of women and children would go into the forest looking for food. With the increase of rice and flour in the diet, people sought wild tubers only as supplements or for special reasons. For example, one day a few women—together with one man and some children of both sexes—dug tubers because their children had diarrhea, which, they said, was aggravated by rice. Some women said they disliked digging tubers because it was hard work and because it took them into areas where they might encounter tigers. Apparently tubers were also somewhat harder to find than they had been in earlier years because some of the most prolific areas, in the low hills near the Aring River, had been incorporated into the oil palm plantation. Also, judging by the large number of holes in the ground, people had already picked over the area where they were then living. Women also spent far less time fishing with hook and line, an activity that had once been a favorite pastime. The reason seems to be that the men were producing a steady supply of fish by setting gill nets out in the stream overnight.

Women worked together with men in several phases of the farming process. They helped with cutting the undergrowth and planting crops, and they intended to do weeding and harvesting after we left. Men alone did the heavier and more dangerous work of felling trees and burning them after they had dried. Women generally worked less in the fields than men. People said this was because it was difficult to prevent children from following their mothers to the fields, and they worried that children would get sick from too much sun. They said that the first time they tried farming on a significant scale, in the late 1960s, eight people died from the heat, seven of them children. In order to avoid putting children at risk, women limited the amount of time they spent in the fields.

Women in the farming group took little part in collecting trade goods in 1990. Occasionally a woman helped her husband by carrying in a small load of rattan, but women seldom went after it in their own right, as several had done in 1975–76. Sometimes wives and children accompanied men making extended rattan-collecting sojourns in the upper Aring or Relai rivers, but the women did not generally collect rattan themselves. They said the work was too hard. Indeed, collecting rattan was more strenuous than it had been in 1975–76 because there were no navigable streams flowing to the collection point at the clearing. Instead of rafting the rattan downstream, people had to carry heavy loads long distances over the hilly terrain.

Women generally left the search for *gaharu?* wood, which entailed long treks through the forest, to the men as well. Occasionally, after a man had cut down a *gaharu?* tree, a few women would join the work party that went back to chop the veins of resin-impregnated wood out of the trunk. On one such occasion, the work party included five men of varying ages, a woman about sixty-five years old, and a young mother with a nursing baby. Like the other workers in such a group, the women owned whatever *gaharu?* wood they removed; the original finders did not claim rights over any more of the wood than they chopped out themselves.

Other chores took up more of women's time than they had before. Most women with families spent an hour or so every day washing clothes. Although husbands sometimes helped, usually groups of women scrubbed the clothes with purchased soap and brushes or pounded them on rocks or tree trunks that had fallen into the stream. The women carried on casual conversations, and their children played in the water nearby. Cooking and collecting firewood seemed to have become women's responsibilities, although men still did these tasks from time to time.

On the other hand, women seemed to spend less time than before on crafts and house building. Traded sleeping mats and containers of various kinds reduced the need for making pandanus mats and baskets. Purchased clothing and trinkets also replaced, to some extent, the rattan waistbands, leaf armbands, and other adornments that women used to make in their spare time. Women still built the family's lean-to shelters, but using sheets of plastic instead of thatch for the roofing greatly reduced the amount of time it took. Overall, women seemed to have more leisure time than before. Although they looked after their younger children continuously, they spent more time resting and visiting back and forth than they did when they lived in the forest.

Men's activities were somewhat more varied than women's. According to two men, one about twenty-four and the other about fifty, men always began the day preparing the equipment needed for the job to be done. If they were going blowpipe hunting, they would make new darts and might also disassemble, dry, straighten, and reassemble their blowpipes. If they intended to collect rattan or *gaharu?* wood or work on their fields, they began by sharpening their bush-knives and axes with whetstones or naturally abrasive river rocks. When going out for the entire day, they would first eat some substantial food; otherwise tea and scraps of leftovers would suffice. After eating, they went to the forest or the clearing or wherever their work took them that day, returning to camp any time between noon and 7 PM, when darkness fell. They ate a full meal with their families and, in the evening, socialized with other camp members.

The men in the farming group alternated between working on their fields and collecting forest produce for trade, for they needed the food they could obtain through trade to tide them over until their crops were ready. Preparing the fields for planting—chopping down trees, letting them dry, and burning them—took three to four months. Every few days during that period the men would stop work on their fields to spend a day or two making forays into the forest to collect rattan, *gaharu?* wood, or honey. Sometimes they made these all-day trips alone; other times they worked in groups of two or three. Occasionally a small party of men or a few families would catch a ride with a trader to an area that had not yet been exploited and work there for a week or more.

In 1990, hunting of all kinds had become almost exclusively a male occupation. Among both the farming and nonfarming groups of the upper Aring, one or more men from each camp went blowpipe hunting every day, and game was by far the greatest source of animal protein. Men living at Kampung Macang used motorbikes to reach places where there was still some game and to collect the materials needed to make blowpipes and darts. Only a few instances of bamboo rat hunting took place, and the hunters in all cases were men. People explained that there were few bamboo rats to be found in the area because bamboo was relatively scarce. They said bamboo rats were much more common along the Lebir River and some of its tributaries, where we had done our earlier research. Other kinds of hunting women had participated in before, such as cutting down trees to get nesting bats, were not being done in 1990.

Even fishing had become a predominantly male pursuit in 1990. Gill netting and spearfishing had increased greatly in importance, no doubt because people had more money to buy the nets and the rubber strips, iron rods, and nylon cord needed to make spearguns. Most families in the farming group owned gill nets, which were about three feet wide and ten to twenty feet long.

Usually the husband staked out the net in a nearby stream in the late afternoon, and the next morning he, sometimes together with his wife, pulled in the net and collected the catch. While his wife cooked the fish, the husband untangled the net and hung it up to dry. During the day, small groups of men sometimes made expeditions to more distant parts of the stream or to other rivers or streams where they would dive into pools and spear fish with their spearguns. A new method of fishing, which depended on a ready supply of flashlight batteries, was for the fisherman to shine his flashlight into a pool at night to attract fish and then whack them with bush-knives. Another popular nighttime pursuit was catching frogs, both to eat and to sell to a Chinese trader.

Collecting honey both for consumption and trade was still important in 1990. The procedure they used was the same as in 1975–76, but the composition of the work parties was different: in 1990 very few women participated.

Men predominated in trade in 1990. Unlike the short-term contracts men and women entered into with various traders in 1975–76, men now held ongoing accounts with particular traders, and many had continuing debts. It appeared that as trade became more institutionalized, it became a relationship between males, probably because Malay and Chinese traders preferred to deal with men.

Men's and Women's Contributions to the Food Supply

The pattern of work in 1990 resulted in men supplying almost all the food for the upper Aring farming group, either by direct food-getting activities or by collecting forest produce and trading it for food. Because of the complicated nature of the economy in 1990, we were unable to obtain complete data on the amounts of food provided by men and women. However, we did manage to record the kinds of work done by all camp members during a sample of twenty-eight days between April 18, when people were still cutting trees for their fields, and June 22, when they were burning the trees and brush in the clearing. Comparing the number of instances of food-getting and non-food-getting work done by men and women over that period gives a rough measure of the contributions of males and females to the total food supply.

In the following tables we consider food-getting activities to include hunting and gathering of wild resources, collecting forest products for trade, and making gardens. We classify as non-food-getting activities such activities as cooking, getting firewood, washing clothes, looking after children, caring for the sick, traveling, and making shelters and houses. We counted such responses as "sat in camp," "rested only," and "slept all day" as one instance of a non-food-getting activity on the assumption that those people probably engaged in at least one non-food-getting activity during the day.

Table 6.1 shows that over three-quarters of men's work activities contributed to the food supply, in contrast with just over one-quarter of women's work activities. The discrepancy in the actual amounts of food supplied by these activities is actually far greater, because most instances of women's food-getting

Table 6.1   Ratio of Food-Getting to Non-Food-Getting Work by Sex

	No. of Instances of Food-Getting Work	No. of Instances of Non-Food-Getting Work	Percent of Food-Getting Work	Percent of Non-Food-Getting-Work
Men	410	111	79	21
Women	94	247	28	72

activities produced only a small amount of food, such as a few fish or a handful of tubers, while many instances of men's food-getting activities, especially collecting rattan and *gaharu?* wood to trade, produced large amounts of food.

Table 6.2 shows that men performed food-producing activities at a rate of just over one per day, while women did food-producing jobs fewer than once every three days. The data in tables 6.1 and 6.2 lend support to our general impression that men's work provided almost all the food consumed by the farming group in the first half of 1990.

Table 6.2   Number of Instances of Food-Getting Work per Person per Day by Sex

	No. of Instances of Food-Getting Work	No. of Person-Days of Work Recorded	No. of Instances of Food-Getting Work per Person per Day
Men	410	363	1.13
Women	94	311	0.30

While men were supplying most of the food during the period of study, they shared it freely with the women and children. As before, husbands and wives pooled all the food they obtained. When men had cash from the sale of forest products, they shared it too with their wives, who sometimes bought food items directly from the traders. The food-sharing network between families also remained in full effect and still applied to traded as well as foraged foods. Game and fish brought into camp were still doled out to as many families as they could feed. Any family that ran short of rice could obtain some from those families that still had a supply. A striking example of this occurred when a family arrived from Pahang with two large bags of rice they had obtained by trading *gaharu?* wood. Within a week the rice was gone, eaten by other camp members who did not have any of their own at the time. The husband explained this with a smile. "It is just the Batek way," he said. Men never expressed any resentment that women were supplying so little of the group's food, nor did women show any signs of feeling beholden to men.

Batek Views of Men's and Women's Work

In 1990 five Aring men told us that it was prohibited for women to hunt with blowpipes, except a little bit in play, and for men to make pandanus mats and baskets, although they could cut the pandanus leaves for their wives. Violating these prohibitions was considered *pəmali?* (Malay *pemali*, "taboo, forbidden act"), an act that would anger the original bear, who would send an ordinary bear to attack the offender.

The idea that men and women must not do the jobs usually associated with the other sex was a departure from previous views of Batek in the Aring area. In 1973, Penghulu Sele', a prominent Aring man, told Kirk that women *could* hunt with blowpipes if they studied how to do it, but that they usually did not, because their breath was too weak. It is not clear why this change in the Aring people's conceptualization of the gender division of labor arose, but it was probably due to the influence of Batek Teh (Mendriq), with whom Aring Batek had interacted at Post Lebir since the early 1970s. The Batek Teh had an elaborate system of *pəmali?* prohibitions, while the upper Lebir Batek did not use the term at all.

In 2004 Kirk visited some of the Lebir Batek we had known in 1975–76, including Chinloy, who had been a keen blowpipe hunter before she had children. Chinloy confirmed that she used to hunt a lot. She did not mention any prohibition against women hunting with blowpipes, and she talked as if they could still do it if they wanted to. In 2004 Kirk also discussed blowpipe hunting with some Batek living on the Tembeling River in Pahang, a few miles above the National Park headquarters at Kuala Tahan. At that camp some residents were making money by, among other things, making and selling miniature blowpipes, together with darts and quivers, to tourists. Husbands and wives were working together at making all these items. One man explicitly said that there was no prohibition on women blowpipe hunting, but that they were simply not very good at it. "They can only get birds," he said.

It appears, then, that the prohibitions on men's and women's work described by Batek of the upper Aring in 1990 represented a localized variation in thinking about gender roles rather than a widespread change in Batek culture.

Gender Relations

Even though the women of the farming group and, to a lesser extent, those of the nomadic group living in the upper Aring River valley were relying upon men for their food in 1990, they retained the autonomy and demeanor we had seen among the upper Lebir Batek in 1975–76. Women were still self-assured and confident as they went about their activities, whatever their activities might be. Women living at Kampung Macang and Post Lebir seemed perfectly comfortable at the weekly market in the Malay village of Kampung Lalok. Often whole families, all dressed in their best clothes, went together, and everyone enjoyed shopping and sampling the delicacies in the food stalls. The conjugal family continued to be the most significant autonomous social unit, and husbands and wives shared equally in decision making. Although the increased importance of trade meant that most of the family's income came from the husband's efforts, spouses decided together how to spend the money. It was not uncommon to see men receive money from traders and immediately hand it to their wives; the partnership of spouses was very much in evidence. Residence patterns also revealed that women were continuing to assert themselves: several couples were living where the wife wanted to be, even when the husband would have preferred to live somewhere else. This was strikingly illustrated in the cases of several Batek Teh men from Post Lebir who had married Batek women. The men were used to a more settled life and lacked some of the foraging skills of the Batek, but they stayed with the most nomadic group of Aring people because their wives wanted to be in the forest and near their parents. The incident in which a woman left her husband behind—and took the plastic roofing from the family shelter with her—when she wanted to visit her son showed clearly that women were not playing a subservient role to their husbands.

Decisions about marriage and divorce remained individual matters in 1990, and women's wishes carried as much weight as men's. We heard of a couple of cases in which parents arranged marriages or persuaded their children to marry, but people said that if there had not been mutual attraction between the individuals, the marriages would not have taken place, regardless of the parents' wishes. Girls seemed very much in control of their marriage choices. Once a couple of young men living at Kampung Macang complained that there was a shortage of marriageable girls among nearby groups. They said that a few years earlier they had gone to Kuala Tahan in Pahang looking for wives, but the girls there refused them, saying that they had become too much like Malays.

Batek women who divorced did not rush into new marriages. Two young divorced women, one childless and the other with one son, were living with the upper Aring group. Both of them had had offers of marriage, but had turned them down. They lived on food they procured themselves and food they received from others through the sharing network. One of the women also collected and traded small amounts of rattan.

Another indication that women retained their autonomy in matters of love and sexuality was the fact that a number of young Batek women had had affairs with Chinese loggers during the previous decade, sometimes in defiance of their husbands or parents. One father constantly fretted over his two teenaged daughters who kept running off to a logging camp where one of them had a lover. At one point he fetched her from the logging camp and moved his whole family deep into the National Park, in hopes that it would discourage her from returning to her lover. The father was afraid that the Chinese man would abandon her, possibly pregnant, once the logging was finished. At least two Batek women had babies by their Chinese lovers, and another woman had married a Chinese man, settled with him in a house near his logging camp and had several children by him. People said that this man treated his wife well and was also kind and helpful to her family and other

Batek. Officials from the JHEOA strongly disapproved of the relationships between Batek women and Chinese men, but neither they nor other Batek could prevent the women from following their own desires.

Leadership in the upper Aring was in flux in 1990. One long-time official headman, Penghulu Sele', was about seventy years old and in failing health. The other headman who had previously been associated with the upper Aring, Penghulu Kepayang, had moved to Pahang to avoid pressures from outsiders. An officer from the JHEOA wanted to replace them, and he asked the Batek to advise him on who the next headman should be. Everyone assumed he would appoint a son of one of the previous headmen, following Malay custom. Although Batek referred to most of the middle-aged sons of the retiring headmen as pəŋhulu⁷, none of these men seemed to want the job. We were told that being the official headman entailed a lot of work, stress, and criticism from Batek and government officials alike, and the pay was too low to make it worthwhile. After Tanyogn died, the JHEOA appointed one of her sons, Galas, to succeed her as pəŋhulu⁷. In 2004 Galas told Kirk that he had given the job up after only a few years because of the aggravation. Meanwhile, Hek, the most worldly-wise son of Penghulu Sele, had replaced his father and was still a pəŋhulu⁷ on the upper Aring in 2004.

No natural leaders, either male or female, with influence beyond their extended families were in evidence in 1990, although such leaders emerged temporarily in connection with specific projects. For example, when a windstorm toppled a tree branch on a newly built ceremonial shelter, one man dreamt that the superhuman beings had caused the storm to express their anger at the group for not having performed a singing ceremony for several years. Because the superhumans told him in the dream to rebuild the shelter with new materials, he took the lead in the rebuilding effort. A woman could just as well have initiated such an activity if she had had the dream. Experts in certain processes, such as burning bees' nests, often took the initiative in those activities, but others participated or not according to their own inclinations.

Although there were no influential female leaders in the upper Aring region in 1990, there were possible signs of one emerging on the upper Lebir in 2004. Sikan—a young, recently divorced mother in 1975–76—had become a prominent figure, wife of the JHEOA-appointed headman of the group and mother of six children. She joked that her husband is only the "downstream headman" (Malay penghulu hilir), while she is the "upstream headman" (Malay penghulu ulu), as her aunt Tanyogn had been. She said, with a laugh, that she tells people when to go to work and not to be too slow. Although Kirk did not have long to observe her behavior, he noticed that when a car full of unknown Malays appeared on the road above the settlement one day, it was Sikan who went up to find out who they were and why they had come, just the sort of thing Tanyogn would have done. The avenue for an assertive woman to play a leadership role still seemed open in 2004.

Both men and women still participated fully in religious rituals in 1990. The most renowned shaman, Penghulu Sele', was no longer active due to his advanced age and poor health, but four younger men, including two brothers, had achieved prominence for leading singing sessions in which they tranced and communicated with the superhuman beings controlling seasonal fruit and disease. During the singing sessions in March, one of the brothers led the singing, but the leading singers in the sessions in May were another man and his wife, one of Penghulu Sele''s daughters. Women also contributed to singing sessions by making decorations, singing, drumming, and dancing. During severe thunderstorms women still performed the blood sacrifice more often than men. As before, both men and women used their individual knowledge and skills in efforts to cure the sick. In one typical example, we saw two women massaging the ailing Penghulu Sele' with cooling water, which contained herbal medicines and blood drawn from two other women's legs. A man had also said a spell over the water.

Both women and men continued to play important roles in funeral ceremonies as well. When a baby girl died, women dressed the body, put leaf bracelets on her wrists, lit incense near her, and surrounded her with fragrant leaves. Her mother soaked a cloth with milk and placed it beside the baby's mouth so she would not go hungry in the afterworld. Men carried the corpse to the burial tree, built a platform and shelter among the branches, put the body in the shelter, and said spells around the tree to keep tigers away.

The only difference in gender relations we saw in 1990 were among a few Batek families who maintained houses at Kampung Macang and were committed to a sedentary way of life. Although wives still had a say in family decisions, such as what goods to buy at the market in Kampung Lalok, they acted somewhat subservient to their husbands in their homes. The more elaborate houses at Kampung Macang had a living room in which guests were entertained, a separate sleeping room, and a kitchen at the back. In those houses wives and their female friends often gathered in the kitchen while husbands entertained male friends in the living area. Husbands sometimes ordered their wives to make tea for the assembled men, and at meals husbands, male guests, and children ate first, in the living room. The women ate later in the kitchen. The behavior of the young wives obviously mimicked Malay rituals of hospitality and the gender roles associated with them, and, indeed, the Batek families who behaved in this way were among those that had at least nominally converted to Islam. In addition, there seemed to be a tendency at Kampung Macang for the men to socialize together in the evening on the porch of one house while the women gathered on the porch of another house, in sharp contrast with the random visiting back and forth between shelters that was common in forest camps.

The deferential behavior of the Kampung Macang women may have been the beginning of a change toward Malay-style gender relations among the Batek who were most committed to sedentary living in proximity to Malays. However, the preponderance of evidence is that it was situational, associated only with Kampung Macang and the presence of guests. Among the people living in the upper Aring in 1990—both nomadic and semi-settled families—husbands, wives, and children normally ate together, as they stated in describing their daily routines. One of the couples that ate separately at Kampung Macang in 1990 also spent time in a forest camp on the upper Aring, and there the wife behaved the same as the other women in camp. Also, one couple that ate separately at Kampung Macang in 1990 told Kirk in 2004 that they only did so when they had guests. They said that their whole family normally eats together. Therefore, it is doubtful that the Malay-style eating and socializing practices we observed at Kampung Macang in 1990 indicated a profound change in Batek gender relations.

Conclusion

The comparison between the Batek in 1975–76 and 1990 does not provide a definitive answer to the question of what conditions were crucial to their gender egalitarian concepts and behavior. This is because, despite major destruction of the environment, the Batek economy and settlement pattern changed very little. The proportion of time spent collecting forest products for trade increased, while the proportion devoted to gathering wild tubers, fruits, and honey declined, but hunting wild game and fishing continued to be their main sources of animal protein. Their pattern of nomadic movements became modified to the extent that they established and used base camps in accessible places, including Kampung Macang, but they spent most of their time actually living in traditional camps in the forest. These changes didn't alter the basic set of ethical principles that guided social life, including the important obligation to share food with those in need whether the food was obtained by foraging or through trade.

At the same time, gender concepts and relations between the sexes continued much as before. Although women were not bringing in substantial amounts of food, they had not become dependent on or subordinate to particular men. The sharing network continued to ensure that all people received food. Women retained their foraging skills and were ready to put them to use again if necessary.

The 1990 study does show that at least in the short run women did not need to bring in much food in order to remain on an equal footing with men. This is to be expected, since integrated systems of beliefs, values, and practices could not change every time women or men brought in more food than the other. It is possible, however, that over the long run, an economy based on men as the sole food-providers could generate social changes that would cause gender inequalities. Scholars have shown that hunter-gatherers who settle down and adopt a full-time farming or herding economy eventually give up the practice of generalized reciprocity because it prevents individuals from reaping the rewards of the labor they put into growing their crops and tending their herds (see, e.g., Lee 2003), and this in turn undermines gender equality. Whether this will happen to the Batek who have settled down remains to be seen.

Chapter 7

Understanding
Batek Egalitarianism

The preceding chapters have shown that the Batek were remarkably egalitarian in the social and cultural treatment of the sexes. This was so as recently as 2004, despite economic changes due to government-sponsored development projects. There was no area of Batek culture or social life in which men controlled women or subjected them to asymmetrical systems of evaluation. Batek concepts of males and females recognized the physical differences between the sexes without imposing evaluative or symbolic significance on them. In daily social life, men and women had equal control over themselves and an equal voice in the affairs of the camp-group. Men and women were equal partners in marriage: the choice of spouse was left to the individuals involved, husbands and wives cooperated economically but were not exclusively dependent upon each other, decision making was a shared responsibility, and divorce could be initiated by either spouse. The political system did not favor men over women except in the headmanship system imposed by outsiders. In the economic sphere, males and females had equal access to the sharing network, which included the foods brought in by both men and women. Neither sex was prohibited from participating in any activity, except for the prohibition among a few Aring River people in 1990 against women doing blowpipe hunting and men weaving pandanus. The contributions by each sex to the food supply differed between 1975–76 and 1990, but in both periods both sexes contributed to the material well-being of the group, and neither sex group thought it was being exploited by the other. Socialization to gender roles occurred without coercion or preferential treatment of either sex.

In this chapter we attempt to bring out the features of Batek culture and circumstances that fostered their gender egalitarianism. We think of these fea-

147

tures as leveling mechanisms that prevented the rise of male dominance, for we accept the premise that in societies in which there is competition for control, males are at an advantage because of their greater physical strength and their freedom from childbearing and nursing. We do not mean to imply that the conditions enabling the Batek to be gender egalitarian are the only conditions that could do so. Gardner (1991) argues that a number of different combinations of cultural and natural circumstances can lead to individual autonomy—which we see as a key feature of gender equality—in hunting and gathering societies.

The Bases of Batek Gender Egalitarianism

In chapter 1 we defined a gender egalitarian society as one in which neither sex has overall control over the other or greater cultural value than the other. Control can be based in the economic system (e.g., the ability to withhold a resource necessary for survival), the system of authority (authority may be vested in such areas as political offices, kinship relationships, and religious ideologies), and in direct force. With these possible bases of control in mind, let us turn to a consideration of how the Batek prevented men from gaining control over women.

Economic Security

We believe that the key economic reason Batek men did not dominate Batek women is that no woman was dependent on a specific man—such as a father, husband, brother, or son—for survival (cf. Leacock 1978). Women were economically secure, surviving through their own foraging efforts and through direct participation in the camp-wide food-sharing network. In 1975–76 most of the staple foods in the Batek diet, including rice and flour obtained in trade, could be procured by both men and women using skills, knowledge, and tools that were readily available to all. No rights of exclusive ownership over resources restricted women's access to any foods or other necessities, and the flexible division of labor permitted them to harvest any resources they came upon. Women also had full rights in the food-sharing network, and they retained these rights even when men obtained most of the food, as was the case in 1990. By contributing to and drawing from the food-sharing network, women could usually be certain of getting some food—including the foods ordinarily obtained by men, such as honey and arboreal game—even when they were ill or when their own food-getting efforts failed. Thus, the economic security of Batek women was based on their being able to depend upon the group as a whole in addition to their own efforts. Although Batek women—and men—could survive by their own efforts alone for limited periods of time, they were not economically *independent* like Hadza and Paliyan women (Woodburn 1978, 1979; Gardner 1966), who gathered most of their own food and shared little even with their husbands.

Because Batek women were economically secure, women could withdraw from unsatisfactory marriages without suffering economic hardship. Both in 1975–76 and in 1990 we saw divorced women with children living happily for extended periods without remarrying, even when they had persistent suitors.

Some scholars have claimed that external trade and other economic processes that involve a delay between when the work is done and when the reward is received undermine the autonomy and equality of women in hunting and gathering societies. Leacock argues, following Engels (1972), that when hunter-gatherers begin to produce commodities for trade, in addition to goods for consumption, families become isolated from each other, and women come to depend on their husbands and sons for survival, rather than on the group as a whole (1954, 1972, 1981). Woodburn contends that "delayed-return" economic processes, which include collecting goods for trade, enmesh women in a system of binding commitments that place them under the authority of men (1978:10).

Why, then, hasn't trade led to male dominance among the Batek? The answer is certainly not that trade is a recent innovation; there is good reason to suppose that the ancestors of the Batek have traded forest produce to horticulturalists for cultivated foods and other goods for the last 3000–4000 years (Dunn 1975), and commercial trade goes back at least to the 1930s (Endicott and Bellwood 1991). Rather, the reason seems to be that the Batek practiced trade in ways that were compatible with the general conditions ensuring women's economic security. Among the Batek, both men and women could and did collect and trade forest produce in 1975–76, although men generally spent more time at it than women. Trade in forest produce was just one of several sources of food for the Batek, and it was compatible with the other forms of food getting they practiced and with their general nomadic, egalitarian way of life. Most importantly, they shared all food obtained by trade just as they shared all food obtained directly from the forest. Thus, women benefited from external trade in the same way as men (K.M. Endicott 2005).

Dispersed Authority

Another characteristic of Batek society that seems to have inhibited the development of male dominance was the broad dispersal of authority (see, e.g., Leacock 1978; Begler 1978; Woodburn 1979). What little authority existed was spread among all adult men and women and consisted mainly of the authority to govern oneself and one's young children. Leadership was based on persuasion; there was no possibility of coercion. In these circumstances it was the qualities of the individual—including eloquence, intelligence, and tact—that determined what, if any, influence a person had over others. Group decisions were usually based on open discussion, and individuals had the right to ignore the consensus and follow their own desires. Batek ethics promoted extreme respect for personal freedom, constrained only by a

general obligation to help others—as exemplified by the food-sharing requirement. Men, women, and children could all express their ideas and wishes
and act on them as they saw fit.

Nonviolence

Another feature of Batek culture that seems to have inhibited male dominance was their suppression of all physical aggression. Like the horticultural
Semai Orang Asli, who also appear to be gender egalitarian (Dentan 1968;
Gilmore 1990), the Batek abhorred violence and claimed that they would
abandon anyone who was habitually aggressive. They regarded violent
behavior as a sign of madness. They were usually successful at defusing
potential violence through their methods of conflict resolution, and they took
great pains to teach their children to avoid all aggressive behavior. Because no
aggression was tolerated, Batek women were safe from coercion based on
physical force or the threat of physical force.

Is Batek Culture a Result of Encapsulation?

The conditions we have identified as making gender egalitarianism possible among the Batek are largely cultural. Some scholars would go further to
the question of why the Batek culture took the form it did in the first place.
Why were Batek nomadic forager-traders and why were they organized in a
fashion that permitted egalitarian relations between the sexes?

A number of scholars have argued that basic cultural features of some
contemporary foraging peoples—including egalitarian gender relations
where they exist—result from the societies being "encapsulated," surrounded
and politically dominated by more numerous and powerful people. The
Batek and other Semang could be categorized as encapsulated because they
are surrounded by Malays. The encapsulation theory implies that egalitarian
relations in foraging societies are an "abnormal" social condition and did not
exist before the societies came under the influence of more powerful neighbors. Although the various proponents of the theory agree that the influence
of the surrounding society shapes the culture of the foraging group, they do
not agree on exactly how this takes place.

In an early formulation of this idea, Gardner (1966) describes the foraging Paliyan of India as being extremely individualistic, noncompetitive, nonviolent, noncooperative (to the point of not even sharing food with spouses),
independent, and egalitarian even between the sexes. They show little emo-
tion for others, and they hold idiosyncratic rather than shared views about
the world. He postulates that these characteristics are due to the Paliyan having been subjected to centuries of abuse, threats, exploitation, and contempt
from surrounding peoples. He argues that the relative helplessness of the
Paliyan "made withdrawal or subservience more realistic than attempts at

retaliation" (1966: 400) and that their repression of aggressive impulses led to their particular cultural characteristics. He claims that a whole category of similarly surrounded and subordinate foragers ("refugee gathering peoples") share similar characteristics.

Testart (1981) defines a category of hunter-gatherers as *chasseurs-cueilleurs enclaves*, "enclaved hunter-gatherers," who are surrounded by more numerous and powerful farmers or herders with whom they trade. He says that the political domination of the outsiders promotes nomadism among the foragers: they keep moving to escape their tormentors. The foragers are egalitarian, he asserts, because continuous exploitation in trade equally impoverishes all of them. Woodburn also examines the relations between foragers and surrounding peoples. He asks: "Have their sharing and egalitarian leveling mechanisms developed in opposition to domination by outsiders? Have we here a sort of moral oppositional solidarity of low-status groups, akin to the egalitarian solidarity manifest in some working-class or millenarian movements?" (Woodburn 1988:62). Some writers (e.g., Schrire 1984; Wilmsen 1989) have argued that the cultures of most if not all contemporary foraging peoples are predominantly shaped by their position in the larger surrounding society. The cultural characteristics of a people such as the Ju/'hoansi of southern Africa, they contend, are determined by their position as an impoverished rural proletariat in the class-stratified societies of Botswana and Namibia.

Could it be that the Batek were gender egalitarian because they were encapsulated by Malays? We think the answer is no. In fact, Malays could never have exercised real control over Semang as long as the latter were nomadic, economically self-sufficient, and had a vast empty forest to hide in (see K.M. Endicott 1983; Lye 1997). Even before Malay villages were removed from the Lebir watershed, local Malays were far from numerous enough or well-organized enough to have politically dominated the Batek. In recent years the Malaysian government, with all the resources of a modern nation-state, has been unable to exercise control over them. And the Batek never depended on trade with Malays for their survival (Endicott and Bellwood 1991), so trade with Malays was voluntary for both parties. If Batek had been coerced or abused by traders, they could have moved to remote areas or to areas near more congenial Malay villagers.

However, the Batek case does support Testart's claim that abuse or the potential for abuse by a more numerous and powerful people may reinforce the nomadism of some foraging groups. Frequent movement was probably the most effective defense the Semang had against the slave raiding that went on in some areas into this century (K.M. Endicott 1983). But the Batek economy also required nomadism, and there is no reason to suppose that they would have—or could have—settled down had there been no threat from Malays. Most Batek remained nomadic as recently as 1990, even though slave raiding ceased in the 1920s.

The Batek culture did not show the kinds of distortions and gaps that would suggest that they were merely a subdivision of the larger surrounding society, like some of the Indian foraging groups that appear to be occupational subcastes of forest produce collectors within Hindu society (e.g., Fox 1969). The Batek had a strong sense of unity and a complete and distinctive culture, including a separate language, religion, and way of life. They considered Malays to be the archetypical "outsiders" with whom they often contrasted themselves. There is no reason to doubt that the Batek could have existed as an independent society with much the same form of culture before the Malays came on the scene.

In our opinion the most plausible reason that the Batek were nomadic forager-traders, with a culture supporting egalitarian relations between the sexes—and the reason that most closely resembles the Batek's own views of why they live the way they do—is that they were filling an ecological and social niche that provided them with a relatively secure and satisfying way of life, one that had some advantages over swidden horticulture, the main alternative possibility in their environment (K.M. Endicott 1979b, 1984). For example, foraging was a more reliable way of getting food than farming in the deep forest, where birds, monkeys, wild pigs, elephants, and crop diseases could easily destroy the results of an entire season's labors. As Benjamin argues (1985, 1987), the Semang are probably the descendants of the Hoabinhians who, after the advent of agriculture in the Malay Peninsula, opted to pursue a way of life based on nomadic foraging combined with trade with their farming neighbors. Until the arrival of the Malays in the interior in the last few hundred years, those neighbors were mainly Senoi Orang Asli, the descendants of other Hoabinhians who opted to concentrate on horticulture. Both groups became skilled specialists who shared the fruits of their respective modes of adaptation by means of trade. Pursuing complementary ways of life reduced the possibility of intergroup friction that could have arisen had they been competing for the same resources.[1] No doubt there have been individual crossings back and forth across the Senoi–Semang boundary (Dentan 1968), especially when intermarriage has been involved, but the two ways of life have nevertheless remained distinct into the twenty-first century. As we have shown in this book, egalitarian relations between the sexes were an integral feature of the foraging-trading mode of adaptation the ancestors of the Batek chose.

Note

[1] Headland and Headland (1997) borrow the concept of "competitive exclusion" from ecology to explain why nomadic hunter-gatherers seldom become farmers. The general idea is that farmers and foragers can live peacefully side-by-side because they do not compete for the same resources, but if the foragers try to adopt farming, they begin to compete with the existing farmers for arable land, thus leading to conflict and suppression of the outnumbered and politically weak foragers (see also Headland 1986).

Appendix

Batek Kinship Terms

The following list gives the Batek reference terms and their genealogical specifications. The terms can also be used as terms of address instead of names. Asterisks indicate terms that distinguish gender.

*1. *pa?*—father (*?ɛy* is used occasionally)

*2. *na?*—mother

*3. *bah*—father's brother, mother's brother, father's sister's husband, mother's sister's husband, mother's husband (if not the father), all other parents' generation males

*4. *bə?*—father's sister, mother's sister, father's brother's wife, mother's brother's wife, father's wife (if not the mother), all other parents' generation females

*5. *ta?*—all grandparents' generation males

*6. *ya?*—all grandparents' generation females

*7. *kəsuy*—husband

*8. *kəneh*—wife

9. *to?*—elder brother, elder sister, mother's elder brother's child, mother's elder sister's child, father's elder brother's child, father's elder sister's child, all other members of ego's generation who are older than ego

10. *bɛr*—younger brother, younger sister, mother's younger brother's child, mother's younger sister's child, father's younger brother's child, father's younger sister's child, all other members of ego's generation who are younger than ego

11. *?awã?*—child, wife's child, husband's child

12. *?awã? sadara?*—brother's child, sister's child, all other members of children's generation who are not one's own children

13. *kaŋcɔ?*—all members of grandchildren's generation

153

14. *kənʔac*—husband's father, wife's father, husband's mother, wife's mother, all parents of former husbands and wives

15. *mənsaw*—child's husband, child's wife, all former husbands and wives of children

16. *habaŋ*—wife's brother, husband's brother, wife's sister, husband's sister, brother's wife, sister's husband

17. *yaŋ*—all members of great-grandparents' and great-grandchildren's generations

18. *yik*—all members of great-great-grandparents' generation

19. *dɔn*—all members of great-great-great-grandparents' generation (also means "ancestors")

20. *mɔyaŋ*—all members of great-great-great-great-grandparents' generation (also means "ancestors")

References Cited

Begler, E. B.
1978   "Sex, Status, and Authority in Egalitarian Society." *American Anthropologist* 80: 571–588.

Bellwood, Peter
1997   *Prehistory of the Indo-Malaysian Archipelago*. Revised edition. Honolulu: University of Hawai'i Press.

Benjamin, Geoffrey
1968   "Headmanship and Leadership in Temiar Society." *Federation Museums Journal* 13 (New Series): 1–43.
1985   "In the Long Term: Three Themes in Malayan Cultural Ecology." In *Cultural Values and Human Ecology in Southeast Asia* (eds. K. L. Hutterer, A. T. Rambo, and G. Lovelace). Ann Arbor: Center for South and Southeast Asian Studies, University of Michigan, pp. 219–278.
1987   "Ethnohistorical Perspectives on Kelantan's Prehistory." In *Kelantan Zaman Awal: Kajian Arkeologi dan Sejarah di Malaysia* (ed. Nik Hassan Shuhaimi bin Nik Abd Rahman). Kota Bharu, Malaysia: Perbadanan Muzium Negeri Kelantan, pp. 108–153.

Boehm, Christopher
1999   *Hierarchy in the Forest: The Evolution of Egalitarian Behavior.* Cambridge, MA: Harvard University Press.

Brown, Paula, and Georgeda Buchbinder
1976   "Introduction." In *Man and Woman in the New Guinea Highlands* (eds. Paula Brown and Georgeda Buchbinder). Washington, D.C.: American Anthropological Association, pp. 1–12.

Bulbeck, F. D.
1985   "Appendix 2: The 1979 Gua Cha Skeletal Material." In "The Re-excavation of the Rockshelter of Gua Cha, Ulu Kelantan, West Malaysia" by Adi Haji Taha. *Federation Museums Journal* 30 (New Series): 96–97.

Burbank, V. K.
1989   "Gender and the Anthropology Curriculum: Aboriginal Australia." In *Gender and Anthropology: Critical Reviews for Research and Teaching* (ed. Sandra Morgen). Washington, D.C.: American Anthropological Association, pp. 116–131.

155

Burkill, I. H.

1966   *A Dictionary of the Economic Products of the Malay Peninsula.* Two volumes. Kuala Lumpur: Ministry of Agriculture and Co-operatives. First published 1935.

Butler, Judith

1990   *Gender Trouble: Feminism and the Subversion of Identity.* London and New York: Routledge.

Carey, Iskandar

1976   *Orang Asli: The Aboriginal Tribes of Peninsular Malaysia.* Kuala Lumpur: Oxford University Press.

Chagnon, Napoleon

1968   *Yanomamö: The Fierce People.* New York: Holt, Rinehart and Winston.

Chodorow, Nancy

1974   "Family Structure and Feminine Personality." In *Woman, Culture, and Society* (eds. M. Z. Rosaldo and Louise Lamphere). Stanford: Stanford University Press, pp. 43–66.

Clifford, Hugh

1961   "Expedition to Trengganu and Kelantan, Report by Hugh Clifford." *Journal of the Malayan Branch of the Royal Asiatic Society* 34: 1–162.

Collins, Randall

1971   "A Conflict Theory of Sexual Stratification." *Social Problems* 19: 3–20.

Coursey, D. G.

1967   *Yams: An Account of the Nature, Origins, Cultivation and Utilisation of the Useful Members of the Dioscoreaceae.* London: Longmans, Green and Co.

Davis, Adelle

1954   *Let's Eat Right to Keep Fit.* London: Unwin.

Dentan, R. K.

1968   *The Semai: A Nonviolent People of Malaysia.* New York: Holt, Rinehart and Winston.

1978   "Notes on Childhood in a Nonviolent Context: The Semai Case (Malaysia)." In *Learning Non-Aggression: The Experience of Non-Literate Societies* (ed. Ashley Montagu). New York: Oxford University Press, pp. 94–143.

Dentan, R. K., K. Endicott, A. G. Gomes, and M. B. Hooker

1997   *Malaysia and the "Original People": A Case Study of the Impact of Development on Indigenous Peoples.* Boston: Allyn & Bacon.

Draper, Patricia

1975a   "!Kung Women: Contrasts in Sexual Egalitarianism in Foraging and Sedentary Contexts." In *Toward an Anthropology of Women* (ed. R. R. Reiter). New York: Monthly Review Press, pp. 77–109.

1975b   "Cultural Pressure on Sex Differences." *American Ethnologist* 2: 602–616.

1978   "The Learning Environment for Aggression and Anti-Social Behavior among the !Kung (Kalahari Desert, Botswana, Africa)." In *Learning Non-Aggression: The Experience of Non-Literate Societies* (ed. Ashley Montagu). New York: Oxford University Press, pp. 31–53.

Dunn, F. L.

1975   *Rain-Forest Collectors and Traders: A Study of Resource Utilization in Modern and Ancient Malaya.* Monographs of the Malaysian Branch of the Royal Asiatic Society, No. 5. Kuala Lumpur: Malaysian Branch of the Royal Asiatic Society.

Endicott, Karen L.

1979   "Batek Negrito Sex Roles." M. A. thesis, Department of Prehistory and Anthropology, Australian National University.

1992   "Fathering in an Egalitarian Society." In *Father-Child Relations: Cultural and Biosocial Contexts* (ed. B. S. Hewlett). New York: Aldine de Gruyter, pp. 281–295.

Endicott, Kirk M.

1972   "Negrito Blowpipe Construction on the Lebir River, Kelantan." *Federation Museums Journal* 14 (New Series):1–36.

1974   "Batek Negrito Economy and Social Organization." Ph.D. dissertation, Department of Anthropology, Harvard University.

1979a   *Batek Negrito Religion: The World-view and Rituals of a Hunting and Gathering People of Peninsular Malaysia.* Oxford: Clarendon Press.

1979b   "The Impact of Economic Modernization on the Orang Asli (Aborigines) of Northern Peninsular Malaysia." In *Issues in Malaysian Development* (eds. J. C. Jackson and Martin Rudner). Singapore: Heinemann Educational Books (Asia) Ltd., pp. 167–204.

1979c   "The Batek Negrito Thunder God: The Personification of a Natural Force." In *The Imagination of Reality: Essays in Southeast Asian Coherence Systems* (eds. A. L. Becker and A. A. Yengoyan). Norwood, NJ: Ablex Publishing Corporation, pp. 29–42.

1982   "The Effects of Logging on the Batek of Malaysia." *Cultural Survival Quarterly* 6: 19–20.

1983   "The Effects of Slave Raiding on the Aborigines of the Malay Peninsula." In *Slavery, Bondage, and Dependency in Southeast Asia* (eds. A. Reid and J. Brewster). Brisbane: University of Queensland Press, pp. 216–245.

1984   "The Economy of the Batek of Malaysia: Annual and Historical Perspectives." *Research in Economic Anthropology* 6: 29–52.

1988   "Property, Power and Conflict among the Batek of Malaysia. In *Hunters and Gatherers 2: Property, Power and Ideology* (eds. T. Ingold, D. Riches, and J. Woodburn). Oxford: Berg Publishers, pp. 110–127.

1997   "Batek History, Interethnic Relations, and Subgroup Dynamics." In *Indigenous Peoples and the State: Politics, Land, and Ethnicity in the Malayan Peninsula and Borneo* (ed. R. L. Winzeler). New Haven: Yale Southeast Asia Studies, pp. 30–50.

2005   "The Significance of Trade in an Immediate-Return Society: The Batek Case." In *Property and Equality, Volume 2: Encapsulation, Commercialisation, Discrimination* (eds. T. Widlock and W. G. Tadesse). New York and Oxford: Berghahn Books, pp. 79–89.

Endicott, Kirk, and Peter Bellwood

1991   "The Possibility of Independent Foraging in the Rain Forest of Peninsular Malaysia." *Human Ecology* 19: 151–185.

Engels, Frederick

1972   The Origin of the Family, Private Property and the State. New York: International Publishers.

Errington, Shelly

1990   "Recasting Sex, Gender, and Power: A Theoretical and Regional Overview." In *Power and Difference: Gender in Island Southeast Asia* (eds. J. M. Atkinson and Shelly Errington). Stanford: Stanford University Press, pp. 1–58.

Estioko-Griffin, Agnes, and P. B. Griffin

1981   "Woman the Hunter: The Agta." In *Woman the Gatherer* (ed. Frances Dahlberg). New Haven: Yale University Press, pp. 121–151.

Evans, I. H. N.

1937   *The Negritos of Malaya.* Cambridge: Cambridge University Press.

Fardon, Richard
1990   "Malinowski's Precedent: The Imagination of Equality." *Man* (N.S.) 25: 569–587.
Flanagan, J. G.
1989   "Hierarchy in Simple 'Egalitarian' Societies." *Annual Review of Anthropology 1989* 18: 245–266.
Fox, R. G.
1969   "'Professional Primitives': Hunters and Gatherers of Nuclear South Asia." *Man in India* 49: 139–160.
Freeman, Derek
1968   "Thunder, Blood, and the Nicknaming of God's Creatures." *Psychoanalytic Quarterly* 37: 353–359.
Fried, M. H.
1967   *The Evolution of Political Society: An Essay in Political Anthropology.* New York: Random House.
Friedl, Ernestine
1975   *Women and Men: An Anthropologist's View.* New York: Holt, Rinehart and Winston.
Gardner, P. M.
1966   "Symmetric Respect and Memorate Knowledge: The Structure and Ecology of Individualistic Culture." *Southwestern Journal of Anthropology* 22: 389–415.
1991   "Foragers' Pursuit of Individual Autonomy." *Current Anthropology* 32: 543–572.
Gilmore, D. D.
1990   *Manhood in the Making: Cultural Concepts of Masculinity.* New Haven: Yale University Press.
Gomes, A. G.
1982   *Ecological Adaptation and Population Change: Semang Foragers and Temuan Horticulturalists in West Malaysia.* Honolulu: East-West Environment and Policy Institute. Research Report No. 12.
Gregor, Thomas
1977   *Mehinaku: The Drama of Daily Life in a Brazilian Indian Village.* Chicago: University of Chicago Press.
Hayden, B., M. Deal, A. Cannon, and J. Casey
1986   "Ecological Determinants of Women's Status among Hunter/Gatherers." *Human Evolution* 1: 449–474.
Headland, Thomas
1986   "Why Foragers Do Not Become Farmers: A Historical Study of a Changing Ecosystem and Its Effect on a Negrito Hunter-Gatherer Group in the Philippines." Ph. D. dissertation, Department of Anthropology, University of Hawaii.
Headland, T. N., and J. D. Headland
1997   "Limitation of Human Rights, Land Exclusion, and Tribal Extinction: The Agta Negritos of the Philippines." *Human Organization* 56: 79–90.
Helliwell, Christine
1994   "'A Just Precedency': The Notion of Equality in Anthropological Discourse." *History and Anthropology* 7: 363–375.
1995   "Autonomy as Natural Equality: Inequality in 'Egalitarian' Societies." *Journal of the Royal Anthropological Institute* (N.S.) 1: 359–375.
Hertz, Robert
1960   *Death and the Right Hand* (trans. Rodney Needham and Claudia Needham). London: Cohen and West.
Ingold, Tim
1983   "The Significance of Storage in Hunting Societies." *Man* (N.S.) 18: 553–571.

Jimin B. Idris, Mohd. Tap Salleh, Jailani M. Dom, Abd. Halim Haji Jawi, and Md. Razim Shafie
1983 *Planning and Administration of Development Programmes for Tribal Peoples (The Malaysian Setting).* CIRDAP Country Report: Malaysia, Kuala Lumpur: Jabatan Hal Ehwal Orang Asli.

Kelly, R. C.
1993 *Constructing Inequality: The Fabrication of a Hierarchy of Virtue among the Etoro.* Ann Arbor: University of Michigan Press.

Kelly, R. L.
1995 *The Foraging Spectrum: Diversity in Hunter-Gatherer Lifeways.* Washington, D.C. and London: Smithsonian Institution Press.

Kent, Susan
1995 "Does Sedentarization Promote Gender Inequality? A Case Study from the Kalahari." *Journal of the Royal Anthropological Institute* (N.S.) 1: 513–536.

Kessler, C. S.
1977 "Conflict and Sovereignty in Kelantanese Malay Spirit Seances." In *Case Studies in Spirit Possession* (eds. V. Crapanzano and V. Garrison). London: John Wiley, pp. 295–331.

Kuchikura, Yukio
1987 *Subsistence Ecology among the Semoq Beri Hunter-Gatherers of Peninsular Malaysia.* Sapporo, Japan: Hokkaido University Department of Behavioral Science.

Leacock, Eleanor
1954 *The Montagnais "Hunting Territory" and the Fur Trade.* Memoir No. 78. Menasha, WI: American Anthropological Association (Vol. 56, No. 5, Part 2).
1972 "Introduction." In *The Origin of the Family, Private Property and the State* by Frederick Engels. New York: International Publishers.
1978 "Women's Status in Egalitarian Society: Implications for Social Evolution." *Current Anthropology* 19: 247–275.
1981 *Myths of Male Dominance: Collected Articles on Women Cross-Culturally.* New York: Monthly Review Press.

Lee, R. B.
1968 "What Hunters Do for a Living, or How to Make Out on Scarce Resources." In *Man the Hunter* (eds. R. B. Lee and Irven DeVore). Chicago: Aldine-Atherton, pp. 30–48.
1979 *The !Kung San: Men, Women, and Work in a Foraging Society.* Cambridge: Cambridge University Press.
2003 *The Dobe Ju/'hoansi,* Third Edition. Belmont, CA: Wadsworth Thomson Learning.

Lepowsky, Maria
1990 "Gender in an Egalitarian Society: A Case Study from the Coral Sea." In *Beyond the Second Sex: New Directions in the Anthropology of Gender* (eds. P. R. Sanday and R. G. Goodenough). Philadelphia: University of Pennsylvania Press, pp. 169–223.
1993 *Fruit of the Motherland: Gender in an Egalitarian Society.* New York: Columbia University Press.

Linehan, W.
1936 "A History of Pahang." *Journal of the Malayan Branch of the Royal Asiatic Society* 14: 1–256.

Lye Tuck-Po
1997   "Knowledge, Forest, and Hunter-Gatherer Movement: The Batek of Pahang,
        Malaysia." Ph. D. dissertation, Department of Anthropology, University of
        Hawaii.
2004   *Changing Pathways: Forest Degradation and the Batek of Pahang, Malaysia.* Lan-
        ham, MD: Lexington Books.
Malaysian Government
1982   *Malaysia: Federal Constitution.* Kuala Lumpur: Malaysian Government.
Marshall, Lorna
1976   *The !Kung of Nyae Nyae.* Cambridge, MA: Harvard University Press.
Marx, Karl
1896   *Capital: A Critical Analysis of Capitalist Production.* Translated by Samuel Moore
        and Edward Aveling. London: Sonnenschein & Co. First published 1867.
Meigs, Anna
1990   "Multiple Gender Ideologies and Statuses." In *Beyond the Second Sex: New
        Directions in the Anthropology of Gender* (eds. P. R. Sanday and R. G. Goode-
        nough). Philadelphia: University of Pennsylvania Press, pp. 99–112.
Mikluho-Maclay, N.
1878a   "Dialects of the Melanesian Tribes in the Malay Peninsula." *Journal of the
        Straits Branch of the Royal Asiatic Society* 1: 38–44.
1878b   "Ethnological Excursions in the Malay Peninsula—November 1874 to Octo-
        ber 1875 (Preliminary Communication)." *Journal of the Straits Branch of the
        Royal Asiatic Society* 2: 205–221.
Montagu, Ashley
1978   "Introduction." In *Learning Non-Aggression: The Experience of Non-Literate Societ-
        ies* (ed. Ashley Montagu). New York: Oxford University Press, pp. 3–11.
Moore, H. L.
1988   *Feminism and Anthropology.* Minneapolis: University of Minnesota Press.
1999   "Whatever Happened to Women and Men? Gender and Other Crises in
        Anthropology." In *Anthropological Theory Today* (ed. Henrietta L. Moore).
        Cambridge: Polity Press, pp. 151–171.
Morgen, Sandra
1989   "Gender and Anthropology: Introductory Essay." In *Gender and Anthropology:
        Critical Reviews for Research and Teaching* (ed. Sandra Morgen). Washington,
        D.C.: American Anthropological Association, pp. 1–20.
Morris, Rosalind C.
1995   "All Made Up: Performance Theory and the New Anthropology of Sex and
        Gender." *Annual Review of Anthropology 1995* 24: 567–592.
Morrison, Kathleen D., and Laura L. Junker, eds.
2002   *Forager-Traders in South and Southeast Asia: Long-Term Histories.* Cambridge:
        Cambridge University Press.
Mukhopadhyay, C. C., and P. J. Higgins
1988   "Anthropological Studies of Women's Status Revisited: 1977–1987." *Annual
        Review of Anthropology 1988* 17: 461–495.
Murphy, Yolanda, and R. F. Murphy
1974   *Women of the Forest.* New York: Columbia University Press.
Nagata, J. A.
1984   *The Reflowering of Malaysian Islam: Modern Religious Radicals and Their Roots.*
        Vancouver: University of British Columbia Press.

Needham, Rodney
1964   "Blood, Thunder, and Mockery of Animals." *Sociologus* 14: 136–149.
1976   "Minor Reports Concerning Negritos in Northern Pahang." *Journal of the Malaysian Branch of the Royal Asiatic Society* 49: 184–193.

Ong, Aihwa
1987   *Spirits of Resistance and Capitalist Discipline: Factory Women in Malaysia.* Albany: State University of New York Press.

Ortner, S. B.
1974   "Is Female to Male as Nature Is to Culture?" In *Woman, Culture, and Society* (eds. M. Z. Rosaldo and Louise Lamphere). Stanford: Stanford University Press, pp. 67–87.

Osmond, Anita, and Winifred Wilson
1968   *Tables of Composition of Australian Foods.* Canberra: The Australian Institute of Anatomy.

Peletz, M. G.
1996   *Reason and Passion: Representation of Gender in a Malay Society.* Berkeley: University of California Press.

Reid, Anthony
1988   *Southeast Asia in the Age of Commerce 1450–1680. Volume 1. The Land Below the Winds.* New Haven: Yale University Press.

Robarchek, C. A.
1977   "Semai Nonviolence: A Systems Approach to Understanding." Ph. D. dissertation, Department of Anthropology, University of California at Riverside.

Rosaldo, M. Z.
1974   "Woman, Culture, and Society: A Theoretical Overview. In *Woman, Culture, and Society* (eds. M. Z. Rosaldo and Louise Lamphere). Stanford: Stanford University Press, pp. 17–42.

Rousseau, Jean-Jacques
1992   *Discourse on the Origins of Inequality; Polemics; and, Political Economy.* Translated by Judith R. Bush. Hanover, NH: University Press of New England. First published 1753.

Sacks, Karen
1974   "Engels Revisited: Women, the Organization of Production, and Private Property." In *Woman, Culture, and Society* (eds. M. Z. Rosaldo and Louise Lamphere). Stanford: Stanford University Press, pp. 207–222.
1976   "State Bias and Women's Status." *American Anthropologist* 78: 565–569.
1979   *Sisters and Wives: The Past and Future of Sexual Equality.* Westport, CT: Greenwood Press.

Sahlins, Marshall
1972   *Stone Age Economics.* Chicago: Aldine-Atherton, Inc.

Salzman, P. C.
1999   "Is Inequality Universal?" *Current Anthropology* 40: 31–61.

Sanday, P. R.
1974   "Female Status in the Public Domain." In *Woman, Culture, and Society* (eds. M. Z. Rosaldo and Louise Lamphere). Stanford: Stanford University Press, pp. 189–206.
1981   *Female Power and Male Dominance: On the Origins of Sexual Inequality.* Cambridge: Cambridge University Press.

1990   "Introduction." In *Beyond the Second Sex: New Directions in the Anthropology of Gender* (eds. P. R. Sanday and R. G. Goodenough). Philadelphia: University of Pennsylvania Press, pp. 1–19.

Schärer, Hans
1963   *Ngaju Religion: The Conception of God among a South Borneo People* (trans. Rodney Needham). The Hague: Martinus Nijhoff.

Schebesta, Paul
1928   *Among the Forest Dwarfs of Malaya* (trans. Arthur Chambers). London: Hutchinson.
1954   *Die Negrito Asiens: Wirtschaft und Soziologie.* Vienna-Mödling: St. Gabriel-Verlag. Partially translated by Frieda Schütze, Human Relations Area Files, 1962.
1957   *Die Negrito Asiens: Religion und Mythologie.* Vienna-Mödling: St. Gabriel-Verlag. Partially translated by Frieda Schütze, Human Relations Area Files, 1962.

Schlegel, Alice
1977   "Toward a Theory of Sexual Stratification." In *Sexual Stratification: A Cross-cultural View* (ed. Alice Schlegel). New York: Columbia University Press, pp. 1–40.

Schrire, Carmel
1984   "Wild Surmises on Savage Thoughts." In *Past and Present in Hunter Gatherer Studies* (ed. Carmel Schrire). Orlando, FL: Academic Press, Inc., pp. 1–25.

Shostak, Marjorie
1981   *Nisa: The Life and Words of a !Kung Woman.* Cambridge, MA: Harvard University Press.

Siegel, James
1969   *The Rope of God.* Berkeley and Los Angeles: University of California Press.

Skeat, W. W., and C. O. Blagden.
1906a   *Pagan Races of the Malay Peninsula, Vol. 1.* London: Macmillan and Co.
1906b   *Pagan Races of the Malay Peninsula, Vol. 2.* London: Macmillan and Co.

Slocum, Sally
1975   "Woman the Gatherer: Male Bias in Anthropology." In *Toward an Anthropology of Women* (ed. R. R. Reiter). New York: Monthly Review Press, pp. 36–50.

Strathern, Marilyn
1987   "Conclusion." In *Dealing with Inequality: Analysing Gender Relations in Melanesia and Beyond* (ed. Marilyn Strathern). Cambridge: Cambridge University Press.

Testart, Alain
1981   "Pour une Typologie des Chasseurs-Cueilleurs." *Anthropologie et Sociétés* 5: 177–221.

Tiger, Lionel
1969   *Men in Groups.* New York: Random House.

Tocqueville, Alexis de
1998–   *The Old Regime and the Revolution.* Translated by Alan S. Kahan. Chicago: Uni-
2001   versity of Chicago Press. First published 1856.

Turnbull, C. M.
1965   *Wayward Servants: The Two Worlds of the African Pygmies.* Garden City, NY: The Natural History Press.

Voss, Barbara L.
2000   "Feminisms, Queer Theories, and the Archaeological Study of Past Sexualities." *World Archaeology* 32(2):180–192.

Waterstradt, John
1902   "Kelantan and My Trip to Gunong Tahan." *Journal of the Straits Branch of the Royal Asiatic Society* 37: 1–28.

White, Isobel
1974   "Aboriginal Woman's Status: A Paradox Resolved." In *Woman's Role in Aboriginal Society,* second edition (ed. Faye Gale). Canberra: Australian Institute of Aboriginal Studies, pp. 36–49.

Widlock, Thomas
2005   "Introduction." In *Property and Equality 1: Ritualisation, Sharing, Egalitarianism* (eds. Thomas Widlock and W. G. Tadesse). New York and Oxford: Berghahn Books, pp. 1–17.

Wilmsen, E. N.
1989   *Land Filled with Flies: A Political Economy of the Kalahari.* Chicago: University of Chicago Press.

Williams, W. L.
1986   *The Spirit and the Flesh: Sexual Diversity in American Indian Culture.* Boston: Beacon Press.

Woodburn, James
1978   "Sex Roles and the Division of Labour in Hunting and Gathering Societies." Unpublished paper presented at the First International Conference on Hunting and Gathering Societies, Paris.
1979   "Minimal Politics: The Political Organization of the Hadza of North Tanzania." In *Politics in Leadership* (eds. W. A. Shack and P. S. Cohen). Oxford: Clarendon Press, pp. 244–266.
1982   "Egalitarian Societies." *Man* (N.S.) 17: 431–451.
1988   "African Hunter-Gatherer Social Organization: Is It Best Understood as a Product of Encapsulation?" In *Hunters and Gatherers 1: History, Evolution and Social Change* (eds. Tim Ingold, David Riches, and James Woodburn). Oxford: Berg Publishers, pp. 31–64.

includes DVD!

The Headman Was a Woman

A comprehensive ethnography of one of the few remaining hunting and gathering peoples of Southeast Asia, *The Headman Was a Woman* presents the gender concepts, roles, and relations of the highly egalitarian Batek of Peninsular Malaysia. Based on longtime field-work, the book describes the lives of Batek men and women in the tropical rainforest, and includes discussions of fieldwork, hunting and gathering, social organization, religion, gender, nonviolence, and cultural persistence in the face of a changing landscape.

*R*ich in detail yet clearly written, *The Headman Was a Woman* introduces readers—from first-year anthropology students to hunter-gatherer specialists—to an egalitarian people whose way of life is both thought-provoking and rare.

*T*he ethnography is accompanied by a 37-minute DVD, *The Batek: Rainforest Foragers of Kelantan, Malaysia.* Footage shows vivid highlights of camp life and social activities as well as all of the important economic processes described in the book.

Waveland Press, Inc.
www.waveland.com

ISBN 13: 978-1-57766-526
ISBN 10: 1-57766-526-0

9 781577 665267

90000

P9-EBI-648